Southeast Asian Identities

Culture and the Politics
of Representation in
Indonesia, Malaysia
Singapore, and Thailand

Southeast Asian Identities

Culture and the Politics of Representation in Indonesia, Malaysia Singapore, and Thailand

edited by **Joel S. Kahn**

ST. MARTIN'S PRESS, New York

INSTITUTE OF SOUTHEAST ASIAN STUDIES, Singapore

Published by
Institute of Southeast Asian Studies
30 Heng Mui Keng Terrace
Pasir Panjang Road
Singapore 119614
Internet e-mail: publish@iseas.edu.sg
World Wide Web: http://www.iseas.edu.sg/pub.html

First published in the United States of America in 1998 by
St Martin's Press
Scholarly and Reference Division
175 Fifth Avenue
New York, N.Y. 10010

Library of Congress Cataloguing in Publication Data

Southeast Asian identities: culture and the politics of
    representation in Indonesia, Malaysia, Singapore, and Thailand/
    edited by Joel S. Kahn.
        p.   cm.
    Includes bibliographical references and index.
    ISBN 0-312-21343-3 (cloth)
    1. Asia, Southeastern--Politics and government--1945- 2. Asia,
Southeastern--Ethnic relations.   3. Nationalism--Asia, Southeastern-
-History.   I. Kahn, Joel S.
    DS526.7.S687   1998
    306' .0959--dc21   97-49584
                                                                         CIP

ISBN 981-3055-78-2 (softcover, ISEAS, Singapore)
ISBN 981-3055-79-0 (hardcover, ISEAS, Singapore)

For the USA and Canada, this hardcover edition (ISBN 0-312-21343-3) is
published by St Martin's Press, New York.

For Europe, a hardcover edition (ISBN 1-86064-243-8) and a softcover edition
(ISBN 1-86064-245-4) are published by I. B. Tauris & Co. Ltd., London.

Typeset by International Typesetters Pte Ltd
Printed in Singapore by SNP Printing Pte Ltd

Contents

The Contributors

Chua Beng Huat is currently Associate Professor in the Department of Sociology, National University of Singapore. A regular social commentator at home, his most recent publication is *Communitarian Ideology and Democracy in Singapore* (London: Routledge, 1995).

Rachel Bloul has a Ph.D. in Anthropology and Comparative Sociology. She is currently teaching Sociology at the Australian National University. Her research interests and main publications are in the fields of ethnic and gender relations, with a focus on Muslim cultures and Muslims in the West.

Nirmala PuruShotam is a Lecturer in the Department of Sociology, National University of Singapore. She holds a Masters degree from the Tata Institute of Social Sciences, Bombay, India, and a Ph.D. from the National University of Singapore. She is currently finalizing a monograph on "Language Negotiations and Ethnic Constructions: The Case of Singapore".

Joel S. Kahn is currently Professor in the School of Sociology, Politics & Anthropology at La Trobe University in Melbourne, Australia. His most recent book is *Culture, Multiculture, Postculture* (London: Sage, 1995).

Goh Beng Lan is a graduate of Universiti Sains in Penang, and Ochanomizu Women's National University, Tokyo, Japan. She has carried out extensive research on urbanization in Penang and has recently obtained a Ph.D. from Monash University.

Ariel Heryanto has postgraduate degrees from the University of Michigan and Monash University. He currently teaches in the Southeast Asian Studies Programme at the National University of Singapore.

Wendy Mee is a doctoral candidate at La Trobe University, Australia. Her Ph.D. research investigates the role of information technology in contemporary constructions of Malaysian modernity. This research provides a comparative perspective to the research she has conducted at Telstra (formerly, Telecom) Research Laboratories into the impact of information technology on the character of Australian work practices, community life and institutions.

Craig Reynolds is Reader in the Asian History Centre, Faculty of Asian Studies at the Australian National University. He previously taught at the University of Sydney and was a research fellow in the Research School of Pacific and Asian Studies at the ANU. He is currently writing a book on the culture and intellectual history of modern Thailand, and his research project with Tony Day on the State in Southeast Asia recently received funding from the Australian Research Council.

Albert Schrauwers recently completed a Ph.D. in the Graduate Department of Anthropology, University of Toronto, with a thesis entitled "In Whose Image? Religious Rationalization and the Ethnic Identity of the To Pamona of Central Sulawesi". He is currently a temporary lecturer in the Department of Anthropology at the London School of Economics.

chapter one

SOUTHEAST ASIAN IDENTITIES
Introduction*

JOEL S. KAHN

In the last ten to fifteen years, we have stood witness to a remark-able world-wide resurgence of cultural politics. The rise of what are commonly termed nationalisms in Eastern and Central Europe, com-munalisms in Asia, tribalisms in Africa, racial and ethnic movements in North America, movements for the rights of indigenous peoples in Australasia and the Americas, conflicts over the consequences of immigration for the national cultures of Western Europe, to say nothing of renewed religious- and/or civilization-based sensitivities on a global scale, all contribute to the sense — shared by the vast numbers of academics, journalists, intellectuals, theologians, corporate executives and politicians — of a world in the grip, to the point of obsession, of what the philosopher Charles Taylor has called "the politics of recognition" (Taylor 1992).

Contrary to the impression generated by the majority of observers of contemporary Southeast Asia — of a region whose peoples are dedicated entirely to the single goal of economic development — matters cultural are never very far down anyone's agenda. Against the presumption of an earlier generation of "mod-ernization" theorists and political economists, it seems to be that cultural particularist rather than cosmopolitan goals have come to the fore for a large number of Southeast Asians. There are these days no national leaders who can avoid, even if they wanted to, cultural issues, most articulating visions of a future shaped by the twin goals of economic growth *and* moral or cultural integrity, rather than either one of these on its own. And no nation in the region can credibly claim cultural homogeneity. Everywhere, the evidence of cultural diversity is overwhelming, if only because it is forcibly brought to our attention either by political élites, or by the spokes-persons for groups disempowered by race, culture, religion, gender or distance from the political centre. It may well be, as the leaders of Malaysia and Singapore frequently remind us, that cultural conflict in Southeast Asia has thankfully not led to the levels of open violence manifest elsewhere in the world, although this may be an overly sanguine view of both Southeast Asia's past and its possible futures. However, it is undeniable that the culturalization of the political landscape, as well as of everyday life for the majority of Southeast Asians, is as much a fact of life in the region as it is elsewhere in the world.

The relatively scant attention paid to these issues in much of the recent scholarly literature on Southeast Asia is probably suffi-cient justification for a volume which takes as its central theme the exploration of culture and identity politics in a variety of Southeast Asian contexts. But this volume does not represent an exhaustive inventory of cultural identities in contemporary Southeast Asia. There is a fair coverage of the region, with chapters by Chua Beng Huat and Nirmala PuruShotam on Singapore, Albert Shrauwers and Ariel Heryanto on Indonesia, Craig Reynolds on Thailand, Wendy Mee and Goh Beng Lan on Malaysia, as well as a chapter on Malaysia, but taking the globalization of Islamic discourses as its theme, by Rachel Bloul. But clearly these chapters deal with only selected aspects or regions of these countries. There are unfortunately no chapters on the Philippines, Myanmar, the countries of Indochina or Brunei, all of which in different ways would be necessary to a more complete picture. Rather, contributions have been selected not just for their regional focus, but for the ways they shed light on a number of central questions to which any contemporary analysis of cultural politics gives rise. Of these questions, four might be singled out as of particular significance:

1. To what extent can we speak of identity politics as global — in other words, can we generalize about the nature, and implications, of the kinds of cultural conflicts summarized above?[1]
2. What are the causes of the turn to culture and identity in the contemporary world?
3. How accurate is it to speak of a *resurgence* of cultural politics — in other words, are we witnessing a re-emergence of Eastern European nationalism, or African tribalism or whatever? Or are these identities in a significant sense *new*? In particular, we need to ask whether there are important differences between contemporary forms of culture conflict and the conflicts over sovereignty generated by nationalist movements that emerged in post-Napoleonic Europe in the nineteenth century, or in the colonial world in the first half of the twentieth.
4. What should we, not just as analysts, but as citizens, make of claims for cultural recognition? This is a particularly vexing question for those with more traditional universalist and cosmopolitan notions about what constitutes progressive politics.

Selected for the way they have made important analytical as well as documentary contributions to the understanding of cultural politics in Southeast Asia, the chapters, while all written by social scientists — anthropologists, sociologists and historians — also draw on insights deriving from recent debates in cultural and literary theory. There are a number of reasons for this, not least the fact that those who have chosen to thematize the linguistic and discursive dimensions of modern existence have been better placed to offer insights into the processes of cultural representation and hence of identity formation and cultural politics that are so significant in the contemporary world than have been disciplines more strongly committed to the metanarratives of classical modernist social theory.

The contributions here, however, suggest three things: first, that out of this encounter with cultural theory, the social sciences

may be re-emerging, although in a modified form, to make a contribution to the understanding of contemporary cultural processes;
secondly, that, in particular, this has been made possible by a renewed commitment in the social sciences to examining comparative
and global, rather than merely local situations; and, thirdly, related
to this, the re-invigoration of the social sciences has taken place,
at least in part through the intervention of what are perhaps too
facilely called "post-colonial intellectuals" into social scientific debate.
That five of the contributors live and work in Southeast Asia is no
accident — a central aim in putting this volume together was to
bring together "insiders" and "outsiders" in a fruitful dialogue.

The chapters in this volume address these issues from the
perspective of particular forms of identity politics in different parts
of Southeast Asia. The volume begins with four papers that focus on
the ways in which dominant discourses seek to construct distinctive
forms of cultural identification below the level of the nation. They
also describe the fate of such imperial forms of "ethnic" identification
with the end of empire and, perhaps also, the waning of counter-
imperial nationalism.

The chapter by Chua Beng Huat on "Racial-Singaporeans" is
subtitled "Absence after the Hyphen", a reference to the relative
(cultural) emptiness of the "Singaporean nation". Singapore is an
interesting case because it shows quite clearly how universalist
themes — such as anti-colonialism, class politics and/or socialism,
or capitalist economic modernization — on their own are, or at least
are perceived to be, insufficient for a "proper" national culture.
Singaporean national culture has, of course, been shaped by all three,
in particular by what Chua calls the "inscription of the culture of
capitalism" through a productionist orientation, the development of
a deep sense of competitiveness, a strong ideology of "meritocracy",
and a cultural emphasis on "individualization". The Singapore state,
as a consequence, relies heavily on developmentalist rhetoric as a
mode of legitimation — an effective strategy, given Singapore's
tremendous developmental record.

However, capitalist economic success on its own has proven to
be inadequate grounding for a national identity, and like other modern
nation states, the Singapore state has experienced pressures to define

itself in particularistic or culturally-unique terms, engaging as a result in various projects of "culture building". These have included, most significantly, an official multiracialism that has in fact had a disempowering effect, and various attempts to construct the Singapore nation as a unique reservoir of "Asian values", as embodying, in Chua's words, "the 'essence' of the communitarian cultures of Asia'". Among other things, therefore, the chapter by Chua Beng Huat shows how even in a place like Singapore, with no single "traditional" ethnic community which could give a culturally-particularistic shape to its national identity, and which probably more than anywhere else in Southeast Asia has been thoroughly interpenetrated by universal or global (or even "Western") cultural influences, the discourse on national identity has been highly particularistic. Singapore shows perhaps more clearly than anywhere else in the world that universalism and particularism, cosmopolitanism and primordialism are necessarily interconnected rather than separate cultural processes in the modern system of nation states.

"Disciplining Difference" by Nirmala PuruShotam traces the "multiracial" construction of Singapore to the period of the British empire, providing us with a detailed analysis and critique of the way that the British colonial government and subsequently the post-colonial state of the Republic of Singapore have constructed and continue to construct a "multiracial" citizenry.

After Singapore was opened up to the global economy by Stamford Raffles it had a highly diverse population made up of the descendants of people already in place at the time of the coming of the British and large numbers of immigrants. How, asks PuruShotam, did this extremely diverse population come ultimately to be forced into a classificatory system comprising four discrete "racial" groups" — Chinese, Malay, Indian and Other (CMIO) — into which all Singaporeans today are forced to insert themselves? By examining colonial census reports that appeared between 1871 and 1947, and that included extensive commentaries on the (changing) census categories, she shows how this "Orientalist" classificatory system was gradually constructed by various "experts", most of whom were of course British. It is impossible to do justice to this careful analysis of an emerging system of social classification. But what the chapter shows is precisely how this surprisingly complex history led to the development of a highly specific set of concepts that served to construct Singaporeans as radically different from each other so successfully that most Singaporeans today have almost entirely internalized what was at the outset a highly arbitrary system of racial and cultural classification. Once again, in one of the societies most open to global economic, political and cultural influence, cultural particularism has flourished.

Ariel Heryanto, in his chapter entitled "Chinese Indonesians in Public Culture: Ethnic Identities and Erasure", also looks at the formation of an ethnic identity, this time of Chinese in Indonesia. Moreover, in examining the changing representations of Chineseness in Indonesian public and/or popular culture, he suggests that perhaps this particular identity is being de-ethnicized.

Throughout Southeast Asia, ethnic politics inevitably calls forth images of conflict between "indigenous" peoples and the largest immigrant group among them, the "overseas Chinese". For example, Malay nationalism from the outset relied heavily on a strong image of the Chinese as (threatening) other, and indeed since well before independence, Malaysian politics has been characterized by a more or less strict organizational separation on racial or "communal" lines.

In Indonesia too, there has been a history of antagonism between groups constructed as "indigenous" (*pribumi*) and others classified as Chinese, a classificatory system that emerged first in colonial times. In Indonesia, however, there has been an added dimension. As Heryanto shows, this system of ethnic classification was reworked during the period of the so-called New Order regime of President Soeharto whose rule has been legitimized by its claim to having rescued (and continuing to rescue) the country from the threat of communism. Moreover, given the official narrative of significant involvement by the Indonesian Chinese in the activities of the Indonesian Communist Party, together with a belief that the People's Republic of China was involved in what the regime likes to call the "abortive communist coup" of 1965, this othering of the Indonesian Chinese played a role in the horrendous massacres that followed Soeharto's rise to power.

As a result, argues Heryanto, the myth of Chinese otherness, combined with the language of communist threat, has been an important legitimizing myth of the New Order regime, which can at the same time rely on the co-operation of ethnically-Chinese economic élites and still disenfranchize the Chinese community as a whole. Here, cultural particularism becomes embedded in the legitimization of a modern authoritarian regime, reminding us that nationalism based on the unique cultural characteristics of its constituents also involves processes of othering and demonization of non-nationals.

Having demonstrated the extent to which the politics of cultural representation has been central to the rise of modern authoritarianism in Indonesia, Heryanto also suggests that evidence of its decline is at the same time evidence of the weakening of the New Order's grasp on power. Here, challenges to the essentialist images underpinning a system of ethnic classification may at the same time be challenges to the power of an authoritarian state.

While so far we have focused largely on internal factors in the emergence of discourses of cultural uniqueness and cultural alterity, global cultural influences have never been out of sight. Indeed, especially during the colonial period, local languages of culture and difference were thoroughly hedged in by the interests and imaginations of the colonial powers. Moreover, there is the sense that current national forms of culture building are as much a consequence of the imperatives of the global system of nation states as they are of particular states in Southeast Asia.

The next three contributions introduce notions of globalization more explicitly. In his chapter on "Globalization and Cultural Nationalism in Modern Thailand", Craig Reynolds writes of the impact of globalization on cultural identities in Thailand. Reynolds draws attention to the ways in which the phenomenon of cultural globalization differs from earlier forms of cultural imperialism when the hegemony of metropolitan cores (whether in the West, or in Thailand itself) almost inevitably resulted in the domination if not the extinction of peripheral cultures. The effect of globalization in Thailand has been ambiguous, as likely to support previously dominated indigenous cultures as to wipe them out, as likely to support new social/cultural movements as to undermine them. The paradoxical result of this is that, in his words,

> [a]s cultural flows import more and more from "out there", whether "out there" be Hong Kong, Tokyo, Taiwan or San Francisco, new regional and ethnic identities are being forged.

One reason both for the relatively high porosity of Thailand to global cultural influences, and for the ability of Thais at the same time to preserve the old and to create new distinctive cultures and identities, may be the history of "openness and receptivity to the world generally", a sort of cosmopolitanism that nonetheless does not take the form of a slavish imitation of other ways, Reynolds suggests.

In his discussion of Thai reactions to global influence Reynolds also draws our attention to another important dimension of the processes of identity formation, namely, the significant role played in these developments by intellectuals. Neither mere puppets of imperial or local state power, as some of the post-colonial critics would have it, nor speakers of the unmediated voices of the subaltern, as they themselves often imply, intellectuals in places like Thailand (and, indeed, in the West), on the one hand, have their own particular voices and agendas and, on the other, are very often the most sig-nificant social group in the production and consumption of cultural identities, new and old. By looking at recent public debates, Reynolds shows how, in the Thai case, intellectuals, many of whom come from a radical, leftist background, are playing a crucial role as the mediators of global culture. Indeed, globalization is itself a central trope of Thai intellectual discourse, as Reynolds' discussion of debates over what the Thais call *lokanumwat* shows, something that suggests that in speaking of cultural globalization we must take into account the fact that it is as much an emic as an etic category.

Reynolds' rich discussion of issues raised both by globalization theory and by cultural politics in contemporary Thailand deserves careful reading. But one thing it demonstrates quite clearly is that our earlier understandings of global cultural flows which envisaged a culturally homogeneous world as its evolutionary endpoint (the classical understanding of "cosmopolitanism") or a world culture produced almost entirely through Western cultural hegemony needs to be substantially revised as we recognize that globalization is as likely to generate difference, uniqueness and cultural specificity as it is to produce a genuinely universal or homogeneous world culture.

This is of course reminiscent of the important work of the anthropologist Arjun Appadurai, who has reminded us that the current state of global culture is characterized by disjuncture and difference as much as it is by sameness and a one-way cultural hegemony. In contrast to the period of European imperialism, now the variegated ideoscapes, ethnoscapes, finanscapes and technoscapes, to use Appadurai's catchy terms, channel cultural influences in a criss-crossed pattern across the globe (Appadurai 1990). As just one example of this change, sometimes just as important to Southeast Asians' perception of the world as the images emanating from the Western-controlled media, are those that come through the medium of Indian or Hong Kong film, or the products of the Japanese communications industries.

In "Gender and the Globalization of Islamic Discourses", Rachel Bloul demonstrates how Southeast Asian discourses on gender are also shaped in significant ways by a "non-Western" globalized discourse, this time that of a world Islamic movement. Describing the debates that took place among the participants at a conference on "Islam and the 'Woman Question'" held in the Malaysian city of Penang — debates that made frequent reference to the local and particular nature of Islam — Bloul argues that in fact they testify to the emergence of a global Islamic language on gender and identity.

Bloul's chapter is important for two other reasons. Firstly, she shows clearly how a particularistic discourse (in this case, one that stresses the distinctiveness of Islamic, as opposed to "Western", discourses about femininity) becomes universalistic, or perhaps better reified under a globalizing impulse. Hence, what may start out for Malaysian Muslim intellectuals as a language of Malay particularism becomes subsumed under global categories like "Islamic womanhood".

Secondly, Bloul's chapter tackles directly what is implicit in a number of other chapters, namely, the extent to which these new discourses are inevitably gendered. Consequently, concepts such as an "Islamic society" imply, almost as a matter of first principle, distinctive gender roles and modes of behaviour. The importance of gender and gendering in relation to recent cultural and identitarian discourses in Southeast Asia is evident in most of the other contributions to this volume. Thus, for example, in her discussion of the construction of "multiracialism" by the Singaporean state, PuruShotam shows how each "race" can only be completely represented by its related, and yet at the same time differentiated, males and females. In a somewhat different way, imperial representations of Asians were also frequently gendered. A clear example of this is seen in the way British writers on the Malays not only wrote of "typical" gender roles among the colonized peoples, but in classic imperial fashion also constructed feminized images of the Malays which contrasted with the "masculine" world of both the colonizers, and that of the more "modern" Chinese.

Theorists of the global condition have tended to argue that a significant determinant of contemporary forms of cultural politics is the nature of the new communications technologies that have developed in the last decade or more. While ideas about cultural globalization first emerged particularly in analyses of the impact of televisual technologies, in the last few years, the transmission of electronic data by means of what has come to be known as the Internet has generated renewed interest in the intersection between local cultures and identities, on the one hand, and the global situation, on the other. While scholarly research on this new technology has been focused largely on the West, and particularly the United States which shapes information flows in significant ways, there is little doubt that, perhaps because of rapidly increasing levels of technical sophistication in Southeast Asia, culture and society in the region are already being shaped in significant ways by the linking of (some of) its citizens both to each other and the outside world by means of the Internet. A volume dealing with the intersection of the global and the local in the Southeast Asian context would be incomplete without a consideration of the role played by these electronic networks on cultural politics in the region.

The chapter by Wendy Mee, an Australian researcher who has spent a number of years examining issues of cultural and techno-logical change in Malaysia, fills this gap. In her lively discussion of the impact of new communication technologies in particular on national identity in Malaysia, she suggests right from beginning that the nation is always adaptive, changing, elastic, multiplex, pluralistic and "is not dependent on homogeneity". She then goes on to argue that globalization does not inevitably bring about the demise of national/local cultures.

In looking at the way that, through the Internet, "Malaysians construct 'modern' Malaysian identities and representations of Malaysia which are both … global and particular", Mee also challenges some of the ideas we hold about nationalism. While most theorists have concentrated on images of the nation which are more civiliza-tional, formalistic, and conventional in character, many of the images circulating about Malaysia on the Internet are of a more popular, vernacular, mundane sort: the serious images compete with and are displaced by the informal ones.

Finally, Mee, along with other contributors to this volume, points to the significant role played by particular groups of people in the construction and reconstruction of national imaginaries. In Malaysia, it is mostly middle class and "technologically-literate" Malaysians who use the Internet, and from her own observations it seems that by far the majority of these are male, professional and under forty years of age. Thus, when speaking of a "Malaysian identity" as con-stituted through new communication technologies, it should be noted that, as always when representation is implied, it is from a quite specific viewpoint or range of viewpoints, rather than the discourse of a homogenous "nation".

That discourses of identity and debates over cultural represen-tation are not just disembodied forms of intellectualizing is a theme of the final two chapters in the volume. By presenting close-grained ethnographic analysis of particular local conditions, Goh Beng Lan and Albert Schrauwers show clearly the extent to which the forging of cultural identity is never the smooth, homogenizing process that it is assumed to be in the eyes of the region's èlites, and indeed in those of many local intellectuals and academics as well. Instead, they demonstrate two things: firstly, that cultural identity and identification is, to use a fashionable term, inevitably contested; in other words, that people do not blithely accept identities given to them, as it were, by either tradition or the blandishments of those in power, but that they often struggle against their interpellation by dominant discourses, or rework identities to make them fit their own circumstances; and, secondly, that identity politics, as these two cases also show, is about more than identity, in that the conflict over representation has to be understood as having a materiality that is frequently ignored by cultural theorists.

The first of these case studies, about the construction of new urban spaces and "cityscapes" in a Southeast Asian context, is Goh Beng Lan's chapter on "Modern Dreams: An Enquiry into Power, Cityscape Transformations and Cultural Difference". This wonderfully detailed analysis of urban development and conflicting urban imaginaries in the rapidly "modernizing" city of Georgetown, located in the State of Penang, shows how the politics of representation in contemporary Malaysia embodies a contest for control of the contours of urban space. One participant is the Malaysian state which, through its various instrumentalities, in addition to its conspicuous economic planning function, is strongly committed to a cultural mission, namely, the forging of a new Malaysian culture and hence of a new kind of Malay(sian) — global, modern, confident, assertive, and enthusiastic in embracing new technologies and capable of fostering competitiveness with the older ("decadent") West. On the other hand, many of these new Malay(sian)s are in fact property developers, driven by the more instrumental imperatives of the burgeoning property market to build new housing, shopping centres and the like as fast as possible. Finally, there are the residents of Georgetown's many "ethnic" enclaves seeking either to ward off rapacious urban re-developers or, at least, to obtain from them adequate compensation for the loss of their property. These local residents too become bound up in a complex system of identity politics, since it seems that only by representing themselves as culturally unique groups are they able even to enter the contest.

Goh's chapter reports on the results of research on one such group, the "Portuguese-Eurasian" residents of one of Georgetown's many urban *kampung*. Unlike many writers on these issues, Goh was actually there to witness the struggle between *kampung* residents, property developers and various instrumentalities of the Malaysian state, the outcome of which was not just a conflict over material compensation, but a heightened rhetoric of culture and identity, reflecting at the local level the intertwining of cultural and economic objectives found in the speeches of Malaysia's political élite. But here we see that while the national goals of Malaysia's political leadership continually have reference to a homogeneous set of "Malaysian values", in fact at the local level these values can be seen to be fragmented and contested, pitting the modernist imaginaries of developers and political élites against the particularistic visions of other groups. Nor, as Goh shows clearly, is it a simple case of two voices — an élite or hegemonizing one versus a local or subaltern one. The situation in Georgetown is, in fact, far more complex — a surprising conclusion being that the principal spokespersons for a Portuguese-Eurasian, rather than a homogenizing national, identity were not the disenfranchised residents of the urban *kampung*, but instead members of a growing professional urban middle class who had their own stake in Malaysia's cultural arena.

The second of these localized case studies is Albert Schrauwers' account of the "ethnicization" of a relatively small group of rural cultivators on the island of Sulawesi in Indonesia. Indonesia, so goes the cliché, is not one nation but many, a conglomeration of hundreds, if not thousands, of separate and discrete ethnic groups, each with its own culture. The "problem" of Indonesian nationhood has, as a consequence, almost always been seen as a problem of maintaining "unity in diversity", which is, interestingly, the national slogan in Indonesia just as it is in the United States. Even that most sophisti-cated analyst of Indonesian nationalism, Benedict Anderson, appears to take it for granted that while the Indonesian nation may be "imagined", its local cultural communities are not (see Anderson 1983).

Very few analysts have recognized that just as Indonesian-ness is a constructed or created identity, so are the lower-level ethnicities of the Balinese, the Javanese, the Minangkabau, and so forth. A clear case of this phenomenon, which Schrauwers calls "ethnicization", is the Indonesian obsession with what Pemberton has called "mini-ization" (see Pemberton 1994), a term he derives from Indonesia's mother of all cultural theme parks, Taman Mini in Jakarta, in which each of Indonesia's supposedly discrete "cultures" is represented by means of a display of "traditional" architecture, "traditional" dress, "traditional" ceremonies, and the like.

Schrauwers' discussion of the ethnicization of the group that has come to be called the *To Pamona* of Sulawesi begins appropriately with a local example of mini-ization, the building of a site for the "Lake Poso Festival" in the town of Tentena along the Trans-Sulawesi Highway. He then asks why it should be that the Indonesian state seems always to construct ethnicity in terms of "local, timeless, 'authentic' traditions", a feature of many of the discourses of culture and identity in the region.

This observation allows Schrauwers to problematize the particular ethnic identity "assigned" to one group in Central Sulawesi, the *To Pamona*, not to demonstrate that a somehow more authentic cultural tradition can be recovered, but that any form of ethnic consciousness in Indonesia is bound to be reifying. And he does this by looking at the, in fact surprisingly, recent history of the very category of *To Pamona*.

Like Goh, Schrauwers finds that the notion of a unique cultural group is and has been contested from the outset. And like Goh, he also finds that this contestation cannot be understood simply as a conflict between the élite and the mass, or between the rulers and the ruled. Instead, cultural politics in Central Sulawesi has been more complex, perhaps because of the definitive conflict between State and Church both in the colonial period and in the decades since independence.

In tracing this complex history, and in linking that history to politics and the economy in Sulawesi today, Shrauwers produces a fascinating narrative that involves not just the subjects of his ethnographic research, but also colonial liberals, the anti-liberal architects of the so-called "ethical policy" who did so much to shape Dutch colonial policy and practice in the twentieth century, the *adat* law experts and ethnologists whose representations of Indonesian cultures have made such a significant impact on the way more recent ethnographers have represented Indonesia's cultures, officials of an independent republic shaken by the regional uprisings in Sulawesi towards the end of the 1950s, and, finally, representatives of the New Order's twin authoritarian and developmentalist tendencies seeking greater control of local-level political processes on the one hand, and expanded tourism on the other. Perhaps the most interesting revelation in all this, something missed in many other accounts of Dutch colonialism in the Indies, is the extent to which the "culturalistic" tendencies of Dutch rule stemmed from a (conservative) religious critique of the civilizing imperial mission of typical nineteenth century Western liberalism — a debate that has done more than most to shape Indonesia's current cultural landscape.

If there is a single question that has exercised the contributors to this volume more than any other, it concerns the implications of the problematic nature of the notions of culture and identity. In other words, while the authors represented here have approached the processes of culture and identity formation in contemporary Southeast Asia in a variety of ways and from a number of different perspectives, in one way or another they take on board two ideas that have been developed largely, but not exclusively, within contemporary cultural theory. The first of these is that human subjectivity and human identity is inevitably constituted through and by culture. The second is that we need to adopt a certain scepticism towards the cultural essentialism that appears to lie behind both traditional approaches to the phenomena of ethnicity, nationalism and the like, and the claims of those players on the stage of cultural politics who "speak for" one or another cultural group, however defined.

This is not the place for a detailed theoretical exegesis. Nonetheless, because these ideas constitute an often unstated starting point for most of the contributions to this volume, it is necessary to say a few words on each. The first, that our identities are shaped by culture, refers at the most basic level to the now fairly widespread critique of (early) modern/Western philosophical ideas about the ultimate autonomy of the individual human subject, and notions about freedom and emancipation that spring from them. Cultural theorists draw on a variety of sources of evidence — from non-Western ideas about personhood to studies of the West that point to the specificity of Western "individualism" — to suggest that far from being the basic building blocks of all human society and culture, autonomous, rational, self-creating subjects are culturally and temporally bound constructs. This leads to the more general position that notions of personhood and the self are everywhere and always culturally and historically contingent, that, therefore, human subjectivity must be determined by cultural context in significant ways, marking off the analyses offered here from earlier voluntarist theories that tended to see in identity politics a cloak for the somehow more "real" instrumental (economic or political) goals of maximizing individuals.

At the same time, as I have suggested, our contributors have maintained a sceptical stance towards cultural essentialism. Here, the best contrast is with traditional theories of ethnicity or nationalism that see identity as stemming directly from an already existing culture. Hence, for example, in his important writings on nationalism, the sociologist Anthony Smith speaks of the *ethnie* that have inevitably constituted the basis for modern nations (see Smith 1990). This can be usefully contrasted with the influential assertion by Benedict Anderson that nations are, on the contrary, *imagined* — that is, that they do not stem from *real*, pre-existing cultural communities, and indeed that these cultural communities are themselves cultural constructs. Here it is Anderson rather than Smith who displays that scepticism that serves to distinguish contemporary from traditional cultural theory.[2] For Anderson (and for most contributors to this volume), but not for Smith, there is no objective sense in which we can speak of a "true Germanness" or a "true Chineseness" for that matter — both are imaginary, not because they are false, but because they are the product of discourse, that is, they are constructed or created out of concrete social and historical processes.

For the authors represented here, it is precisely this kind of scepticism that constitutes the starting point for analysis. Hence Albert Schrauwers writes: "[M]y aim ... is to deconstruct the very notion that an 'authentic' *To Pamona* culture can be uncovered." In a very different context, Goh Beng Lan shows that in Malaysia none of the prevailing notions of a unique "Portuguese-Eurasian" culture arise out of a discrete and timeless set of beliefs and practices inherited from a timeless past. Instead, all claims to "Portuguese-Eurasianness" stem from, and in one way or another are shaped by contemporary political practices. Such a view of identities, and the "underlying cultures" upon which they claim to be based — as in some sense, constructed — can be found throughout this volume.

This scepticism extends also, or even primarily, to scholarly or journalistic "analysts", who in presenting supposedly objective accounts of their own or other cultures can be seen to be as much entrapped in the processes they describe as are the supposed bearers of the cultures they seek to describe. Nirmala PuruShotam argues convincingly that even the taken-for-granted ethno-racial categories "Chinese", "Indian" and "Malay" — categories to which the vast majority of Singaporeans unquestioningly assign themselves — are in a very real sense arbitrary, having acquired their contemporary parameters not largely from objective cultural markers, but from the advice given to colonial census-takers by British scholars and orientalists during the colonial period.

If the language of cultural uniqueness is not a false trail laid down by those actually pursuing instrumentalist politics, but is instead somehow constructed, rather than pre-given, then the task of the analyst becomes twofold: firstly, it requires asking how subjectivities in the particular cases examined are actually constituted by specific sets of cultural practices; and, secondly, it calls for an investigation of the social and historical processes that have generated those cultural practices. This is a task undertaken with some success for a variety of Southeast Asian contexts by the contributors to this volume. And in this they stand on their own, requiring no caveats or qualifications on the part of an editor. Instead, in the final part of this introduction, I would like to offer some concluding remarks on the nature of contemporary identity politics in Southeast Asia with a view to raising a number of issues for future consideration.

Difference, Postmodernism, Post-nationalism
There is an immediate objection to the assertion that the cultures of modern Southeast Asia are in some sense constructed. For no matter how nuanced our approach is, no matter how much we appeal to the phenomenological reality of the "imagined community", no matter

how much we may rail against reductionism, we are left with the considerable problem of understanding the very real power of those beliefs which underpin it. The dilemma is evident in the oft-quoted passage from *Imagined Communities* in which Anderson points to the imaginary, but at the same time very "real" dimensions of national identity:

> [the nation is always imagined] as a *community*, because, regardless of the actual inequality and exploitation that may prevail in each, the nation is always conceived as a deep, horizontal comradeship. Ultimately, it is this fraternity that makes it possible, over the past two centuries, for so many millions of people, not so much to kill, as willingly to die for such limited imaginings. (Anderson 1983, p. 16.)[3]

If the nation exists (only) in the imagination, how is it that it seems so real to those caught in its thrall? Is the "reality" of the observer the yardstick against which the nation is declared imaginary, any less imaginary? Is there any basis for distinguishing between the "rational" constructs of social scientists and the "irrational" languages of the rest of humanity?

I do not presume to offer a resolution to this age-old theoretical dilemma here. Instead, in these concluding remarks I want to approach it indirectly from a somewhat different angle, by asking about the conditions which have given rise to it. If it took the "discovery" of the constructed, and hence problematic, nature of culturalist discourse to produce theories, rather than historical, empirical or ethical accounts of identity politics, and if this seems to have taken place in the social sciences from the late 1980s, then the question needs to be asked: what is it about this period that led so many different observers to view cultural identity as a theoretically problematic rather than a straightforward category? To some extent, this problematization of cultural identities can be explained by reference to theoretical developments, many of which have taken place outside the social sciences. As I have already suggested, some of the most significant contributions to the study of identity formation have taken place in literary theory and the relatively new fields of cultural and post-colonial studies. Given the concern here with issues of representation, it is perhaps not surprising that theories of identity influenced by these new theoretical trends should have taken the form that they have.

But to treat theory as if it was somehow abstracted from the world, as if theories influence other theories in a kind of vacuum, would be a mistake. Certainly, what can be read in this collection of studies about the contemporary discursive processes through which individuals and groups construct their cultural identity in Southeast Asia — a region that has spawned some of the world's best-known and most influential nationalist movements in the twentieth century — is that nationalist projects, at least in this regional context, and at least as they have been conventionally conceived, are presently under challenge, if not even declining in influence. Or, to put it in another way, perhaps the problematizing of cultural identities in theory is part of a more general process of what might be loosely termed "post-nationalization."[4] Evaluating such a proposition allows us, firstly, to assess more readily the extent to which current forms of identity politics in Southeast Asia are, in some sense, new phenomena rather than a resurgence of earlier kinds of nationalist and ethnic "sentiments"; and, secondly, to reflect on the actual relationship between social theory and the social processes by looking at the deconstructive project of the contributors to this volume (and, we could add, of other intellectuals as well, both in Southeast Asia and elsewhere) as part of a wider cultural process that aims to counter the essentializing discourses of political élites in Southeast Asia (and the West).

To assess the extent to which earlier nationalisms are being superseded in Southeast Asia ideally requires a comparison between the language of culture and identity mobilized in earlier nationalist movements in the region which is beyond the scope of an introduction such as this one. Suffice it here to suggest that classical modern forms of nationalism contain within them two apparently contradictory languages — first, a universal language of rights, national sovereignty and citizenship, and secondly, a particularistic language of, to use Appadurai's terms, blood and territory. Seemingly contradictory, in fact nationalism appears to have always required both cosmopolitan and primordial elements.

I would suggest then that we might speak of post-nationalism when we have evidence that either one or both of these elements of national identity is/are breaking down. And we can, I think, see evidence of a burning of the classical nationalist candle at both ends, as it were. On the one hand, there are now a large number of instances in which the universal language of rights and sovereignty has come under attack for being Eurocentric. As many of Southeast Asia's political leaders are fond of pointing out, far from being truly modern or universal, this language is in fact itself particularistic, a Western discourse unsuitable to Asian realities. There is a sense that the development of local ideologies of an Islamic or a Confucian or an Asian trajectory of modernization is almost inevitably linked to a critique, even demonization, of "the West", and hence the claim, implicit or explicit, that Southeast Asians have discovered a civilizational path that quite literally supersedes modernity. The point here is not so much whether or not we agree with this critique, but whether the national imaginaries of a Lee Kuan Yew or a Mahathir Mohamad are any longer shaped by modern/Western universalism.

On the other hand, there is also evidence to support the contention that the primordial dimensions of classical modern nationalism are also being eroded. For example, there appears to be what some have called a postmodernization of cultural identities in the region in the sense of an increasing dominance of signifiers of identity, of what one might call, extending Baudrillard's use of the term, cultural simulacra. By this I refer to the sense that the kinds of cultural identities documented by the authors in this volume are established by reference to a rather limited set of signifiers — dress, items of diet and the like — rather than cultures in the anthropological (romanticist) sense of "ways of life". Consider, for example, PuruShotam's account of the almost shorthand portrayal of Singapore's different races in various national celebrations, or of the significance of a "heritage house" to certain members of Penang's Eurasian community, discussed by Goh Beng Lan.

Postmodernization in this sense might in turn be linked to the quantitative increase in the levels of circulation of signs associated with the communications revolution, which in turn can be linked to the greatly increased levels of commodity circulation associated with the development of the global economy. As observers like Jonathan Friedman have pointed out, higher levels of global commodification do not necessarily spell the end of cultural politics. On the contrary, it is precisely the uses which contemporary cultural movements make of commodities that allow them to establish their cultural uniqueness (see Friedman 1994).

Finally, post-modernization might be linked to the feeling of a decline of the overtly political projects of classical nationalism in the region, pointing instead to the strengthening of the ties joining together culture, identity and the economic sphere. Southeast Asian regimes, for example, have increasingly turned, as we have noted, to indicators of economic "development" for their legitimation. Moreover, oppositional movements seem increasingly concerned with questions of cultural heritage (for which we can often read rights to dress in "traditional" ways or eat "traditional" foods, or exercise ownership rights over "traditional" designs, and so forth) rather than political sovereignty.

But many cultural theorists see in the postmodernization of identities something which appears to be absent in most forms of representational politics in Southeast Asia, namely, a self-consciousness about the "constructedness" of cultures and boundaries, a playfulness or even transgressiveness, encouraged by the fact that the markers of identity are now "merely simulacral". For one thing, to the extent that we have long recognized the arbitrariness of the relationship between signifiers and signified, identities have always been simulacral and hence postmodern. Why therefore should the current construction of cultural boundaries be more susceptible to critique and transgression? For another thing, there is little to suggest that identity politics in contemporary Southeast Asia are anything less than serious, even "dead serious". This calls attention to the importance of the kinds of cultural critique being pursued by many of the contributors to this volume. For it makes their attempts to "deconstruct" at least the kinds of hegemonic discourses of identity formation, which are so central to the legitimation of all regimes in the region, seem all the more important.

Finally, theorists writing of other parts of the world have suggested that we are witness to new kinds of "post-national" identity politics at a global level. The perception of post-national trends in the "global order of nation states" is as yet somewhat vague and fragmented. No one, for example, has seriously suggested that the nation state is about to disappear. At the same time, there are indications that other organizational and discursive forms currently pose considerably stronger challenges to the system of nation states than has been the case in the past. What are some of these challenges and alternatives, these current "strains in the union of nation and state" (Appadurai 1993, p. 413) in Southeast Asia?

One indication that this union of nation and state in Southeast Asia is coming apart is found in the number of political regimes in the region which have pulled back from the close identification of state with nation, and hence from the cultural projects of nation-building so typical of the nationalist period of their history.

And yet, even with the apparent triumph of economic instrumentalism, the felt need for a distinct national identity has apparently not disappeared. As in Singapore, in Malaysia intellectuals closely associated with the ruling faction within UMNO (United Malays National Organization) have been recruited to the task of constructing a new kind of Malay (the so-called *Melayu Baru*), a concept which now seems to be extended to all of Malaysia's constituent "racial" groups. Moreover, in spite of the government's attacks on what it brands as Islamic "extremism" (the opposition Muslim party PAS, and members of so-called *dakwah* groups like Al Arqam), there is also a strong sense that Malaysia's political élites are moving towards the implementation of a new kind of Islamic State (see Hussin Mutalib 1993; and chapter by Bloul in this volume).

There is also a sense of significant changes in Thailand. Reynold's account of the "globalization" of Thai identities is a case in point, as is a recent discussion of the transformation of Thai identity in a fashion reminiscent of the cultural processes of post-modernization described for the West.

We might also point to a somewhat different trend, but one which has the similar effect of breaking the blood–territory equation of classical nationalist (and subnationalist) movements, and that is the formation of globalized movements for cultural identity, described by Appadurai in the following terms:

> Recent ethnic movements often involve thousands, sometimes millions, of people who are spread across vast territories and often separated

by vast distances. Whether we consider the linkage of Serbs separated by large chunks of Bosnia-Herzegovina, or Kurds spread across Iran, Iraq and Turkey, or Sikhs spread through London, Vancouver, and California, as well as the Indian Punjab, the new ethnonationalisms are complex, large-scale, highly coordinated acts of mobilization, reliant on news, logistical flows, and propaganda across state borders. They can hardly be considered tribal, if by this we mean that they are spontaneous uprisings of closely bonded, spatially segregated, naturally allied groupings (1993, p. 416).

This leads us conveniently to a final reason to speak of a post-national phase in Southeast Asian history. For increasingly, processes of cultural identity and identification in the region are becoming international or global in orientation, in the sense that they have reference to what many have termed "diasporas" rather than local-ized cultural or national groups. We might, for example, mention the global dimension of movements to encourage the speaking of Mandarin in Singapore, or attempts to envisage an "overseas Chinese" community, or to re-invent a "Malay civilization" that crosses the current political boundaries in the region, or the vision of a trans-national Tai-ness of which Craig Reynolds writes, or movements to protect the rights of the region's indigenous peoples as a whole, or, perhaps the most frequently cited case of such global identification in Southeast Asia, that of membership in a global Islamic *ummat* (the subject of the chapter by Rachel Bloul). It needs to be emphasized that a global Islamic identification is not just the goal of those oppo-sitional groupings labelled "fundamentalist" in places like Indonesia, Malaysia, southern Thailand and the Philippines. It is also, in a somewhat different sense, a goal at least of the Malaysian state.

In short, the radical economic and political transformations taking place in the Asia-Pacific region are being accompanied by sig-nificant shifts in the discursive processes through which individuals and groups construct cultural identity. While the various ethnic and nationalist projects that have their roots in the colonial period continue to define lines of identification and cleavage, they have in recent years been more or less rapidly overtaken by new kinds of cultural movements and hence new forms of "politics of recognition" (see Taylor 1992). This is, in itself, a very important observation for it suggests — contrary to the predictions of nineteenth century "cosmopolitanism", or twentieth century notions of the triumph of Westernization and/or the end of history — that far from dissolving into a homogeneous mass of self-interested and autonomous individual subjects, humanity continues to be fragmented and human subjectivity continues to be determined by principles of cultural, religious, and linguistic identification, although these principles may be new ones. It needs to be recalled that many of the negative evaluations of nationalism, whether in Europe or elsewhere, shared a belief that a post-national world would also be a cosmopolitan world — a world, to borrow a phrase used to describe Herbert Spencer's utopia, devoid of sociological (and one might add, cultural) furniture, a world made up entirely of enlightened individuals. In its proliferation of new cultural identities and movements, contemporary Southeast Asia certainly does not support such a conclusion.

As a result of the emergence of these competitors for the loyalties of the citizenries of the world's nation-states, Appadurai suggests, national loyalties and imaginaries are in decline. But, in fact, post-nationalization of this kind implies an even more basic transformation of cultural identities, whether they be national or regional, for they appear to be producing a rupture in the earlier nexus between cultural identity and locality, producing instead identities that are diasporic, that is to say, effectively de-territorialized. Therefore, what we have called cultural identity and identification is decreasingly "primordial" — whether at the level of the nation or of the "tribe" — that is, the tribal metaphor of unity of blood, territory and community is increasingly invalidated by the diasporization of the world. This has implications not just for nations, but for all forms of cultural identification. Therefore, if we are moving beyond nations, we are also moving beyond ethnicities as previously understood.

But before we rush to embrace the grandiose language of the new theorists of post-nationalism, it is worth asking whether the novelty of the new global order is, in fact, being overplayed. On the one hand, as I have already suggested, the "old" primordialisms themselves cannot be understood merely as premodern leftovers in a then newly emerging global order of "rationalized" nation-states.

In an important sense they were themselves a precipitate of the processes of nationalization and rationalization, a set of negative constructions or critiques of those rationalized nationalisms of the early nationalist heroes like Soekarno and Nasser, rather than the irrational outcry of traditional communities being merged into new nations. If this was the case in the early decades of this century, then we should not be surprised to find that primordialism has also not died in the contemporary global cultural order. Appeals to blood, territory, race continue to characterize cultural conflict at all levels in Southeast Asia and beyond. Rather than being always critiques of an old universalism, based on the simplistic cosmopolitanism of emancipatory rhetoric, they may now be rejections of the new kinds of cosmopolitanism favoured by observers such as Appadurai. For a close reading of much of what now passes for globalization theory can be seen to be a defence of at least certain dimensions of the American dream. In this, Appadurai is himself a significant figure, arguing that the particular relationships being forged among diasporic communities in the United States might be the model for the world in the future. This subtle re-insertion of the United States back into the world sounds suspiciously, to this observer at least, like those older arguments for the superiority of Britain, Holland and France, based on the universality of their value systems when compared to the parochialism and particularisms of Asia. Might it not make more sense to pay careful attention to the way Asians in Asia are grappling with these issues, than continually turning to the recommendations of Americans, even if the latter are now claiming a diasporic connection to Asia?

Perhaps the best evidence of an emergent post-nationalist and/ or post-colonial sensibility in Southeast Asia is provided not by the spread of theories from the West, but by the emergence of a new generation of post-colonial intellectuals in Southeast Asia, some of them represented in this volume. For ideas developed by cultural theorists elsewhere in the world, designed to "empower" previously hegemonized cultural minorities — notions like multiculturalism, anti-orientalism, diasporic cultures — have come to play very different roles in Southeast Asia. Rather than empowering or emancipatory, such notions are all too often embedded in new languages of state power. In this respect, Southeast Asian intellectuals and activists have a unique perspective on cultural developments in their region. And to the extent to which, like many of our contributors here, they are prepared to speak out against and combat the kinds of essentialized readings of culture and identity that are increasingly being mobilized by economic and political élites in the region, they also provide us with insights into cultural "modernization" and cultural particularism in the region that cannot be drawn from general observations about globalism, post-colonialism, post-nationalism and the like.

Notes

* I would like to acknowledge the invaluable assistance of Frank Formosa and Beth Robertson in the preparation of the manuscript, and of the anonymous readers appointed by the Institute of Southeast Asian Studies who offered many helpful suggestions. I would also like to thank all the contributors who bore with my endless editorial suggestions with good humour and patience.

1. A number of influential commentaries on culture conflict in the contemporary world rest on this assumption, that wherever they occur, such conflicts are similar. A good argument is presented by the political scientist Samuel Huntington who subsumes geographically-dispersed conflicts under a single heading. They are all manifestations, he suggests, of a global conflict of civilization (see Huntington 1993). But, of course, this kind of generalization is found widely, notably in the work of those who focus on processes of cultural globalization (cf. Robertson 1992; Appadurai 1993).

2. Here, it should be noted in relation to Anderson (1983) that, while his theory of national identity formation is in some ways unique, he nonetheless shares with other recent theorists the view of the nation as a problematic formation rather than a primordial given (see also Gellner 1983; Chatterjee 1986, 1993).

3. This dilemma recalls the problem encountered — but, it must be said, never satisfactorily resolved — by most earlier (post-war) theorists of how it is possible to reconcile the co-presence of the rational and the primordial, the universal and the particular, the cosmopolitan and the parochial in all existing nationalisms. See Chatterjee (1986) for a definitive critique of various liberal "solutions" to this dilemma.

4. Elsewhere, I have described the new discourse on culture and identity as "postculture" (see Kahn 1995).

References

Anderson, Benedict. *Imagined Communities: Reflections on the Origin and Spread of Nationalism.* London: Verso, 1983.

Appadurai, Arjun. "Disjuncture and Difference in the Global Cultural Economy". *Public Culture* 2, no. 2 (1990): 1–24.

———. "Patriotism and its Futures". *Public Culture* 5, no. 3 (1993): 411–29.

Chatterjee, Partha. *Nationalist Thought and the Colonial World.* London: Zed Books, 1986.

———. *The Nation and its Fragments: Colonial and Postcolonial Histories.* Princeton: Princeton University Press, 1993.

Friedman, Jonathan. *Consumption and Identity.* London: Sage Books, 1994.

Gellner, Ernest. *Nations and Nationalism.* Oxford: Basil Blackwell, 1983.

Huntington, Samuel P. "The Clash of Civilizations". *Foreign Affairs* 72, no. 3 (1993): 22–49.

Hussin Mutalib. *Islam in Malaysia: From Revivalism to Islamic State?* Singapore: Singapore University Press, 1993.

Kahn, Joel S. *Constituting the Minangkabau: Peasants, Culture and Modernity in Colonial Indonesia.* Oxford and Providence: Berg, 1993.

———. *Culture, Multiculture, Postculture.* London: Sage Books, 1995.

Kahn, Joel S. and Francis Loh Kok Wah, eds. *Fragmented Vision: Culture and Politics in Contemporary Malaysia.* Sydney: Allen & Unwin, 1992.

Pemberton, John. *On the Subject of "Java".* Ithaca, NY: Cornell University Press, 1994.

Roberston, Roland. *Globalization: Social Theory and Global Culture.* London: Sage Books, 1992.

Smith, Anthony. "Towards a Global Culture?" In *Global Culture: Nationalism, Globalization and Modernity,* edited by Mike Featherstone. London: Sage Books, 1990.

Taylor, Charles. *Multiculturalism and the "Politics of Recognition".* Princeton: Princeton University Press, 1992.

chapter two

RACIAL-SINGAPOREANS
Absence after the Hyphen

CHUA BENG HUAT

As in all nations that are dominated by immigrant populations, Singapore is "multiracial" in demographic composition. If bonds of solidarity among citizens of modern nation-states were built on the "universalization of a shared civilization or ethnic tradition in the minds of equal and autonomous individuals as a condition for its continued survival" (Chun 1994, p. 50; see also Gellner 1983), then nations like Singapore have an endemic problem of finding a "common bond" to bind its population to a sense of shared identity and destiny. Alternatively put, there are serious obstacles to formulating the cultural "substance" that may lend materiality to the "imagined" community called a nation. These difficulties are compounded in the Singapore case by particularistic conditions at its inception as a "nation".

Singapore was granted internal self-government by the British colonial administration in 1959. It was nevertheless difficult for the Singapore population to push on to the obvious next political step because an independent Singapore was thought to be "a foolish and absurd proposition" (Lee Kuan Yew, quoted in Drysdale 1984, p. 249) for several reasons: politically, because Singapore had been administratively part of peninsular Malaya until the latter's independence in 1957; economically, because under the prevailing belief in import substitution as the best development strategy for decolonized states it was deemed that as an island without a large domestic market Singapore was non-viable; demographically, because Singapore's population consisted almost entirely of immigrants (even the island's Malays were immigrants from neighbouring areas); and culturally and ideologically, because these immigrants were oriented less to Singapore than to their "homelands" of China, India and emerging Malaya. Under such conditions, the population could only see its continuing existence as part of peninsular Malaya, especially economically.

Then, in 1963, the possibility of communist rule on the island prompted the Malayan political leadership, who had been unenthusiastic about a "merger" with Chinese-dominant Singapore, to move quickly to form a Malaysian Confederation with Singapore and the British colonial territories of Sarawak and North Borneo, subsequently renamed Sabah. Membership proved difficult for Singapore, leading to its separation from Malaysia after two brief years. In 1965, political independence was thrust upon the population by fiat, under the People's Action Party (PAP) government. The "absurd" had become the reality.

Until 1965, Singapore as an independent political entity was an "absence"; it was not an idea which a population was trying to realize. This "absence" accounts for the successive attempts to "define", to "substantiate" and to eventually "realize" a national identity at every level of social and political life. Unlike economic development, however, success in identity building has been elusive — the ontologically real has tended to continuously and cunningly slip away from all attempts to represent it.

The Hegemony of Economic Discourse
The supra-racial governmental structure of British colonialism and subsequently of Malaysian federalism was dismantled as a result of independence. A "reason" for the new state[1] had to be found and Singapore was severely impoverished in ideological/symbolic resources for this task.

Being a settlement of immigrants, Singapore had no indigenous tradition and structure of government that could be resurrected. Of the three races, the Chinese were the most numerous and best organized through multiple layers of clan and trade associations, culminating in umbrella organizations such as the Hokkien Association and the Chinese Chamber of Commerce. However, they could not morally claim any special or exclusive political and social right over the new island nation. Furthermore, the geopolitical condition of archipelagic Southeast Asia placed them in a region of overwhelmingly Malay-speaking populations of Malaysians and Indonesians, who were unlikely to accept a Chinese nation in their midst with equanimity. The Malays, though regionally indigenous, constituted a numerical minority which was unable to dominate politics in the new state. Finally, the Indians were doubly disadvantaged because, on the one hand, they were fewer than the Malays and, on the other, they were immigrants like the Chinese. Thus, the conditions necessary to forge what could be called a "shared" cultural heritage as the basis of this new nation did not seem to exist at that time.

Denied of myths of shared traditions, the state sought and found an alternative "reason" and source of legitimation in "universal" concepts thought to be capable of concurrently transcending and suppressing ethnic differences. Through their ability to incorporate all members of the population as individuals, regardless of racial/cultural affiliation, such universal concepts were deemed to hold the potential for the establishment of social bonds based on horizontal solidarity among the newly enfranchised citizens of a "Singapore" understood now as a nation. Candidate universal concepts available at the time were, among others, anti-colonialism, class politics and socialism/communism, and capitalist economic modernization.

Anti-colonialism played a useful role in the processes through which Singapore gained independence (Chan 1984). However, Singapore's status as an independent nation was achieved without a revolutionary struggle, which might have testified to the presence and expression of a "collective will" among the population and which, subsequently, might have also been elevated to the level of a "founding" myth of the new nation, as was the case in Indonesia (Yong 1992). As for class politics, the left had by the time of independence been politically suppressed and decimated by the emergent People's Action Party (PAP) government. Furthermore, the case for "communism" was by then increasingly conflated with radical segments of the Chinese population, particularly with those groups of secondary and tertiary students that were highly mobilized politically, including the undergraduates at Nanyang University, the Chinese-language university that was founded in the mid-1950s. The PAP's own history as a coalition of a group of English-educated, professionally-trained social democrats and a populist left faction that was well embedded in the "outlawed" radical trade unions had transformed the former group, who inherited the political fortune of the party, into staunch anti-communists.[2]

The obvious discursive grounding for the new state was, therefore, capitalist development. With the monopoly of state power in hand, a reconstituted PAP government turned to the persuasive material promises of capitalism for the new "Singaporeans". Political separation, which led to the apparent collapse of the anticipated larger Malaysian market for Singapore's fledgling industrialization, might be said to have placed the economic viability of the island nation in serious jeopardy. The PAP government astutely seized upon this apprehensiveness, turning it into an ideological means with which to highlight the problem of guaranteeing the "survival" of the new nation and how this could only be achieved through economic development. The legitimation of the state and of the whole national project was thus from the very outset cast in economic rather than symbolic terms.

Politics was reduced to economics: "[p]olitical problems ulti-mately mean the problem of how we make our living, how we can give everyone a fair and equal chance to study and work and have a full life" (Lee 1962, p. 83). The "survival" of the new nation, defined in economic terms, in turn came to be entwined with the problems of how individual citizens "make a living" (Goh 1976). National economic growth and improvement of the population's material life became both the rational basis for organizing the new nation and the criteria by which the performance of the regime was to be defined, assessed and legitimated. Sharing in this material progress became the entitlement of citizenship.

The Inscription of the Culture of Capitalism

Capitalist economic development requires for its success the active proletarianization of the population into a disciplined industrial work-force (Offe 1987) through the inscription of a set of requisite cultural attitudes and values. Cultural development in the new state, therefore, had to abide by the dictates of the logic of capital. The following are some of the cultural concomitants of capitalist development in Singapore.

First, a productionist orientation at the work-place had to be promoted through an ethos of "mutual trust and co-operation" between labour, employer and the state in order to maximize production from the workers, profit for the enterprise and economic growth for the nation. "Trust and co-operation" were not, however, left to the uncertain outcome of cultural exhortation, but were secured institutionally by acts of legislation introduced in 1968, 1982 and 1984 with the aim of creating and maintaining stable industrial relations. The overall result has been, on the one hand, increased discretionary power for employers and, on the other, reduced "benefits" for employees in terms of working hours, paid holidays, and so on. However, it should also be noted that this framework of industrial relations has not frozen wages to past levels, but has actually allowed them to increase in step with national economic growth.

Secondly, it was essential to develop a sense of competitiveness in people, and this was done by sustaining a desire among Singaporeans for attaining comparative advantages in material consumption. The entrenchment of this is reflected in the economic-instrumental orientation towards education that is generally exhibited by Singaporeans. In this context of generalized "competitiveness", individuals have been encouraged to use education principally as a means of attaining higher income levels and other materialistic and status rewards. Education has thus become effectively a compulsive "paper chase", culminating in what could be called the "certification of the self". Incidentally, it should also be noted that this growing demand for education, training and professional qualifications has turned Singapore into a lucrative source of fee-paying students that is being increasingly exploited by universities in many Western countries.

Thirdly, competitiveness had to be itself ideologically under-pinned by rules of "fairness" and "individual merit" — that is, it had to be underwritten by an ideology of "meritocracy". The government's ideological refrain that "no one owes another a living" was extended to cover the many services that the state provides to citizens. For example, access to public housing by a family has come to depend entirely on the ability to pay rather than on any non-monetary criterion of measuring needs.

Fourthly, by advocating that each citizen's social and economic circumstance is supposedly determined by a combination of his/her industry and natural endowment and no other cause, formal "meri-tocracy" has enabled the state to rationalize the consequential in-equalities of class under capitalism by "individualizing" failures and successes. Hence, this meritocratic discourse has come to play a significant role in the identity formation of individual Singaporeans by acting like an ideology of self-justification for those who are successful, and of self-deprecation for those who are not.

Finally, "competitiveness" and "meritocracy" have been them-selves steps in the progressive "individualization" of the self in the new state; in instituting these values as part of an economically determined national culture/ideology, the state itself has become an agent of "individualization", consequently reinforcing the requisite individualism of capitalism.[3]

The aggregate cultural effects of the social inscription of the above values has been the emergence of an everyday life-world characterized by a high level of privatization of largely financially defined interests associated with an increasingly better educated and well disciplined work-force which embodies a high level of com-petition for material consumption. The achievement or absence of material success, such as one's children's performance in school and one's ability to afford private housing and cars, have become the anxieties that define the everyday life of the majority of those who live on the island.

On the whole, the government has been successful in delivering the material promises of capitalism to the population in the past three decades. The epitome of this achievement has been its promise to enable every household to own, at least, a public housing flat of decent quality and size. This success has imparted to the new state a measure of "nationhood" and to its population a measure of identity as "Singaporeans". It has given to both a sense of "pride of achievement" which contributes to a positive self-image (Thumboo 1989); economic success has become synonymous with Singapore (Drysdale 1984; Sandhu and Wheatley 1989). Thus, the universalizing tendency of capitalist growth should not be underestimated as a rationality of the state. However, as we shall see, capitalist economic success at both the individual and the national levels may constitute weak grounds for the building of bonds of national identity.

Multiracialism and the Disempowering of Race

Significantly, the economy-determined characteristics of everyday life are strategically excluded from the state-generated discourse of culture in Singapore. This exclusion is managed through the "universalization" and "naturalization" of capitalism, which is unavoidable and necessary to the very physical survival of the population. Its "essential" nature is positively reinforced by its ability to fulfil not only the demand of "making a living" for each citizen but, beyond this, the expansion of material comfort as the desired realization of "a full life". By naturalizing the "dull compulsion of the economic", the cultural consequences of capitalism are ideologically conceptualized as necessities and, as such, placed outside the cultural sphere, where preferences rule.

The ideological exclusion of the economy-determined everyday life as culture is facilitated by foregrounding the "cultures" of the three races through the concept of "multiracialism" as cultural policy.[4] Understood in terms of cultural policy, multiracialism makes reference to, but goes beyond, the ontology of race in its political effects. Through it, race is essentialized as an unchanging feature of the population so as to ground various specific ways of disciplining the social body. The issue here concerns the double question of how the ontological given of different races living in Singapore is to be discursively thematized and, in the process, transformed as a relevant phenomenon in political discourses which rationalize strategies of social administration?

Race is essentialized in the following manner: officially, one's race is defined strictly by patriarchal descent; one's race supposedly determines one's culture (multiculturalism); this race-culture is assumed to be embedded in the language of the race. Thus, race is assured continued existence through compulsory school instructions in a "mother tongue" language (multilingualism), as a second language after English.[5] In this set of discursive processes which constitute individuals as members of distinct racial groups, differences among the population are radically reduced. For example, in the discursive formation of the Chinese as a "single" group, dialect differences which had sharply divided them in the past are suppressed by abolishing dialects in the mass media and by the promotion of Mandarin as the "language of the Chinese".[6] Similarly, differences among the Malays are reduced under a common "Malay" language, and in this particular instance, the "group" is additionally defined by Islam. Finally, language differences among Indians were initially suppressed by privileging Tamil, the south-Indian language spoken by more than 60 per cent of the Singapore-Indians, as the "group" language. Subsequently, responding to protests from other language speakers, other Indian languages are now made available as acceptable mother tongues, including Hindi, Punjabi and Bengali. This reduction of differences is, of course, tantamount to the suppression of some constitutive components of individual and collective identities within the population itself. The result is that the three discursively produced groups — "Chinese", "Malays" and "Indians" — become the relevant administrative racial categories that are used to rationalize government policies and political practices (Siddique 1989).

In practice, these groups are made observable through their "cultural" activities. For example, official annual public holidays are dedicated to cultural/religious celebrations such as Hindu (Indian) and Muslim (Malay) festivals and the Chinese (multireligious) new year. The officially sponsored racial/cultural categories in turn generate activities organized by the racial groups themselves, giving rise to the impression that the "cultures of Singapore" are frozen in three respective "traditions". While such a conception may be considered mistaken from an anthropological viewpoint (Benjamin 1976; Clammer 1985), it is an effect of official "multiculturalism" and one which is promoted by the government for precisely these very political and ideological advantages.

This intentional discursively produced race has at least one clear political consequence. It undermines the value of race as a political currency. By promoting "group rights" in a cultural sphere which is restrictively circumscribed by racial boundaries, the state is able to claim for itself a "neutral" stance towards all racial groups, without prejudice or preference (Kuo 1985; Siddique 1989). Thus, except for "protecting" the "mother tongues" in schools, the responsibility for promoting racial/cultural activities is entirely dependent on individual and/or collective efforts of each officially constituted racial group.[7] The cultural vibrancy of each group is dependent entirely on its members, with the state providing equal administrative support; no preferential claim can be made on any state agency on the basis of race.

Significantly, within the kinds of cultural discourses that have emerged in Western contexts, it is believed that what has come to be called multiculturalism is a means for "empowering" minority ethnic and other groups by redressing discriminatory practices against them. In Singapore, on the other hand, what has come to be called "multiracialism" functions effectively as a means of disempowerment because it erases the grounds upon which a racial group may make claims on behalf of its own interests without ostensibly violating the idea of group equality that is the foundation of multiracialism itself. In Singapore, multiracialism pushes race out of the front-line of politics while according it high visibility in the cultural sphere.[8]

Race and the Social Organization of Welfare

While the ideologically hegemonic economic sphere may be excluded in the official discourse on culture, political management of the consequential social inequalities of a capitalist economy cannot be excluded. The inequalities stand in the way of elevating capitalist economic success as the basis of national identity formation for all citizens, as noted earlier.

Of course, one way of managing the inequalities would be to institute policies to promote greater equality of income. However, for the Singapore state to do so it would have to tamper with and risk undermining the ideas of individual competitiveness, meritocracy and private accumulation — that is, the logic of capital itself. To avoid such ideological contradictions, the people at the bottom of Singaporean society can instead be simply transformed into individual households "who need help". And once this transformation of the less privileged has taken place, their welfare will then come to depend upon the moral largesse or altruism of the larger community of which they are members. Ideological room is thus created for the different racial groups to "help" their own kind, a process that can be rationalized as being both constitutive of and constituted by the racial groups as "communities". This is the PAP government's strategy to reduce social inequalities generated by capitalism.

In 1981, admitting to the generally low economic position of the Malays (Zoohri 1990), the PAP government sponsored the establishment of Mendaki, a Muslim organization under the leadership of Malay Members of Parliament (MPs).[9] Ten million dollars of public funds were donated as an inauguration fund. Mendaki aims to enhance the academic performance of Malay students, so as to improve the long-term employment and financial prospects of the Malays as a whole. In 1989, a similar organization, the Singapore Indian Development Agency (Sinda), was set up by Indians to help their own "low achievers". Given the logic of multiracialism, a Chinese agency was inevitable and hence, the launching of the Chinese Development Assistance Council (CDAC) in April 1992. However, in the latter two cases, no inaugural funds were provided by the government.

These agencies are officially called "community self-help organizations". The term "community" is narrowly drawn around the discursive boundaries of the three official races and concretized in the same way in which funds are raised: every Singaporean worker contributes to improve the educational performance of the children of needy families in his or her "own" racial group. The state lends an administrative hand. Contributions are deducted monthly from the employees' compulsory social security savings in the government-managed Central Provident Fund. No cross-racial contributions are permitted in this basic deduction.[10]

In principle, contributions are voluntary. However, in contrast to the conventional practice of charity, contribution is presumed unless one intentionally opts out. Given the obvious good cause and the paltry monthly contribution, few opt out. Those who do, are usually against the "opt-out" practice, preferring to preserve the right to decide whether and how much to contribute. Others argue that this strategy of caring for the less able will in effect intensify racial divisiveness, which is detrimental to the formation of a Singaporean identity and national unity. They prefer a national institution for the needy which defines community in national rather than racial terms, adding often that the setting up of "self-help" organizations is but the state's way of reducing its commitment to and responsibility for the social welfare of the people.

The government's response to these charges evinced its essentialist position on race and its conception of the role of the state in social welfarism. First, it argues that "race" is an essential constitutive element of a person's identity that will not be erased and that governments attempt to erase it at their own peril. Secondly, it argues that by expanding social welfarism, the state in developed capitalist nations has usurped the "communitarian" role of local communities and is thus destructive of community itself. Significantly, this is also consistent with the ideological commitment to the family as the "fundamental" social unit and the first institution of "self-help" and welfare maintenance for members of the national community. Again, this ideological position on the state and welfarism is not without substantive and conceptual support. Social democratic Sweden, with its generous welfare state, is a case in point. It could not avert the contradiction of undermining its ideological commitment to local community through the expansive and expensive state provision of welfare goods (Kemeny 1992).

The institutionalization of racially constituted self-help organizations puts in place a series of divergent, if not contradictory, ideological tendencies in the social organization of race in Singapore. First, it prominently inserts race in the management of the overall social welfare of the nation; its limited educational role can always be expanded to absorb other functions. This insertion stands alongside the encasing of race within the private spheres of religious and festival practices while keeping it politically ineffective. Secondly, the communitarian emphasis of these organizations contradicts the individualizing tendencies entrenched in the hegemonic economic sphere. Perhaps it is because of this latter contradiction that contribution to the self-help organizations must be extracted through presumed contribution rather than left to individual decisions. That there are divergences and/or contradictions in the ideological sphere of Singapore is unexceptional, nor do they necessarily signify the presence of an ideological impasse or crisis, because the ideological system is always only relatively, rather than systematically, coherently organized (Althusser 1971). The divergences placed in the ideological terrain by these organizations suggest the presence of a larger ideological frame.

The Asianization of Singaporeans

In spite of the fact that Mendaki has been in existence since 1981, the self-help organizations received full ideological rationalization only in 1990, with the explicit promotion of a national ideology by the government. However, because the PAP government has always prided itself for being "pragmatic" and free of ideological encumbrance (1995), the national ideology has come to be known as "shared values". These shared values are: nation before community and society above self; family as the basic unit of society; regard and community support for the individual; consensus instead of contention, racial and religious harmony. A White Paper on Shared Values was adopted by Parliament as, presumably, the guiding principles for the ongoing governance of Singapore.[11]

Examining the shared values, one readily notes that what motivates them is the desire to privilege "collectivity" over individuals. This is represented by the government as the "essence" of the "communitarian cultures of Asia", or "Asian communitarianism". Self-help organizations find their ideological justification within the auspices of this "communitarianism", as in "society before self" and "regard and community support for the individual".[12] This rediscovery/reinvention of Asian communitarianism is itself the consequence of a larger and long-standing ideological project to forestall the supposedly "corrosive" effects on the population of

Western cultural and consumer industries, manifest in an emerging "hyper-individualism".[13]

The "West", used ideologically and intentionally, is cast as a single homogenous cultural entity which embraces liberal individualism in its cultural core. To this individualism is attributed the dubious credit for all the perceived ills of contemporary Western nations, including the relatively high rates of divorce, crime and unemployment; high levels of state social welfarism which allegedly undermines work ethics; the ruinous fiscal deficits which result from each successive government's over-extended attempts to satisfy welfare demands, to win electoral office (Chua 1992); all of which contribute to the decline of both the economy and social order.[14] A set of counter-values in the social body was initiated in the early 1980s by the PAP government to check the "insidious" penetration of liberal individualism and its attributed social consequences.

Initially, religious education in secondary schools, including Confucianism for Chinese students, was used as the vehicle to teach a counter-individualistic ideology. This was abandoned when it was discovered that such education heightened religious commitment and rigidified religious/racial divisions (Kuo et al. 1988).[15] Subsequently, an integration of selected elements of the so-called "traditional" values of Chinese, Indian and Islamic cultures was proposed and consecrated as the cultural essence of "Asia". The three traditions were radically distilled and reduced to the above-mentioned set of five shared values and appropriated by the state for the ideological reinscription of Singapore as an "Asian" society and Singaporeans as "Asians" (White Paper 1991, p. 1). There is a beguiling simplicity in the way these values are formulated. Against the West, Asia is privileged; against rights and entitlements of individuals are juxtaposed the interests of the "collective"; against individualism is pitched community and family. What emerges is a simple dichotomy of morally "good" Asian communitarianism against morally "decadent" Western liberal individualism.

The formulation of "Asian communitarianism" is a new threshold in the long and anxious process of a public discourse which has as its objective the containment of modernization within an "Eastern" context (Koh 1980). Its formulation, with apparent self-assuredness, is part of the self-confidence that has emerged in various Asian nations, including Singapore, as a result of the rise of capitalism. This self-confidence in turn incites the various arguments, promoted by both Asians and others, that the Asian cultural inheritance is the determinant of and explanation for the rise of Asian capitalism (Vogel 1979; Berger and Hsiao 1988). In the case of Singapore, the requisite cultural entailments of capitalism, discussed above as the active proletarianization of the population, are thus absorbed into a cultural discourse of Asian communitarianism. It thus follows that cultural continuity through the inscription of this communitarianism will be the best guarantee of continuing social cohesion and economic success in Singapore.[16]

This cultural discourse of Asianization is apparently being conducted without due consideration being given to what is now commonly known as the "new international division of labour", which denotes a different structuring of global capitalism resulting from changes in technologies of production and communication. These changes have led, since the 1960s, to a massive flow of Western capital into Asia in search of greater profit from lower labour costs. To tap into this capital flow, governments in the region have been actively organizing infrastructure development and transforming the attitude of their respective populations into disciplined workers, so as to facilitate rapid industrialization. These are necessary processes within the logic of long-term capital accumulation and may largely explain the rise of capital in Asia, which must, therefore, be taken into account alongside any cultural explanation.[17]

The "Asianization of Singaporeans" is an intentional discursive distillation and reformulation of vastly different traditions and their respective discontinuous histories into simple formulas of cultural continuity. It constitutes the current ideological conjuncture in the PAP government's attempt to "fill in" the absence of a defining or definitive national character for Singaporeans, which it hopes will ideologically homogenize the differences among the population and unify them as a "people" in the collective imaginary. Against the background of prolonged recessions in the North American and Western European economies and the concurrent rise of Asian capitalism, the discourse of "Asianization" has met with "intuitive" ideological resonance in segments of the population in Singapore.

Where is the Singaporean?

As discussed above, the whole trajectory of attempting to inscribe a Singaporean identity discloses the many difficulties that have been involved in the discursive or allegorical formation of a Singaporean "nation". This is a trajectory constituted simultaneously by processes of exclusion and invocation. Excluded from this identity construction are the cultural, social and political consequences of capitalist economic development, which, in aggregate, constitute the predominant part of the "culture of everyday life". Invoked are the figures of family, race (as community) and Asians, in which the idea of Singaporean, both as an adjective and as a noun, remains conspicuously absent.

It can be readily demonstrated that it is precisely what is excluded from the official narratives of the nation that constitutes the actual "shared" experiences of all who live in Singapore. The anxieties of living under the demands generated by a highly market-driven yet highly state-managed capitalist regime are, with few exceptions, the central concerns of all. Without irony, these anxieties are mixed with the measures of pride in being part of an incorruptible system which is efficacious in generating economic growth, in improving material consumption for all, in maintaining a clean and efficient city and, finally, in maintaining social stability and public security. This pride is reinforced by constant comparison with the "decadence", "chaos" and "irrationalities" that apparently surround this island of "rational planning". These comparisons are repeated in the speeches of national leaders, circulated widely by the national media, and in the popular sphere, directly "experienced" by Singaporeans in their travels.

Indeed, it is with these comparisons that a "Singaporean" differentiates himself/herself from Others. For example, Malays in Singapore distinguish themselves from Malays in Malaysia and Indonesia in terms of the level of economic development, the difference in the levels of corruption of public officials and — the most mundane of all comparisons — the level of public cleanliness in the neighbouring countries. Similar comparisons are made between Singapore and other nations, including China and India. Identity being an unavoidably relational concept, it is via these comparisons that a sense of being Singaporean, a Singaporean identity, is constructed. Comparisons with Chinese, Malays and Indians in their respective countries add to this identity building process, for the differences enable Singaporeans of Chinese, Malay and Indian background to distance themselves from whatever claims that their "lands of origin" may still make on them.

This distancing at the popular level is reflected also in the stance of the Singapore state in international relations and diplomacy. Recent examples of its assertion of difference and, subsequently, also of independence, include the government's insistence that the state-led investment drive in China is motivated entirely by the opportunities for profit, in which racial-affinity is but grease to the cause. Moreover, in the immediate aftermath of the Medan riots in May 1994, the Singapore Government chastized the People's Republic of China (PRC) for its comments on the racism of the rioters towards the ethnic Chinese in Indonesia. In distancing itself from the PRC and in defending the "domestic" realm of Indonesia, the Singapore state inserted its own claim to independence.

It should be abundantly clear that a Singaporean identity — of the nation and of its people — can be discursively constructed through the thematization of the modern. The Singaporean perception of the dedication, systematicity and efficiency of the PAP government and of the "success" of the collective effort in battling inauspicious conditions for the survival of the nation, pushing it to the pinnacle of Asian capitalist development behind only Japan, has reached "mythic" proportions. These are surely ideological resources for the construction of national myths.

Ironically, it is precisely because of the modernist features that Singapore politicians are being engaged internationally to provide a cultural explanation for the rise of capital in Asia. In such explanations, the PAP government chooses to either exclude or subsume these features into a cultural discourse which reinvents a particular version of "Asian" culture. This version reduces the complexities of the different cultures of Asia to a single dimension of "communitarianism".

From the point of view of the traditions invoked, such a reduction may be deemed a caricature of the cultures themselves; and hence, not acceptable. The question then arises as to why the latter strategy is preferred by the PAP government over that of projecting an identity of modern dimensions which, given the nature and strength of the development that has taken place in Singapore, would stand a greater chance of success than any invocation of "Asian" identity.

"Communitarianism" as a Formulation of the Future

Although the state-generated discourse on Singaporean identity claims to be derived from a "search" for the cultural roots of its constitutive population, the resultant formulation based on the institutionalized notion of shared values is aimed at "bringing back a future". This is not surprising because, as Chun (1994, p. 51) points out, nationalism as a search for new kinds of "bounded community" is always a project of the future. In the case of Singapore, this "future" is itself formulated by the government's understanding of modern democratic society and polity, read through the extant social problems of Western liberal democracies. Indeed, it is this desire to prevent the future development of liberal democracy in Singapore that motivated the search for a set of counter-values in the first place. The shared values are to be inscribed in the social body as measures to forestall the insidious penetration of liberal individualism. Given this motivation, the discursive connections to past traditions made for the shared values is but an alibi for the institutionalization of a blueprint for the future.

As such, the active inscription of communitarianism in the social body must be read as expressing a desire to develop the nation in a direction different from the industrial nations of Europe, North America and Australia, so as to avoid the perceived or actual excesses of liberal democracy and the social welfare state. It is this intentional channelling of future development away from liberal democracy that critics object to, as they see this in terms of "social engineering" and anti-liberal "authoritarianism" (Wong 1991; Rodan 1992). These charges are not without substance.

There is a tendency among politicians and a segment of intellectuals in Singapore to equate democracy with liberal democracy as practised in the United States. Seeing the latter as the only and unavoidable form of democratic polity, they have come to accept that communitarianism as national ethos is only possible under "soft authoritarianism" (Chan 1992). "Soft authoritarianism" is a narrowly defined political sphere with a formally, popularly elected majority government which concentrates power and centralizes all decision-making in the Cabinet and the civil service and which engages in stringent policing activities in areas such as religion, race relations and the arts through various censorship agencies, all in the name of protecting public interests. This view of the élite obviously lends substance to criticism of authoritarianism. It is a view that requires immediate political analysis, commentary and contestation.

To the extent that the actual practices of liberal democracy and extensive social welfarism have inflicted serious, if not excessive, social costs on those nations that embody them as dominant ideological and political forms, the PAP government's desire to avoid such costs is reasonable. Therefore, analytic and critical attention should be paid to the shape of the society and polity which has been envisaged in the recent discourses on "communitarianism" and "Asianization" in Singapore. Not to do so means to remain caught up in a debate about the nature of Asian culture that continues to be firmly planted on the ideological ground of essentialism.

Conclusion

Up till now, the Asianization of Singaporean identity has not displaced the entrenchment of multiracialism as a cultural policy, neither has it affected the unrelenting drive towards even greater capitalist economic development, which in the current conjuncture is embodied in the way the pursuit of "excellence" is promoted as a national ethos. The potential and actual disjunctures and contradictions between communitarianism, multiracialism, individualism and capitalism are likely to continue to co-exist for they may never be resolved. For example, given the intimate connection between capitalist economic growth and individualism, suppression of the latter has severe limits. Hence, the inscription of communitarianism in Singapore's population will always be partial. Such is the relative coherence of the ideological sphere that disjunctures and contradictions will be managed in an ad hoc fashion when the need arises. Issues of racial and national identity are strongly embedded in such a relatively coherent and self-adjusting system. Similar disjunctions and contradictions will be embraced by individuals, who will be reflexively and contextually Chinese, Malay or Indian; or perhaps Singaporean; or even Asian but, unavoidably, units of capitalist human resource. There is no formal solution.

It is precisely because there can be no possibility of a formal or permanent solution to these issues that Singaporeans, individually or in groups, may strategically appropriate for their own interests, or for their own contestatory purposes, as the case may be, the discursive contents of the attempts by the state to "realize" an identity on their behalf. Thus, for example, the initiation and celebration of racial/ cultural activities and racially-based self-help organizations have provided various opportunities for those who hold political aspirations of "community" leadership. On the other hand, as mentioned earlier, the cultural, social and political consequences of capitalist economic development constitute an alternative cultural resource for those others who choose to locate themselves in these spaces and even contest the state's attempt to either racialize or Asianize them, as in the case of certain civil society organizations.[18] Unfortunately, space limitation does not permit the analysis of the potential and actual strategies of individual Singaporeans to be taken up here.

Notes

1. As Foucault suggests, the term "reason of state" is now treated with conceptual and political suspicion and evokes "arbitrariness" or "violence"; yet, before this suspicion set in, the term referred equally to the "rational" basis, including rational knowledge of the art of governing a state (1990, pp. 74–755).
2. For a history of repression in the early years of the PAP regime, see Bloodworth (1986).
3. According to Foucault, the political rationality for the state has as its inevitable effects both individualization and totalization (1990, p. 85).
4. Substantively, it may be argued that the political experiences of the PAP leadership, during Singapore's brief membership in Malaysia, might have predisposed them to the course of multiracialism. This would be consistent with their championing of a "Malaysian Malaysia" in contrast

to the model of Malay dominance promoted by the United Malays National Organization (Siddique 1989, p. 572).

5. Only a brief statement will be made about language policy in Singapore because of space limitation. It is argued that in order to tap into global capitalism, the population must have facility in the English language, the language of international commerce, science and technology, repeating the universalizing theme. The overwhelming economic advantage of English effectively wiped out education in other languages. According to the government, the "natural" demise of community-based vernacular schools was made complete by the institutionalization of a national education system in 1987, with English as the primary medium of instruction and the languages of the different races as "second" languages.

6. Reflecting the policy of multiracialism, Mandarin in Singapore is known as the "language of the Chinese" (*huayu*), in contrast to being known as the "national language" (*guoyu*) in Taiwan, and "the common language" (*putonghua*) in the People's Republic of China.

7. It should be noted that the fixing of the "mother tongue" of a child is often a difficult issue. For example, a child with a Chinese father and an Indian mother is generally given Mandarin as his/her "mother tongue" language in school because of the patrilineal descent criterion in the fixing of one's race (see Purushotam 1989).

8. This political side-lining of race reaches a high-point in the intentional dispersion of the Malay population through a quota system in the allocation of public housing flats (Chua 1991).

9. Zoohri asserts, "the inescapable fact is that the Malays have found themselves trapped within a definite vicious cycle. The absence of the right education had made them incapable of associating themselves with modern trade and commerce. They, therefore, had to opt for occupations of low economic status. This inevitably made them poorer than the other communities. It is this vicious cycle syndrome that had entangled them for over a century" (1990, p. 9).

10. David Brown (1993) has read this process of the constitution of racial groups as equivalent to the government-sponsored formation of interest groups which can then be given proper operating space within the inclusive corporatist sphere of the PAP regime.

11. The White Paper on Shared Values was submitted and "accepted" by the Parliament on 2 January 1991.

12. It should be noted that even Mendaki, which was founded before the institutionalization of the shared values, was justified by the Prime Minister in terms of its potential contribution to the welfare of all Singaporeans. According to him, "If the money is seen to be in aid of

communal ends, then no party, governing on the basis of one man, one vote, will be in a position to go out of its way to give more to a group which says it is going to be more loyal to its ethnic ties than to Singapore society" (Goh Chok Tong, quoted in Zoohri 1990, p. 82).

13. The desire to forestall the cultural influence of the West has a history that dates back to the early days of nationhood when Western liberal culture was labelled as "yellow" culture (Hanna 1973).

14. Space limitation does not allow for detailed documentation of what the government considers as evidence of the negative consequences of rising individualism in Singapore. One of the most ideologically loaded is its formulation of rapid job changes among workers for higher wages within a very tight labour market as job-hopping, which is to be read as absence of company loyalty among the workers, whereas the same phenomenon among executive workers is deemed as seeking one's market worth (Chua and Kuo 1995).

15. For a detailed analysis of the experiment with inscription of Confucianism in the social body of Singapore, see Chua (1995) and Kuo (1992).

16. There is clearly intellectual affinity between the government's and the neo-conservative (Bell 1976) critique of Western liberalism. However, in the latter case, the critics are inclined to disengage the culture of advanced capitalism from its economic underpinning (Chua 1986); whereas in the case of the Singapore Government, the economy is reformulated and absorbed into a new set of cultural practices.

17. For a systematic account of these processes, see Harvey (1988). The cultural explanation is not without its dissidents in Singapore. One very notable instance is the changing of the Institute of East Asian Philosophy, which specialized in Confucianism because of an initial belief that this philosophy may account for Asian capitalist success (Tu 1991) into the Institute of East Asian Political Economy, under the executive chairmanship of Dr Goh Keng Swee, architect of Singapore's industrialization, after he had declared that Confucianism is an agrarian system of thought which has no relevance to industrial societies (Kuo 1992).

18. For an analysis of oppositional forces in Singapore, see Rodan (1996).

References

Althusser, Louis. "Ideology and the Ideological State Apparatus". In *Lenin and Philosophy*. London: Monthly Review Press, 1971.

Benjamin, Geoffrey. "The Cultural Logic of Singapore's Multiculturalism". In *Singapore in Transition*, edited by Riaz Hassan. Singapore: Oxford University Press, 1976.

Bell, Daniel. *The Cultural Contradictions of Capitalism*. New York: Basic Books, 1976.

Berger, Peter, and Michael Hsiao Hsin-Huang, eds. *In Search of An East Asian Development Model*. New Brunswick: Transaction Books, 1988.

Bloodworth, Dennis. *The Tiger and the Trojan Horse*. Singapore: Times International Press, 1986.

Brown, David. "The Corporatist Management of Ethnicity in Contemporary Singapore". In *Singapore Changes Guard,* edited by Garry Rodan. Melbourne: Longman Cheshire, 1993.

Chan Heng Chee. "Democracy, Human Rights and Social Justice: What Comes First?". *Straits Times*, 22 November 1992.

———. *A Sense of Independence: A Political Biography of David Marshall*. Singapore: Oxford University Press, 1984.

Chua Beng-Huat. "Reading Foucault as a Conservative". Working Papers No. 74. Department of Sociology, National University of Singapore, 1986.

———. "Not Depoliticized but Ideologically Successful: The Public Housing Programme in Singapore". *International Journal of Urban and Regional Research* 15 (1991): 24–41.

———. "Australian and Asian Perceptions of Human Rights". In *Australian Human Rights Diplomacy*, edited by Ian Russel, Peter Van Ness and Beng-Huat Chua. Canberra: Australian National University, 1992.

———. *Communitarian Ideology and Democratization in Singapore*. London: Routledge, 1995.

Chua Beng-Huat and Eddie C.Y. Kuo. "The Making of a New Nation: Cultural Construction and National Identity in Singapore". In *Communitarian Ideology and Democratization in Singapore*. London: Routledge, 1995.

Chun, Allen. "From Nationalism to Nationalizing: Cultural Imagination and State Formation in Postwar Taiwan". *Australian Journal of Chinese Affairs* 31 (1994): 49–69.

Clammer, John. *Singapore: Ideology, Society and Culture*. Singapore: Chopman Publishers, 1985.

Drysdale, John. *Singapore: Struggle for Success*. Singapore: Times Books International, 1984.

Foucault, Michel. *Michel Foucault: Politics, Philosophy, Culture*. London: Routledge, 1990.

Gellner, Ernest. *Nations and Nationalism*. Oxford: Basil Blackwell, 1983.

Goh, Keng Swee. "A Socialist Economy That Works". In *Socialism that Works*, edited by C.V. Devan Nair. Singapore: Federal Publications, 1976.

Hanna, Willard. "Culture, Yellow Culture, Counter-Culture and Poly-Culture in Culture-Poor Singapore". *American Universities Field Staff Report*, Southeast Asia series 21, no. 2 (1973).

Harvey, David. *The Condition of Postmodernity*. Oxford: Blackwell, 1988.

Kemeny, Jim. *Housing and Social Theory*. London: Routledge, 1992.

Koh, Tai Ann. "The Singapore Experience: Cultural Development in a Global Village". In *Southeast Asian Affairs 1980*. Singapore: Institute of Southeast Asian Studies, 1980.

Kuo, Eddie C.Y. "Language and Identity: The Case of the Chinese in Singapore". In *Chinese Culture and Mental Health*, edited by W. Tseng and D. Wu. New York: Academic Press, 1985.

———. "Confucianism as Political Discourse in Singapore: The Case of an Incomplete Revitalization Movement". Working Papers No. 113. Department of Sociology, National University of Singapore, 1992.

Kuo, Eddie C.Y., Jon Quah and Tong Chee Kiong. *Religion and Religious Revivalism in Singapore*. Singapore: Ministry of Community Development, 1988.

Lee, Kuan Yew. *The Battle for Merger*. Singapore: Ministry of Culture, 1962.

Offe, Claus. *Contradictions of the Welfare State*. Cambridge, Mass.: MIT Press, 1987.

Purushotam, Nirmala. "Language and Linguistic Policies". In *Management of Success: The Moulding of Modern Singapore*, edited by Sandhu and Wheatley. Singapore: Institute of Southeast Asian Studies, 1989.

Rodan, Garry. "Singapore Leadership in Transition: Erosion or Refinement of Authoritarian Rule?". *Bulletin of Concerned Asian Scholars* 24 (1992): 3–17.

———. "State-Society Relations and Political Opposition in Singapore". In *Political Oppositions in Industrializing Asia*, edited by Garry Rodan. London: Routledge, 1996.

Sandhu, Kernial S. and Paul Wheatley. *Management of Success: The Moulding of Modern Singapore*. Singapore: Institute of Southeast Asian Studies, 1989.

Siddique, Sharon. "Singaporean Identity". In *Management of Success: The Moulding of Modern Singapore*, edited by Sandhu and Wheatley. Singapore: Institute of Southeast Asian Studies, 1989.

Thumboo, Edwin. "Self-Images: Contexts for Transformation". In *Management of Success: The Moulding of Modern Singapore*, edited by Sandhu and Wheatley. Singapore: Institute of Southeast Asian Studies, 1989.

Tu, Wei-Ming. *The Triadic Chord: Confucian Ethics, Industrial East Asia and Max Weber*. Singapore: Institute of East Asian Philosophies, 1991.

Vogel, Ezra. *Japan as Number One: Lessons for America*. Cambridge, Mass.: Harvard University Press, 1979.

White Paper. *Shared Values*. Singapore: Singapore National Printers, 1991.

Wong, Loong. "Authoritarianism and Transition to Democracy in a Third World State". *Critical Sociology* 18 (1991): 77–101.

Yong, Mun Cheong. "Singapore: The City State in History". In *Imagining Singapore*, edited by Ban Kah Choon, Anne Pakir and Tong Chee Kiong. Singapore: Times Academic Press, 1992.

Zoohri, Wan Hussin. *The Singapore Malays: The Dilemma of Development*. Singapore: Singapore Malay Teachers Union, 1990.

chapter three

DISCIPLINING DIFFERENCE
Race in Singapore

NIRMALA PURUSHOTAM

Ethnic Names in Contemporary Singapore

The most commonsensically available ethnic names in Singapore that are applied to self and others are "Chinese", "Malay", "Indian", and "Other". These categories surface and simultaneously create, yet constrain social space in a multitude of ways. Every citizen of the island is required to carry around with him/her an identity card in which there is the entry "Race". The most commonly used, accepted, and recognized categories therein are Chinese/Malay/ Indian/Other (CMIO). The use of the word "race" itself deserves mention. Commonsensically, CMIO is perceived to arise from innate, biological differences between peoples.

On the eve of Singapore's nationhood, the political élite chose "multiracialism" as one of the tenets upon which the republic would be predicated upon. "Multiracialism" in turn rested upon the construction of the population as being constituted of four main racial categories: Chinese, Malay, Indian, Other. Correspondingly, "Race" is associated with a plethora of policies and regulations. Additionally, almost every government-organized national event highlights the existence of this CMIO. Pictorial depictions, even effigies of CMIO that was a highlight of the 1994 National Day Parade, further hammer home the message that the population of Singapore comprises four "racial" types. Standard elements in pictorial depictions are noteworthy also for the stereotyping that they more than hint at.

Thus, the Chinese are represented in yellow-ochre skin tones, with just a touch of pink that gives them a pleasant rosiness. The man will be dressed in trousers and a shirt, but the woman will be clothed in a cheongsam; her children have some varying items that are commonly identified as Chinese, such as the *guàzi mao*, a black Chinese skullcap with red tassels, and a false pigtail to boot. The Malays are always warmly browned, and dressed up in appropriate clothes, namely, in *baju kurong*, with *kain samping* around the waist and *songkok* on the heads of the males, and *slendang* hanging down one shoulder of the females. The Indians are given a richer, darker brown (closer to milk chocolate), with the woman invariably in a *sari* and with a *bindhi* between her eyebrows, the man quite often in a Sikh turban, and the girl child in a long silk skirt and the boy child in *salwaar khameez*. "Others" are one or two shades pinker than the Chinese, and dressed in what would be described, in everyday language, as formal Western dress.

In contrast to this caricature, most men, women and children in Singapore are attired in the latest fashions from Hong Kong garment factories, produced for the American and European markets. Most Indian men in Singapore are not turbaned, unless they are Sikh practitioners, and while many women still hang a cheongsam, *sari*, *sarong kebaya* or two in their wardrobe and also actually wear them on a daily basis, any casual observer would notice at once that for most women daily dress is not a marker of their ethnicities. Still, the caricature does reflect the reality of a fourfold category that encompasses even those who devise ways to try and escape from them.

The difference is not just a matter of surface presentations. A central feature of the 1994 National Day Parade was a dance of "Races in Harmony". In this dance, the audience witnessed a stream of dancers running into the vast stadium field in a variety of dress and symbols marking "Chinese" out from "Malay", "Indian" and "Eurasian" as "Other". Additionally, one of the prominent songs of the day, written precisely for events of national meaning, resounded from the National Choir who were joined by an enthusiastic crowd that packed every seat in the stadium. This song included the potentially loaded refrain, "Every creed and every race, Has its role and has its place".

In kindergarten, a private Montessori school even, my five-year-old son, who had by then learned that the diversity of his background gave him the privilege of being multicultural, was faced with a dissenting Mandarin language teacher. My son tried to argue that he was "multicultural" and that all humans were only of one race anyhow. But the teacher, who thought his arguments to be misunderstandings that arose from the complexities of his background, took pains to make him understand that he was "Indian", even if different from most other "standard Indians", as she put it. In relation to this, one of his assignments in Mandarin class involved him in the work of searching for appropriate pictures — that of a Chinese man in shirt and tie; a Malay woman in *sarong kebaya*; and an Indian man in turban. He carefully pasted these on separate sheets of paper, under which he wrote, in his newly learned Mandarin, "He is Chinese", "She is Malay" and "*I* am Indian", respectively. To my consternation, he also then explained to me, as his teacher had to him, that he *was* "Indian" really.

As an adult with more recourse to arguing against being typed, I find the attempts to reside outside the CMIO categories as barricaded as my son did. Almost all forms in Singapore, whether emanating from public or private offices, have an entry for "Race". I have always entered into the space so provided the category "Homo Sapiens Sapiens". Invariably, I have been asked to explain the term: when I try to insist that racially I belong to this one species I meet with either mirthless laughter or cold annoyance. My efforts are then scratched out and replaced by the term "Indian". Sometimes, however, I am not so easily identifiable: these are at those times in my life when I have had extremely short hair cuts, and dressed in "Western" clothes. At these times, there is some confusion whether I should be entered as "Indian" or "Eurasian". By this time, I merely submit to the answer expected of me, "Indian".

Face-to-face encounters that are not initiated by forms allow me more room to manoeuvre, but for a limited time and in a limited way. They usually run like this: "What are you?" (this is a fairly standard and common question that arises in daily life in Singapore). Most Singaporeans familiar with Singlish know that it is a question about your CMIO ethnicity. When I reply that I am a human being, I am usually met with laughter and the enjoinder "Aiyah, you know what I mean, lah". I have tried a variety of approaches to this: "Singaporean"; "my mother was born in Selangor", "my family is very mixed, even got Hokkien, Cantonese and Ukrainian". Thereafter, I will be subject to a cross-examination that I have yet to develop the skill to fence off. In this, inadvertently, I will refer to roots that reveal that I am also "Indian", but this is then translated to, "Oh, that means you are Indian, lah".

Where have these four names, that powerfully frame all of us in contemporary Singapore, come from? This question, as I shall show, reveals that orientalism as a colonial system of ongoing meanings still exists, albeit in new forms; and more significantly, in our work, so placing us in what might be perceived as neo-orientalism in our daily lives. For these four names are actually deeply rooted in our colonial past. Its applications by the present élite, its acceptance by most people at this time, involve us in some, even if limited, way to consenting to a neo-oriental rule of sorts.

My argument is that these names derive — although they are also reinforced and modified in different ways by other histories that were occurring simultaneously — from the orientalist concern to understand, catalogue and sometimes explicitly explain the "Other". A significant inheritance of the colonial period then is a system of ethnic names and procedures for their achievement that nationalist élites received and worked with. Often, there was little re-examination of the names they had inherited, even when those names were used upon themselves. I should stress that these ethnic names and even some of their meanings could have emerged from what existed prior to colonization. Colonization, however, brought with it immense changes. This included a policy of encouraging immigration into colonized lands. Furthermore, immigration in turn involved the creation of segregated socio-economic niches.

Certainly, the catalogue of names and related meanings were in most part removed from what was of primary significance and meaning to the people so named. They may have been real to the orientalist administrator, scholar and so forth, but in many ways they were rather peripheral and insignificant in the realities of those they were used upon. Yet these irrelevant practices by which "races" were created became and continue to be important aspects of government today. As Said notes:

> The methodological failures of Orientalism cannot be accounted for by saying that the *real* Orient is different from Orientalist portraits of it, or by saying that Orientalists are Westerners for the most part, they cannot be expected to have an inner sense of what the Orient is all about.... Despite its failures, its lamentable jargon, its scarcely concealed racism, its paper thin intellectual apparatus, Orientalism flourishes today... Indeed, there is... reason for alarm... its influence has spread to the "Orient" itself. (Edward Said 1979, p. 322)

Singapore in British Malaya

By 1819, the presence of the British Raj was well established in other parts of the globe, including the Indian sub-continent, the land mass that comprises modern China, and large parts of the Malayan peninsula and Penang island. Accordingly, the British had already recognized certain groups as being of particular relevance and interest to them. It is in relation to this that we have what is still a preferred history of the island: Raffles, it seems, landed on a piece of property whose value had not been understood and so left unexploited by its few inhabitants, who were primarily named as "Malay" and "fishermen".

One of Raffles' first formidable tasks then was to set about attracting inhabitants to his new site of interest. But he was not about to bring in just anyone: spaces were opened up for specific groups, who in turn reflected relevant British interests and orientations.

Raffles, following the rule established in those parts of British Malaya that were already colonized before 1819, recognized the Malays' inability to work in the at once British and modern economy — that is, from the perspective of the British, the Malays were laid back, or more bluntly, lazy. This evaluation derived from their uselessness as severely exploitable labour in tin-mines and rubber plantations. The perspective that the Malays would have found it rather irrational to give up self-owned farms and their relative independence in such work was, of course, inadmissible.[1] In any case, the near slavery conditions that the immigrants could withstand became proof of their inherent natures. Thus, the Chinese ability to withstand the arduous conditions of the tin-mines, run by unscrupulous Chinese managers, underscored their industriousness. The "Klings and other Southern Indians" (the earlier names that the British gave to what would later become condensed into "Indian") who came to tap rubber in the British plantations were receptive to arduously repetitive tasks because of their "docile" nature. The British with their superior intelligence were more innately suited to the all-important work of governing and administering the colony.

In the main, then, with Raffles' expropriation of the island of Singapore came increasing waves of people from various parts of the region and even the world at large, as I shall show. At one dimension, spaces were created, as noted above, for specific groups that the British meaningfully recognized by the shorthand terms "Chinese" and "South Indians". The former signified "industry and economic genius" and the latter the ability to "labour" (Vlieland 1932, p. 8).

The island's "real" population increasingly comprised a much more variegated lot: those already there, long before the arrival of the European colonialists; those for whom movement into regional centres was an established practice befitting the traditional social maps of the area; those who were members of a variety of ethnic groups that were shaded by the categories "Chinese" and "Indian"; those who had newly discovered the East as their colonies; and so forth.

Who of these highly variegated groups of people, with their multiple memberships, were selectively named? By whom were they named? What are the larger socio-historical significances of this, if any? As a corollary to this, what meanings did these names harbour, notionally and/or specifically?

The major source regarding official and élite naming practices are limited to census reports, from 1871 to 1957, pertinent to Singapore as part of the larger realm of British Malaya and/or the Straits Settlements.[2]

There are important reasons for using the censuses, although these are limited insofar as they present to us one realm in which social categories pertinent to naming differences and instituting exclusions were and are achieved. But the focus is on the dominant group's naming and related meaning-making practices. However, at any given time the dominant group is in a dialectical relationship with the others that it controls: to some extent who they name is negotiated, affected, and limited by realities other than those that the élite would like to construct. Unfortunately, as it happens in many historical documents, voices of the ordinary persons are generally stilled — dismissed as too average to be recorded until fairly recently. Even the few British persons who may have entered the discussion, and particularly those who may have resisted it, are quieted. The censuses are the voices of a few British in control of some aspects of life in Singapore at that time. Yet these latter, as I shall show, had to devise procedures to ensure that their ways of naming were the only real and realized ones, specially in relation to discourses they held among themselves as the ruling élite. In this respect, the British pre-figure the work of the present élite in re-producing CMIO *vis-à-vis* the details therein.

Distinguishing "Races": From Tacit Name Gathering Practices to Orientalist Deliberations on the Other

The work of distinguishing "races" in the censuses involved a number of tasks, which were interrelated to each other. These included the collection of "race" names by the population concerned, the screening of such names for authenticity as defined by the census administrator, and the related refinement of such names linked to the construction of the rationale for differentiation, and thus the production of "race" names as potent symbols.

Therefore, there were firstly the names that the census population used on themselves. In daily life experiences, who we are is a matter of common sense, unproblematic. As we move between a range of social worlds marked by varieties of people socioculturally different from us, we have to deal with the issue of "us" and "them" unproblematically enough so that daily life can proceed fairly smoothly. In this respect, ethnic names are an important device —

shorthand references, typifications that immediately assign a complex of meanings without the need to state onerous and specific items attached to them. Which names surface and are socialized in some measure is dependent on the context in which the names are used. The context of the census is, in this respect, very revealing.

First, the census schedule comprised a single sheet of paper measuring 19 inches by 21 inches, with columns for 17 different entries, of which "race" is one. Each person is strained into one line in the schedule. This contrasts with the vastness of ethnicity in the real world, where there are, to begin with, a much longer list of "race" names — for "Us" by "Us", for "Us" as given by "Them", for "Them" as given by "Us", and so forth. Furthermore, these different "race" names are tied to shifting contexts, and hence complex and with shifting meaning systems. In this way alone, the organization of the census form clearly enforces an immense degree of oversimplification. Certainly, one can understand that such a device was and is necessary to suit the enormous task of doing censuses. However, the issue here is that the simplified names with their simplified meanings assume a social significance which has serious implications and consequences for contemporary Singapore.

To compound matters, the administration of censuses ensured that some ethnic references were made more visible than others. First, census forms were administered by male enumerators,[3] who filled in the form with respect to each person in every household. A number of questions easily come to mind. What race names, for example, would thus be omitted? For instance, in the 1947 census, the census superintendent bemoaned the larger than expected number of entries for "Hailam" women. "Hailam" women, he maintained, were subject to onerous customary restrictions which made it difficult for them to migrate. Consequently, Hailam men in British Malaya tended to marry Cantonese or other women. When the husbands filled in their wives' "race", they named them as Hailamese rather than Cantonese.

Secondly, the British favoured the use of specific "races" as enumerators. High on their list were European managers of rubber plantations. They employed large numbers of "South Indian" migrants. Census administrators, as I shall elaborate later, always assumed the European managers' ability to distinguish their labour along "race" lines.

Straits Chinese enumerators appeared to have been favoured highly, where Europeans were not available. They were perceived as more educated and intelligent than the other non-White enumerators. Malay enumerators were also favoured, probably because of the widespread use of Malay as a bridge language among the various ethnic groups of the time. A number of germane, even if unanswerable, questions must be raised. How would a Malay enumerator, for example, enter the "race" of a person? What "race" name would be simply accepted/acceptable and so entered? What "race" name would be "corrected" by him, because the enumerator accepted his own version over that of the householder's response? Alternatively, how would a householder filling in the form himself/ herself name the "race" that he or another household member belonged to, *vis-à-vis* the enumerator he encountered? That is, would he or she use the name that is contextually relevant to, for example, naming "Us" in specific relationship to a Straits-born or Malay enumerator?

The case of "Bengalees and Other Natives of India" illustrates this point well. In the 1921 census, "Bengalees" and "Klings" were popular names for migrants from the North and South of India respectively. But these reflected names used on "Us" by those who were not "Indian". To "Us/Indians", "Bengalees" were from the Bengal Presidency. But to "Us/Indians" *when interacting with those "Them" who do not really know "Us/Indians"*, "Bengalees" referred to Indians from North India. Accordingly, as noted in the 1921 census for instance, Punjabis who would not refer to themselves as "Bengalees" when among other "Punjabis" especially, were inclined to do so when interacting outside strictly Punjabi networks and spaces. I should note, further, that within Punjabi networks and spaces, a more important mode of identification referred to village, caste, sub-caste and the like.

Thirdly, there are recorded instances of the hostility with which the Chinese viewed the census. For them, the census was but a tool of the British administrator who was engaged at that time to control and eliminate the Chinese secret societies that were prevalent then.

The Straits Chinese enumerators who were used to obtain census data were the same identifiable group used by the British as the necessary intermediaries via which the secret societies were policed. Given this scenario, what was the kind of information that the Chinese were willing to give, bearing in mind that the secret societies were importantly linked to ethnic identities?

The names that referred to "Chinese" were broken down into only two types in the first census: "Chinese" and "Cochin Chinese". In the next three censuses, "Chinese" was used as an umbrella category under which separate names were given, such as "Cantonese", "Hokkien", "Hailam", "Kheh", "Straits-born", and "Teochew" tribes. In the 1921 census, there were additions to the latter names: "Hokchiu", "Hokchia", "Hin Hoa", "Kwongsai" and Chinese from the "Northern Provinces" of Shanghai, Beijing, and so forth (Nathan 1921, pp. 77–85). By this time, procedures had been established by which these names could be identified. These procedures were devised because the British census superintendent had learnt, through previous censuses, that the entries for race in the case of the "Chinese" had to be double-checked if they were to be sophisticated enough. I shall examine the practices involved later.

Thus far, then, as a means of collecting information on what "races" there were in Singapore, the census, at one level, was affected by the use of select enumerators and householders and thus their meaningful interpretations of "race". These interpretations can be described as a tacit means of collecting race names for census purposes — that is, such names as were given by enumerators and/ or householders were the accepted entries in the census reports. In this way, naming the other involved a certain tacit reliance on common sense notions and related names. With time, as the censuses became documents to which others referred to, including especially other census superintendents, the tacit mode of giving "race" names gave way to more careful deliberations. Still, some characteristics of tacitness remained: deliberations centred on searching for those entries that were instituted because of the reliance on others, besides the "White races", particularly the British. Thus, the deliberations included a search for and use of experts. In relation to this, principles of organization began to emerge, namely, the device of the place and the device of language. Both devices are crucial in the explication of mother tongue ethnicities in contemporary Singapore.

To reiterate, common sense appears to have been the major mode of giving names in the census of 1871. Thus, with no commentary whatsoever, this first census unabashedly proclaimed the existence of the following "distinguishing races", named and ordered thus: Europeans, and Americans, Armenians, Jews, Eurasians, Abyssinians, Achinese, Africans, Andamanese, Arabs, Bengalis and other natives of India not particularized, Boyanese, Bugis, Burmese, Chinese, Cochin Chinese, Dyaks, Hindoos, Japanese, Javanese, Jaweepekans, Klings, Malays, Manilamen, Mantras, Parsees, Persians, Siamese, Singhalese, Military — British, Military — Indian, Prisoners — Local, and Prisoners — Transmarine.[4] The number of some of these mentioned groups was as small as one person, showing clearly that the list was not reflective of numerical presence alone. There was, at the same time, some attention given to numerical predominance; the population of the island at that time comprized "chiefly of Chinese, Malays, and Klings or immigrants from Southern India".[5]

Still, there were a number of apparent rules, designed by the census administrator, at work. Two main organizing principles appeared to have been used in ordering this list of "race" names. The first gave priority to occidentals and those closely associated with them, in descending order, reflecting perhaps the degree of closeness to the "real" source. Secondly, after these groups were named, the other names were arranged in order of the alphabet of the English language. In addition, the term "nationality" was restricted in use, to refer to the "European, American and Eurasian resident population in the Island"; while the word "races" clearly referred to "the native population".[6]

Ten years later, in the census of 1881, changes were introduced. Forty-seven peoples were distinguished in mostly alphabetical order; the alphabet being invoked after the Europeans and "races" closer to them were listed. These forty-seven types were reclassified in the preceding pages and tables under six main categories, referred to as "nationalities" and "other nationalities" — the first signifying the occidental, and the second signifying all others besides "Us".

These six categories were "European and Americans", "Eurasians", "Chinese", "Malays and Other Natives of the Archipelago", "Tamils and other natives of India", and "Other Nationalities". Once instituted this way, these six divisions were retained in this form for the following two censuses.

Furthermore, under all these categories, with the sole exception of "Eurasian", differentiations were made, which — in some instances at least — clearly signified distinct separateness between the different groups named under the same genera. These different names that were listed remained essentially similar to the list of the 1881 census.

Thus, nineteen classes were distinguished under "Europeans and Americans". They included Americans, Austrians, Belgians, British, Danes, Dutch, French, Germans, Greeks, Hungarians, Italians, Maltese, Norwegians, Poles, Russians, Romanians, Spanish, Swiss, and Turks. The only changes made after 1871 were the exclusion of Maltese, Portuguese and Romanians; and the substitution of "Spaniards" for "Spanish". In 1901, the Portuguese and Romanians were reinstated, and "Bohemians", "Canadians" and "Swedes" were added to the list.

The term "Chinese" was clarified as comprising "Cantonese", "Hokkien", "Hailam", "Kheh", "Straits-born" and "Teochews". There was also the sub-group "Tribe not stated". The usage of "tribe" underscores the perception of a special underlying connectivity among the Chinese, which I shall be referring to later. The 1891 census omitted "Tribe not stated"; but it resurfaced as an item in the 1901 census, to which "Hokchiu" was also added.

This connectivity among peoples from the same land mass was distinctly missing in the categorization of "Tamils and *other natives* of India", which replaced the older version of "Klings and other Southern Indians". In this respect, there was an expansion of the list relating to the land-mass of India. Four groups were now admitted: "Bengalis and etc.", "Burmese", "Parsees", and "Tamils". There were no changes in the next two censuses, except for the addition of "16th Madras Infantry" in 1901.

The term "Other Natives" was also a marker used in the category "Malays and Other Natives of the Archipelago", under which all the decennial censuses from 1881 listed the Achinese, Boyanese, Bugis, Dyaks, Javanese, Jawi Pekan, Malays, and Manilamen. No changes were made at all in the next two censuses.

In the category "Other Nationalities" there was a wide variety that included Africans, Annamese, Arabs, Armenians, Japanese, Jews, Persians, Siamese and Sinhalese. "Egyptian" was added in the next two censuses.

What is important is not the race names *per se*, but the "nationality" classifications under which they were listed. To reiterate, they were "Europeans and Americans", "Eurasians", "Malays and Other Natives of the Archipelago", and so forth. Ostensibly, these were in themselves "race" names: certainly they were at times referred to as such. There is an added dimension that should be clarified. This is that except for the category "Eurasian", which was never in any census deliberated upon and accordingly expanded, these classes arose from a particular reference to the globe. The world was cut up into a select number of blocs.

Thus, the different groups of "nationalities" and "other nationalities" sectioned the global map into identifiable areas: Europe and America; the Malayan Peninsula and the surrounding archipelago; mainland China; and the Indian subcontinent as a whole, incorporating also Burma. This first principle of organization, even if only implicit and possibly arising from the names that arrived in the filled-in census schedule form, was carried into the 1921 census. There was an apparently clearer sense of the notion of place that began to be developed from then on.

Before examining this further, I would like to reiterate that the race names under these six classes, and the six classes themselves, were mostly left unchanged throughout three censuses. But in 1921 there was a sudden rush of new peoples being identified that revealed that naming drew inspiration from searching for places within the territories previously identified. At the same time, in 1921 too, phrases such as "Malays and Other Natives of the Archipelago" were replaced by the less cumbersome "Malays". Yet the corresponding use of these titles to name races indicates that "Malays" was a short form of "Malays and Other Natives of the Archipelago". It is almost as if the longer names had been around for so long that they were recognizable in the shortened way. Thus, there was no need to expand upon what "everyone" understood in the term "Malay" — that is, its broad reference could be tacitly achieved. The new shortened forms were still six in number but renamed "Europeans", "Eurasians", "Malays", "Chinese", "Indians" and "Others" — they were certainly much closer to the ethnic categories used in Singapore today.

Searching for Races with Proper "Expertise": The Devices of Places, Languages and Essential Characters

That the six new classes under which different "races" are now sorted are reminiscent of the 1881 categories is clarified by the broader range and related increase in the number of identifiable races that the 1921 and 1931 censuses developed. "(N)ot one of these (six classes) is one race", notes J. E. Nathan, the superintendent of the 1921 census. Thus, there is a sudden expansion of race names: from an average of forty names in the previous censuses, the 1921 census identified fifty-six races, of which twenty-eight were in "numbers exceeding 1,000" (Nathan 1921, p. 70). C. A. Vlieland continued this expansion, boasting that his deliberations had enabled him to name "over seventy races" in the 1931 British Malayan census (Vlieland 1932, p. 69).

How did this expanded list develop? Searching through all the censuses, and examining the record of debates on "race" that are to be found only in the 1931 and 1947 censuses, I worked out four devices that were used to name "races". It should be stressed that these four devices were used fairly haphazardly, with different emphases at different periods, and for different groups, depending on the superintendents' "expertise" (inclinations).

Before naming these devices, I should first clarify that the word "race"

> is used in a peculiar sense ... is used, for lack of a more appropriate term, to cover a complex set of ideas of which race, in the strict or scientific sense, is only one small element. It would be of little use to the administrator or the merchant .... An attempt at classification by "nationality" or more exactly by national status or political allegiance would be almost equally open to controversy and of little, if any,

practical value. It is in fact, impossible to define the sense in which the term "Race" is used for census purposes; it is in reality, a judicious blend ... of the ideas of geography and ethnography, origin, political allegiance and racial and social affinities and sympathies" (Vlieland 1932, p. 73–74).

Del Tufo, who used the word "race" in like fashion, suggested that perhaps "community" was a better term, although even this was "not free from objection" (del Tufo 1949, p. 71). In sum, as both make clear with similar examples,

> "What is your race?" ... is ... of the same nature as ... "What is that man?" ... In such circumstances, we should be surprised, and possibly annoyed, to be told that a Madras Indian was British or Dravidian, when we wanted to know whether he was a Tamil or a Telegu .... (Vlieland 1932, p. 74).

> (W)e do not want an Englishman to describe himself as, say, Anglo Saxon: we want English; nor do we want a Tamil Brahmin to describe himself as an "Aryan" or a "Brahmin" ... And do not for instance enter "British" because this term describes one's national status, and ... such different peoples as natives of New Zealand, British India, or any Crown Colony" (del Tufo 1949, p. 71).

Thus, a close examination of the censuses shows an increasing if implicit reliance on, first, the six classifications as six blocs of places on a global map, highlighted by the particular conditions, that is, perceptions, values, concerns and such, of the world to the British in Malaya. Secondly, these blocs were clearly further subdivided into more specific places, within which varying conditions sharpened some aspects of these places *vis-à-vis* others. Their precise distinctions depended on which blocs of places were being examined.

Thirdly, there was the added dimension of distinguishing these places as origins of a racial group by the association of place with language: the dominant language in a particular place named a racial space. The primary place was, of course, British Malaya itself, in that it is the peoples that populated it who were the focus of attention in all the above places and spaces: but the naming of these peoples involved a search backwards in time, a search that focused on the named principles by which race became identifiable.

However, British Malaya as a place was also used as a differentiating principle in a highly specific way. Thus, fourthly, the economic and sometimes political spaces within which the differentiated population was located in British Malaya became the means by which essential characteristics were marked out, which in turn acted as further proof of the reason for making the distinctions.

The specifics of how the device of place, language and essential characters which rationalized the creation of racial categories in the censuses differed with respect to the idiosyncracies of each census superintendent. These variations were, moreover, tied to the availability of expertise on different peoples that the census superintendent assumed he had, as well as the experts that he consulted. Hence, the most crucial device, the use of "expert" knowledge, resulted in

> a series of attitudes and judgements... (which) send the Western mind, not first to Oriental sources for correction and verification but rather to other Orientalist works... (therefrom utilising and adding to) a common discourse, a praxis, a library, a set of received ideas, in short of doxology, common to everyone who entered the ranks." (Edward Said 1979, p. 121.)

I should note that an important aspect of using "real" knowledge included the development of procedures by which entries for "race" that were "not correct" were screened out. For, in the words of C. A. Vlieland, the superintendent of the 1931 census, "Oriental peoples have themselves no clear conception of race" (Vlieland 1932, p. 74).

Sources of Verification and Correction

The "Who's Who" list of acknowledged experts is revealing. J. E. Nathan, "Malayan Civil Service, Superintendent of the 1921 Census, British Malaya" was perhaps one of the first in the region — at least where censuses are concerned — to avail himself of the services of orientalist scholars of varying distinctions. Thus, this 1921 census superintendent availed of "Dr. R. O. Winstedt, D. Litt.", deemed to be an expert on the "aboriginal races" and "Chinese" and "Indians" in British Malaya; "Mr. A. M. Pountney, a Chinese scholar"; and a Mr. Shellabear's specialized knowledge on Malacca Babas and the

Baba Malays (Nathan 1921, p. vii). Apart from this, there were also documents such as "The Handbook of British Malaya, the introductory paragraphs of annual Administrative Reports, the Colonial Office List and other publications... written... from the point of view of the historian, the ethnographer and the philologist..." (Vlieland 1932, p. iv).

This later list was cited by the next census administrator. To this he added the expert advice of L. J. B. Turner, Director of Statistics, Ceylon; Professor J. Van Gelderen, Superintendent of Census for the Netherlands East Indies, to whom he was especially grateful for the consequent suspicion he harboured against certain groups of enumerators; and Mr. V. W. W. S. Purcell, M. C. S., Assistant Director of Education (Chinese). To top all this, there were the special credentials he himself brought to the task. For "C. A. Vlieland, M. C. S." was well skilled, by his admission, in "modern scientific geography" that, again by his reckoning, enables, among other things, a better understanding of "race" characteristics. Thus, for example, he explains that the term "Malays" refers to a people who live in a "marine-equatorial climate" — a term that better captures the geography of the region, compared to the terms "tropical" and "monsoonal". In such a climate, the impenetrable forest forces people to live along the coastal regions. Here nature provides them with a bounty that "disinclines" them to labour; one should note, however, that Vlieland graciously submits that this has led many to mistakenly perceive the Malays as lazy!

Vlieland was also the first to come up with a "Manual of Enumeration Procedure for District Assistant Superintendents". This was used up to the last census conducted in 1947, and was one of the few documents in British colonial offices that were not destroyed by the Japanese during the Occupation. (The Japanese found in these records the ideal paper with which to make cigars). "M. V. del Tufo, M. A. Cantab., Malayan Civil Service, Barrister-at-Law of the Inner Temple" cited this as "a discovery of great value" to himself as the 1947 census superintendent.

All these experts were students of the "Other"; there was no need to call upon experts on the Europeans nor the Eurasians. Additionally, most of these experts' knowledge was of the Chinese and Malay, but the fact of their expertise on one area was rather elastic. Pountney, the Chinese scholar, divided the peoples from Sumatra into groups that could be considered "Malays proper" and those that should be treated separately. He was also called upon to help in the classification of "Indians". Winstedt was grandly knowledgeable about aboriginal races, the Chinese and the Indians. Indeed, it did not take much to be an expert, as I have mentioned. Thus, the most important experts on the "Southern Indians" were European managers on rubber plantations, who from early on had "correctly" identified the "South Indians" as comprising Tamils, Telegus and Malayalis. Del Tufo was the only one of the census superintendents who realized in 1941 that he should prepare to learn more about the "Indian" category. To this end, he consulted "Mr. Y. M. Yates, ICS, Superintendent of the All India Census of 1940". But his work had to be postponed because of the Japanese Occupation of British Malaya. By 1946, political events in India signalled the weakness of the once invincible rule of the British Raj there, and this did not enable him to enforce the assistance of Yates. Nor did it enable him to obtain the census list of races in India. Del Tufo saw this as a disadvantage, but nevertheless assumed, again, that the knowledge of the "Southern Indians" as a race was sufficient from the European and other managers. Instead, he concentrated on expanding the list of races that comprised the "Northern Indian" component of "Indians", and noted his apparent satisfaction with the improvements he had done.

Searching for Places of Origin, Language Areas and Essential Characters

The experts' contribution to the racially different groups under each of the six classes, as noted, expanded the list contained within them. In the CMIO categorization that is in force today, the major headings condense differences, and even obliterate them. The major headings at that time, in British Malaya, were certainly not used in this way. The experts cited were consulted precisely to clarify these major headings. They were used, in effect, as references to places they had to "return" to, figuratively speaking, to legitimate whether particular persons belonged to this or that major racial group.

Clarifying "Europeans"

"Europeans", a shortened form of the older version "Europeans and Americans", guided the superintendents to countries within Europe and America. The European countries included Austria, Belgium, Great Britain, Holland, France, Germany, Greece, Hungary, Italy, Malta, Norway, Poland, Russia, Roumania, Spain, Switzerland, and Turkey. Sweden was added to this list in the following census and thereafter. More "races" were distinguished when Great Britain became subdivided further into Wales, Scotland, Ireland, Australia, New Zealand, Canada and, of course, England.

There was a recorded resistance from those who preferred the name "British" to these subdivisions. The superintendents, however, merely noted this as frustrating to them, and unlike the case with the other groups, did not furnish a list or use any procedure to enforce conformity. Indeed, the notion of resistance itself is interesting, for it implied that the entries were made wilfully and not out of ignorance. One superintendent remarked that the problem was that the British were too intelligent! Perhaps it was this assumption of intelligence that ensured that no mention of the need for or the lack of knowledge about the European peoples was ever made in the deliberations that marked the last three British censuses.

Clarifying "Malays"

With the Malay world, the focus of attention was on peninsular Malaya and the surrounding "Malay archipelago". The actual places within them that were named were the Malayan peninsula, Sumatra, Borneo, Bawean, and Celebes. There were two distinct ways of identifying places within this bloc, with a corresponding shift in the races that were thus considered distinguishable.

First, in 1921, Nathan considered peninsular Malaya and parts of Sumatra as associated places, separated from other parts of Sumatra as well as other islands in the archipelago. The connection was to be found in his glib statement that "Sumatra is originally the home of the Peninsular Malay". Accordingly, he used the term "Malays proper" to refer to the peoples of Malaya, whom he saw as originally coming from the island of Sumatra, and the peoples of select districts in Sumatra, namely, "Sumatran Malays" from Jambi, Kampar,

Siak, Menangkabau and Rawa. In this way, all the other "allied races" could be named. Thus, Java is the original home of the Javanese; Benjermassin, a district in the south of Borneo accorded the Banjarese their separate place, although it was noted that they had "long emigrated to Sumatra" (Nathan 1921, p. 75); Bawean Island as the original home indicated the Boyanese, as did Celebes of the Bugis. Achinese, Korinchi and Mendeling, albeit traced to Sumatra as their original home, were considered separately. The Achinese were described as having a language of their own, and being at war "for independence against the Dutch" (Ibid., p. 72). Korinchi were simply noted to "have characteristics peculiar to themselves" (Ibid., p. 72). No mention was made as to what made the Mendeling distinctive.

Secondly, Vlieland drew a separate conclusion. Indeed, he renamed the heading "Malays" as "Malaysia" (Vlieland 1932, p. 75). This signalled a different way of looking at the bloc from which the races that comprised it were named. This "Malaysia", then, constituted the Malay peninsula and the Indonesian archipelago. To some extent, his "modern scientific geographer" mind would not let him ignore that the Indonesian archipelago was the property of the Netherlands Indies Government (Ibid., p. 76). With this division, indigeny in the Malay peninsula, which he attributed to the aborigines, classified them as one racial class (Ibid., p. 75). Those who were born in British Malaya, but not originally from outside Malaysia, were "Malays". Thus, a Sumatran Malay who was born in British Malaya was Malay; but her or his parents, if they were born in Sumatra, were classified as "Malaysian" (Ibid., p. 76). All the others — namely, Javanese, Sumatrans, Boyanese, Banjarese and Bugis — were separated from the "Malays" and came under the common classification "Malaysians".

Thirdly, and coming after Vlieland, del Tufo (1947) reconstructed the heading as "Malays and Other Malaysians". He treats British Malaya as a major component *per se*: Malays then must incorporate all peoples "of the soil". In this respect, the reference "Malay" is considerably broadened. It re-incorporates the claim of 1921, in which "Malays" were perceived as "to a large extent, descended from the East Coast of Sumatra from whom (and particularly the Malays from Menangkabau, Jambi, Rhio, Siak and Kampar) they are ethnographically indistinguishable" (del Tufo 1949, p. 72). To this he added "aboriginal stocks" for their "affinity" with Malays, noting also that "settled aborigines" identified themselves as "Malay" (Ibid., p. 72). But the incorporation of British Malaya as part of the archipelago was clear in the term *"Other* Malaysians", who consisted of "Javanese", Boyanese", "Menangkabau", "Other Sumatran peoples" (for example, Batak, Lampongan, Nias, Banjarese and Bugis) (Ibid., p. 74).

Clarifying "Chinese"
Perhaps the most revealing case under the heading "Chinese" is the "tribe" "Straits-born", later renamed "Baba Chinese". The "Straits-born" appeared in all censuses from 1881 up to the 1921 census when they disappeared, possibly under the term "Hokkien". Based on the expertise of Shellabear, it was agreed that these distinct peoples were the result of a long association between China and the Malay Peninsula, dating as far back as the 1300s (Nathan 1921, p. 77). They comprised immigrants from Amoy, who married Malay women and made the peninsula their home. In this respect, they could well have been grouped under "Malay" or "Malaysian". Alternatively, they could have been incorporated under "Hokkien", as they appear to have been.

Three clear aspects for their presentation as a separate tribe clarify the way the factors of place and language enable a separate "race" to be named. First, the place of origin of the Baba Chinese was traced back to Amoy, despite the long years of settlement and cultural assimilation. Secondly, the lack of facility with Hokkien, and its replacement with "Baba Malay", described as "a wonderful pidgin", set them apart from other Hokkiens (Nathan 1921, p. 77). Thirdly, in contrast to all others in the category "Chinese", they stood out as "the best educated and wealthiest and most intelligent" (Ibid., p. 78).

China, as the place of origin, was broken down into specific provinces and districts, with specific reference to the Chinese population in British Malaya. This is not to say that the average "Chinese" was consulted as to who he really was. Indeed, the reverse was true. Over the years, there was an awareness that the Chinese, as has been mentioned, were not very co-operative with the census enumerators. Furthermore, there was concern about the enumerators' ignorance of the Chinese. Unlike the Indians on estate plantations that were largely run by Europeans, the Chinese were not in any setting where a similar group of supposedly responsible persons could be asked to clarify their distinctions.

The availability of experts, particularly Pountney, "the Chinese scholar", changed this considerably. With him came first the understanding that the word "tribe" was problematic, an understanding that further explains the reliance on language for naming a people as a separate race. Thus, via Pountney, Nathan set a pattern that was largely emulated by his successors. He noted the mistaken use of "dialects" for what were "principal languages" and the dialects of these languages. The uniting factor was the "one uniform character employed in writing" (Nathan 1921, p. 78). It is arguable that it is this conception of language, now reduced to uniform script, that led to the heading "tribe" for those listed under "Chinese". Pountney also made it clear that to ascertain the constituent tribes it was necessary to trace a migrant back to a particular province within China. In sum, Nathan devised:

> Two particulars connected with the question of race ... the translation of the Chinese headings being "What district or Protectorate man are you?" and "When you were young what language did you speak in your family?" to act as checks on each other ... (and) jointly supply all that was necessary for the proper subdivision of the local Chinese population into its constituent tribes (Nathan 1921, p. 78).

Armed with this information on province and district, and language, Nathan compiled a new list of "tribes" under the category "Chinese", one in which old groups remained, but new ones were "discovered". Thus, the list was expanded from Cantonese, Hokkien, Hailam, Kheh, Straits-born (now Baba Chinese), and Teochew. It now included Hokchiu, Hokchia, Hin Hoa, Kwongsai, and Chinese from Shanghai, Beijing, and the more northern parts of China (Nathan 1921, pp. 77–85). It should be noted that Vlieland compiled these names with the apparent omission of "Hin Hoa" and "Baba Chinese", and "Hakka (Kheh)",

> a list of tribes recognized for census purposes, written euphonically in Malay and in English and also in Chinese character.... Many Chinese

who cannot be said to be in any full sense literate, can recognise the written character denoting their "tribe" and the enumerator could often solve the difficulty of an individual's tribe by showing him the list, making him point to the characters representing his "tribe", and entering in the schedule the Malay or English equivalent written against it. (Vlieland 1932, p. 79).

This list was used again in the 1947 census, with the reincorporation of the Hin Hoa, now referred to as Henghwa.

A search through the recorded discussion pertinent to these names reveals, once again, the reference to places within China as a bloc, using languages and essential ideas about groups of persons drawn especially from the economic niche they occupied in British Malaya as the basis for dividing the "Chinese" in the manner just described. It should, however, be noted that del Tufo, writing, significantly, in the pre-war era, and at a time when the invincibility of the Empire was no longer taken-for-granted, bemoaned the essentialist notions that his predecessors had accepted unquestioningly. Thus, he wrote:

> It has been the fashion, since Mr. Nathan set it in 1921, to dilate upon the distribution of the several tribes throughout Malaya and the predilections and aptitudes for this way of life or that which largely determine their distribution. Quite apart, however, from the fact that the writer lays claim to no specialist knowledge of the Chinese he feels that it is pointless to dogmatise upon social and occupational habits, originally brought from China, which are in a process of constant modifications by long residence in Malaya and ...which... owe much to the accidents of history.... (del Tufo 1949, p. 297).

Even so, del Tufo went on to make statements about the occupational preferences of the different Chinese "tribes" in ways reminiscent of his predecessors. In any case, the list that had been compiled was used by superintendents who were not afraid of their dogmatic notions.

Hokkien and Cantonese applied "in local usage" to inhabitants of "certain areas only" of Kwangtung, Fukkien (Hokkien), and Kwongsai Provinces. "Strictly" everyone from these three areas should have been named "Hokkien" or "Cantonese" (Vlieland 1932, p. 78).

Khehs or Hakkas were not traceable to any one part of these different provinces but were rather distributed over several of them: in any case, they are "a race apart", with "their own language and characteristics" (Vlieland 1932, p. 78). These Roman Catholic planters (Nathan 1921, p. 80), "the most rural inclined of all the tribes" were dominant, together with the Cantonese, in tin-mining (del Tufo 1949, p. 78).

The Cantonese were admired for their greater versatility: they could participate in agriculture, urban life and tin-mining. There was in fact a "predilection, if they have one, for mining" (Vlieland 1932, p. 80; and del Tufo 1949, p. 76). Cantonese women were singled out for the observation that the percentage of women in this tribe was "considerably higher than that of any other Chinese tribe, (which) is due in some measure to the fact that practically all the Chinese prostitutes are Cantonese" (Nathan 1921, p. 80).

The Hailamese were from the island of Hainan, which is part of the province of Kwangtung, but their language was "very different" from the Cantonese and their "characteristics" set them apart (Vlieland 1932, p. 78). They were mainly engaged as domestic servants, particularly in European households, or engaged in shopkeeping, when they lived in the towns (Nathan 1921, p. 84; and del Tufo 1949, p. 77).

The Hokchiu, Hokchia and Hin Hoa (later Henghwa) were really "branches of Hokkiens" (Nathan 1921, p. 79). However, the Hokchiu were specifically associated with Fuchow, the capital of Fukien, and the Hin Hoa were from the districts of Fukien (Vlieland 1932, p. 78). The Hokkien *per se* were also from Fukien. The separation could have been in terms of specific places of origin within China and the different occupational niches.

It was noted that the Hokchiu and Hokchia were rickshaw-pullers (Nathan 1921, p. 78) while the Hokkien in the towns were shopkeepers and traders (Ibid., p. 79; and Vlieland 1932, p. 80) — indeed they had a "genius for trade and shopkeeping" (del Tufo 1949, p. 76). The Hokkien were also considered to have a "tendency to permanent settlement", as the case of "Baba ... originally of Hokkien extraction" evidences (Vlieland 1932, p. 80).

The Kwongsai were distinguished in terms of place, having come from the province between Canton and Yunnan (Nathan 1921,

p. 84). The Chinese from the Northern Province were also placed by location of origin, as understood in these censuses: they were described as being chiefly tailors, washermen, dealers in silks and skins (Nathan 1921, p. 85).

Clarifying "Indians"

> The correct division of the Indian population into its constituent races is, as it has been on previous occasions, a matter of no little difficulty. This appears to be mainly because the racial divisions are not understood locally. To the average Malay or Chinese enumerators then, every person of Indian nationality falls into one of two classes, Kling or Bengali (Nathan 1921, p. 85).

Nathan's lament underlines a lack of scholars whose expertise on "Indians" could be called upon. Certainly, Pountney provided some assistance, as did Winstedt, but these men were described as experts on Chinese, and on Chinese and Indians in British Malaya, respectively. In this case, however, to name a race involved tracing the peoples back to British India. Unlike the Chinese situation, where references to protectorates could and were made, the references to British India did not correspond to the map that the British had in mind. As colonial rulers, the latter's map referred to names they had compiled for the land-mass they were ruling. Thus, as Vlieland (1932, p. 84) said,

> It is of little use to instruct an English-speaking enumerator to ask an Indian what "Province" he comes from or instruct a Malay enumerator to enter "Madras, Panjab dan sa bagai nya" (Madras, Punjab, and etc.) in the birthplace and "bangsa" (race) in the race column. As to the birthplace, the result of asking (say) an Indian from the United Provinces where he was born is highly unlikely to be the appearance in the schedule of a recognisable equivalent of "United Provinces". The entry may be a village name, a district name or an actual error, but is still more likely to be an unrecognisable jumble of Roman or Arabic letters, which constitute the enumerator's attempt at representation of a half caught wholly unfamiliar sound. As to race, most Asiatics in Malaya, and certainly the vast majority of those available as enumerators, only recognise two classes of Indians — i.e. "Klings" or Southern Indians of whom the Tamil is taken as a type, and "Bengalis" including all

others. This, in spite of the fact that the Bengali proper is rare in Malaya, and there seems no good reason for classing (say) natives of Calcutta with Punjabis who are numerous in Malaya, and differ markedly in appearance and characteristics from the true Bengali. Even a native of the United Provinces, an Afghan or a Punjabi, if he has been any length of time in Malaya, is as likely as not to describe himself as a "Bengali" in speaking to a Malay enumerator; if on the other hand, he tries to give us what we want, the enumerator will generally write down, in despair, something quite unintelligible, or fall back on the one term he knows — i.e. "Bengali". (Vlieland 1932, p. 84.)

Thus, the lack of access to a place-name within the bloc constituted by the subcontinent of India created a problem that was difficult to overcome. There was an apparent reference to places as markets used by the Indians themselves; but such places did not fit in with the map of British India — they were thus not "what we want". It will be recalled that, to get what they wanted in the Chinese case, the question "what Protectorate man are you" was devised. This was tied to a list that involved euphonic sounds in Malay and English; and in characters distinguishable to the Chinese. This was simplified by the uniform script that the Chinese, regardless of language, used. The "Indian" case was not so easily resolved. What kind of list could be developed that could be used by the Malay or Chinese enumerator for the "Indians"? The former recognized only two main names, and the latter spoke languages that did not involve a common script. Most of all, there was a lack of real expertise, from among the White races, which compounded the problem.

The lack of expertise meant that the only procedure used to elicit a correct answer was the general statement, "Enter the province of birth of natives of India". There was also the instruction, "Enter the race as English, French, Tamil, etc." (Vlieland 1932, p. 83). These instructions were issued in the 1921 census. Consequently, the following race names emerged: Tamil, Telegu, Malayalee (also collectively referred to as "South Indian"); Punjabi (Sikh and Other Punjabi); Bengali; Hindustani, referred to as "a somewhat vague term"; Pathan, Gujerati, Maharatta, Burmese, and Gurkha.

The correlation assumed to exist between the White races and their knowledge of other races is markedly clear in the ease with which the problem was solved for the whole of South India. Thus, from 1921 the "kindred races" from South India were named as "Tamil", "Telegu" and "Malayalee". This compilation of race names was based on the confidence given to "(European) managers of estates who could generally be relied upon to classify them satisfactorily" (Vlieland 1932, p. 83).[7]

Indeed, so definite was the legitimacy given to their knowledge that no effort was made to question these race names in subsequent censuses. This was so even when the geographer in Vlieland enabled him to further differentiate according to place. Thus, Vlieland was the only superintendent to see the place "South India" as having more than racial space within it. Tamils were Madrasis, signalling here the Madras presidency. Telegus "originally came from the hill country of the Eastern Ghats", Malayalee were located in their "racial home ... the Western or Malabar coast" (Vlieland 1932, pp. 82–86). Vlieland also pointed out that immigrants from Coorg, Mysore and Travancore were variously classified as Tamil, Telegu and Malayalee. But, as with Nathan, the trust in the enumerators involved in entering these races in the schedule and, the recognition given to South India as a more relevant place of focus, ensured that this use of the three races to name all South Indians was "tolerably (acceptable)" (Ibid., p. 82).

The problem was with the Indians from the north. How were they to be racially identified when the people themselves made errors in giving proper answers? To compound matters, there was the problem of the ignorance of enumerators who failed to record those proper answers that may have appeared. Certainly, Nathan's device clarified important differences that should be identified. However, the basis for division was not clear enough. Places and spaces were still too vague, still traced through the voices of enumerators and the people themselves without the intervention of proper expertise.

Vlieland's answer was, as in the Chinese case, to devise two particular questions that he believed would provide him with proper place names from which his work could proceed:

Now while it is useless to question the average northern Indian in English as to his "race" or the "State", "Province", "Presidency" or

"District" in which he was born, or in Malay by any of the nearest equivalents of these terms (many of which are not in common use) there are two words which are easily mastered by either a Malay or English speaking enumerator, and have a definite meaning for the average northern Indian — they are "*Zillah*" (approximately = district) and "*Suba*" (approximately = Province). If we could get these data regarding each individual with certainty, a sound classification could be produced (Vlieland 1932, p. 84).

Unlike the Chinese case, Vlieland found it too difficult to construct a list that the enumerators could use — a list by which a point of the finger could provide the right answer with little room for mistakes either by the householder or the enumerator. The Chinese case involved one script; the Indian case involved just too many "various vernaculars" (Vlieland 1932, p. 84).

Thus, there was still need for expertise — the "invaluable" advice and assistance of the Inspector General of Police of the Straits Settlements, the police force being one major niche towards which some North Indians gravitated. To this, Vlieland added his geographical map of North India. Hence, the name "Punjab, etc." which identified Northwest India as an area within which were located the Punjab, Afghanistan, Kashmir, the Northwest Frontier Province and Baluchistan; "United Provinces" which identified people from there; "Burmese" which maintained the distinctiveness of people from the whole of Burma; "Bengal, etc." which named the people originating from Eastern Bengal and Assam; "Bombay, etc." which included people from Sind, Bihar and Orissa; "Nepal" which named the "Nepalese"; while the rest were neatly swept into the practical "Other and Unidentified" (Vlieland 1932, p. 83).

Language was clearly not used as a marker to differentiate those races under the category "Indian". Vlieland especially, but also his predecessor, legitimated the different groups in this category with reference to the distinct economic niches which they occupied in British Malaya.

The Tamils, Telegus and Malayalees were seen as originating from the "great Tamil emigration port — Negapatam (Negapatnam)" (Nathan 1921, p. 87). The majority of these peoples worked in rubber estates, and the labour for this was importantly supplied by "the chief Tamil recruiting centers in Madras" (Nathan 1921, p. 88). Vlieland also acknowledged that their presence in Singapore at the time of the 1931 census was due to the demand for labour in the construction of the Naval Base and general municipal and development work (Vlieland 1932, p. 86).

For Nathan (1921, p. 89), the Punjabis and Sikhs were recognized as occupying military and semi-military jobs, as well as agricultural work, and bullock cart driving. The Bengalis were seen to be employed as clerks, artisans and shopkeepers; the Pathans were seen to be watchmen, bullock cart drivers, or in the police force. There was no word on the occupational niches of the Maharattas, Burmese and Gurkhas.

Vlieland (1932, p. 86) appears to have used the same economic spaces but rearranged them. "North Westerners", who included the Punjabis and Sikhs of Nathan's class, were seen to form a "considerable proportion in the Police Forces. Apart from this they were also extensively employed as watchmen". The group also tended to combine money lending with their other pursuits. The "principal avocation" of peoples listed as "United Provinces" was "milk selling and dealing in bread and other foodstuffs" (Vlieland 1932, p. 86). The "Burmese", he clarified, made up an entire regiment in Taiping.

Despite Vlieland's recorded satisfaction with the new list of groups identified under "Indians", del Tufo was appalled by what he saw as a purely geographical mode of making up this list. His basis for contention in this respect was the use of yet another expert, Mr. M. W. Yates, ICS, Superintendent of the All India Census of 1940.

Yates had devised "lists of *zillahs* and *riasats* as well as principal communities known to emigrate to Malaya". These lists were "printed in phonetic English and Malay as well as in the vernacular script in commonest use in the locality from which each group came... in much the same ways as the lists of Chinese tribes". Del Tufo was confident that with this list he could "secure a reasonably precise classification of Indian race-groups and a more ambitious classification of Indian birthplaces" (del Tufo 1949, p. 77). But del Tufo had to relinquish his plans as events of 1940 quickly overtook him. By 1942 the Japanese had occupied British Malaya. He returned to his work on the census in 1947, after the war. The political events in post-war British India forced him to rely on his own knowledge, "which concerning all but the Southern Indians is trivial" (del Tufo 1949, p. 77).

Again, the assumption of the superiority and sufficiency of knowledge of the South Indians compared to that of the North Indians ensured that only the latter group was screened. But del Tufo poured scorn on Vlieland's presumption of expertise. His predecessor, as was just noted, had placed a great deal of satisfaction in the use of the terms *zillah* and *suba*, albeit without actual lists of these. Accordingly, he claimed that he had got more important information by which the North Indians were duly differentiated. Del Tufo insisted that Vlieland's knowledge was worthless. It did not make such a list available. He was also particularly unimpressed by the collections of peoples and related names such as "United Provinces", which merely reduced race/community to geography.

He preferred the expertise of Nathan instead, and reverting to the earlier census, drafted a list "of principal communities (that) was given to enumerators who were directed to ascertain which of them the person enumerated belonged" (del Tofu 1949, p. 77). This list

> as re-drafted originally comprised Bengalis, Dogras, Gujeratis, Maharattis, Marwaris, Parsis, Pathans, Punjabis, Rajputs, Sindhis, and "Other Northern Indians", but at a later date Dogras, whose numbers here are in any case very small, were replaced by the Sikhs.... (del Tufo 1949, p. 77)

Yet the period after the Japanese Occupation of Singapore was a crucial time in British Malayan history. During the Occupation, the Japanese had ruled the country harshly. What kinds of communities and related identities and affiliations were forged? Additionally, the harsh treatment of the Chinese was particularly remembered and recorded, in part because of the long-standing enmity between China and Japan.

At the same time, the invincibility of the British Raj in India was clearly shaken, to say the least. Events in India, shaped by the aftermath of colonialism, were the context for newly emergent ethnic identities and affiliations. Indeed, del Tufo was furnished with ample proof of this in many of the entries in which the enumerated, as he called them, failed to order their entries against the list he had supplied. In its place were entries such as "Indian", "Pakistani" and "Dravidian" (del Tufo 1949, pp. 78–79). For del Tufo, these were a bother, a failure even, as they had to be swept under the cover of "Other and Indeterminate" when they should have fitted in neatly with his so painstakingly worked out orientalist scheme.

The Disciplinary Potency of Race Names

By now it should be clear that two sets of race names had been created. First, each of the six categories provided the means by which an expanded list of race names was drawn. In this respect, especially in comparison with the CMIO of today, they comprised elaborated race names. It must be stressed, however, that these names were themselves selected and narrowed ethnicities. Each person was assigned one racial name. This ignored the multiplicity of identities and affiliations a single person could have in a plural society, even in the course of a single day.

Secondly, this first list was, as shown, drawn up according to six names that mainly identified blocs of places on a global map. These six place names were also used as highly condensed race names.

Thus, "Malays", "Buginese", "Baweanese" and so forth signalled different races, distinct from each other. Their grouping under "Malays" potentially homogenized them. In this homogenization, they all shared place and space within the bloc "Peninsular Malaya and the surrounding archipelago". Simultaneously, the "Malays" as a particular race comprised the numerical bulk in this group. Solely on the basis of size, the word "Malays" became the condensed race name for all the others from this area of the world.

In the case of the "Chinese", the elaborated race names signified differences between them. Again, "Chinese" was used as a means to homogenize all the variants therein. In this respect, too, the bloc "China" is the unifying term. The essential character draws from the Hokkien genius for trade and shopkeeping, now extended to "Chinese" generally. The language factor added strength to the valid use of the highly condensed name of "Chinese". Different languages, even when recognized as such, retain the notion of being different dialects — a notion that draws strength from a common recognizable script. This quality of the language is not at all like "our" understanding of languages.

In addition, the reality of ethnic tensions and conflicts between Hokkiens, Cantonese, and so forth had been recognized as disastrous for political disciplining. Since the 1900s, reform and revolutionary movements in China had worked to construct similarities by which the differences could be effaced or at least attenuated. Yet at the ground level these differences were crucial: the first racial riots in Singapore were precisely riots between the various "Chinese tribes". Allegiance to "Chinese" as an identity was particularly valuable as a means of constructing a political base. Politicians like Sun Yat Sen understood that their distinct differences could reduce the kind of mass support they could otherwise work towards, without which, in Sun Yat Sen's case for instance, the support would be fragmented to merely a Cantonese base. Lee Kuan Yew's Hokkien/Baba Chinese background, added to his Western-educated background, would have reduced his base considerably if the "Chinese" distinctions were played up over and above the condensed and unifying version of "Chinese".

Concerning the "Indians", despite this condensed name, a strain is evinced and retained till today. Marked by Britain's own social map of India, even the condensed version of "Indian" marked a large labouring pool of South Indians from a smaller, especially prominent by its presence as policing assistants to the British in Malaya, pool of army personnel and policemen from North India. This division marked the Indian subcontinent as almost two distinctive places of origin.

Of the two sets of race names, the more condensed list is mostly used today. At this point, a short summary of the arguments in relation to their further development would be useful.

It should be clear by now that race names are special categories designed from the perspective of an élite "Us" to differentiate, analyse and compare "the Others" with the Western self, and "the Others" among themselves. In this way, race names tame everyday life ethnicities. In everyday life usage, ethnicities — identities and affiliations that claim their bases in primodialities — can be multiple, fluid social phenomena. They partition but do not enclose as rigidly as race names attempt to do. Race names are thus an "apparatus of knowledge" (Foucault 1979, p. 126), applied to multiple identities. Consequently, the multiplicity is ranked and/or erased. The ranked ethnic identities are enclosed into a single class, with their fluid meanings condensed into specific items and sharper details that enhance disciplinary work through them. "Discipline", as Foucault states, "is a political anatomy of detail" (1979, p. 139).

With respect to this, let us now examine the disciplinary potency of the condensed race names that continue from the details they present/specify, namely, the detail of "origin"; the detail of "contribution"; the detail of "essential characteristics" (which co-exist with the vagueness of customary differences); and the detail of language. These details are imbued with meanings, which are important because of "the hold (they) provide for the power that wishes to seize it" (Foucault 1979, p. 140).

The Detail of Origin

"Origin" simultaneously locates peoples in blocs and places within these blocs. By this detail, the population of British Malaya was subdivided into those whose home was originally here and those who came as sojourners or permanent settlers. As British Malaya was a place located in the bloc "Malayan Peninsula and the archipelago", two original peoples were nameable:

First, if the peninsula proper was used as the place of origin, then the only original people were the "aboriginal races". If the peninsula was treated within the bloc it was located in, the "original people" included immigrants from selected districts of Sumatra, or the (Sumatran) Malays, with the all important bracket around Sumatra. Permanent settlers were "of the soil" in this way only by way of their origin from at least within the bloc, as the globe was divided according to British interests.

Origin did not, however, signify rightful occupation of all spaces within British Malaya. Correspondent to the detail of origin was the notion of "indigenous spaces". Aborigines were enclosed within the forested interiors of the peninsula proper, while Malays were placed along the coastal and riverine regions, where they fished and planted rice for their consumption.

In this way, the map of the area left a great variety of un-occupied spaces — imaginary and physically real. European, or British, appropriation of place did not displace. Indigenous peoples had their indigenous spaces. The British penetrated virginal spaces and en-hanced their meaningfulness and value by their superior foresight and administrative skill. Conversely, indigenous peoples did not have the requisite qualities to enable optimal use of a place.

The Detail of Contribution

Optimal use of British Malaya required the rule of the superior White races. These Whites, mainly men, were epitomized in individuals like Stamford Raffles: with imagination and courage they harnessed superior knowledge and reconstructed dormant places into vibrant spaces. Thus, in contemporary Singapore, Raffles remains a figure not of a colonial past that we would critique, but a man to whom we owe our present circumstances.

The vision of the British, however, required the labour of those who could be so yoked. Again, race provided the means. Chinese and Indians, arriving from very difference blocs of origin, opened up new, useful spaces: they developed, they modernized; in a word, they were economically productive. Of the two, the Chinese were singled out as exceptional in their contribution. In part, the Indian contribution was seen as enclosed in the rubber plantations that lay outside the domain of Singapore *per se*. Furthermore, while their labour was acknowledged, the British admiration for the Chinese focused on the trading activities of the Hokkiens in particular. The condensed "Chinese" race name thus obliterated not only differ-ences within the groups that constituted it. At the same time, the different races were ranked in a fairly clear order of contribution: the Chinese were way ahead of the others, particularly the Malay peasant who was seen as not really having laboured, given the bounty of a "marine-equatorial" climate.

The notions pertinent to "origin" and "contribution" present different legitimations concerning the presence of different peoples in different spaces — legitimations that must be renegotiated as the larger historical context shifts British Malaya as colonial property to a nationalist place. But to whom should the colonial property be transferred?

The Tension Between "Origin" and "Contribution"

In nationalism, "origin" is used to reclaim spaces that are seen to have been wrongfully appropriated, rightfully owned by an indigenous "Us". Where the British once harnessed a place in which indigenous spaces continued beside the new spaces they developed, these new spaces are now seen as exploitative, of having denuded and appropriated indigenous spaces. The myth of "contribution" is laid bare. But a twofold orientation arises. The British are clearly distinguished as the appropriators and must be sent home. The non-European races, particularly those condensed as "Chinese" and "Indian", were not so easily replaced in their original countries. At one level, there is the commonality of being yoked to the Occident. At another level, there is the experience of the Japanese Occupation of Singapore, through which a sense of community may well have been forged. This needs further exploration.

In sum, while the British were relatively easily displaced out of the emerging nation, and would in time become placed with the "Others", the Chinese and Indians, and in the Singapore context, the Chinese in particular, posed a problem, precisely because they received notions of "Us" and "Them", and, relatedly, "origin" and "contribution".

The tension then between the right to space via origin and the right to space via contribution is a tension couched in racial terms, even if implicitly. Contribution relates to work that only the "outsiders" did to begin the process of development and modernization. This work is given new lease in the very items that arise in the conceptualization of "nation" in third-wave nationalising countries. Thus, nationalism buys into the image of the "Other" as requiring modernization for a modern economy. The "Other" stares at itself via a borrowed mirror.

In this borrowed mirror, two spaces are imagined: indigenous/traditional spaces within which are prominently located the original peoples of the place; and useful/modernized spaces, within which are the immigrant populations, namely, the "Chinese".

A word about origin and immigrant is necessary. The "Baba Chinese" and "Jawi Pekan" afford a glimpse into the negotiability of origin. Their homeland certainly is Malaya itself. The perpetuation of these communities required in-migration. Back in China and India, these communities could fairly easily have been swallowed up and re-assimilated, or re-asserted themselves, for instance, as a Hokkien community and a Tamil community, respectively. The strict and enclosed meaning given to origin denies tracing place and space in terms of actual birth-place. Thus, in my terms, my birth-place, my homeland, my origins are Singapore. The procedures by which I am racially classified, even today, trace my origins to India. In all seriousness, it could of course go beyond time and place. It has me locked to one single place in a map designed in colonial times. In an important sense, this ensures my status as a sojourner: there is the potential uneasiness as to where home really is. In this respect, the door to emigration from Singapore is always left open to some extent among sufficient numbers of Singaporeans to cause governmental concern.

This uneasiness also perpetuates an uneasy alliance with place, despite the long generational presence of the various "races" in Singapore. This is clarified in a number of instances, not least of which is the rewriting of Singapore history by which the myth that Raffles landed on a sparse island, waiting to be occupied, is perpetuated. So is the need to retain the invisibility of the contribution of the Malay peasant to the region's economy even at the time of British rule. Additionally, there is the maintenance of the notion of the Malay in Singapore, particularly as an immigrant, including immigrants from the Peninsula, thus divorcing the historical links by which Singapore is inextricably tied to the land north of it. Simultaneously, indigeny among Malays, which remains difficult to erase completely, is associated with their long-standing place in the Peninsula and on the island (remembering the few fishermen Raffles found here in 1819). Accordingly, much work has been done to establish that the Chinese have had as long-standing a presence in the island: the artifacts that archaeological work in Fort Canning has thrown up have been used as proof of this.

Thus, instead of redrafting the question of who "We" are in our terms, we have stayed too close to significant items in the orientalist texts. This perpetuates a tension that must be disciplined. If origin remains an issue of legitimation, however implicitly, then contribution must be given as much, if not greater, legitimation than ever before. At the same time, if origin is an issue, then it too must be dealt with, given its space to perpetuate itself.

Disciplining Differences: Correcting Racial Flaws, Enhancing Race-ness

Paradoxically, the promise of nationhood is conjoined to the presence of and the further development of those spaces that were made possible by the efforts of precisely those who did not originate from within the larger place. This marks an essential character flaw in the indigenous peoples: thus, we still have the image of the economically backward Malay in sharp contrast to the economically forward Chinese. This image is not restricted to the island, but affects the style of perceiving the region and thereby regional economics too. At this time, however, my comments will be confined to the island of Singapore *per se*.

The problem in racial terms then is that if economic growth is a nation-building desideratum, the "economic genius" of the Chinese is to be encouraged and given the space to grow. At the same time, the economic backwardness of the Malays must be corrected, via education and changes in orientation. Thus, the underdevelopment of the "Malays" under a colonial economy is both bracketed and perpetuated to some extent, in no small part because racially inherent characteristics can be corrected only so far.

More crucially, the orientalism that undergirds economics as a science and evaluative knowledge is disguised. The question as to what kind of economics we want, indeed what kind of economics we have inherited, never arises. Different orientations to production and consumption may not be stated, or when stated they take on the guise of economic irrationality rather than ethnic difference. In some ways, these irrationalities, when associated with particular ethnic groups, further underscore racial flaws that are in need of correction and therefore disciplining. Indeed, they also signal a continued failure to contribute.

Simultaneously, the continued exclusion of certain races from certain spaces arises from the perceived flaws inherent in a race.

These flaws, because they are racial in nature can never be fully corrected. This acceptance of flaws in the race require the peoples so named to correct them and thus, the mechanism of discipline is achieved. For the races themselves who want to participate in the economy, and judge their performance as a collective along economic dimensions, and failing to see in these judgments the fact of "Us" examining "Them", they perpetuate their need for policing so that they can better develop as a people.

To sum up, orientation to a particular ideology of production and consumption is ethnically differentiable: class and ethnic perspectives overlap in an important sense, but class overrides the omnipresence of racial meanings that underlie it. The ideology of production and consumption is thus divorced from its orientalist texts/roots: it is a human desideratum, and therefore supposedly devoid of its male and ethnic biases. Thus, a different orientation to production and consumption and so productivity as a measure of worthiness is dismissed as traditionalistic — a presentation of a self that will not adapt to modern times.

Thus, for instance, Islamic revivalism in Singapore arose as one counterpoint to an economics that was considered to be alien and alienating, contemporary economics having its roots too in colonization and then modernization. In this revival, the dominance given to the valuation of individuals and collectives in economic terms was questioned. Instead of enabling discourse about the material versus the spiritual, the quantitative versus the qualitative, these questions became a mark of Islamic fundamentalism — that is, economic irrationalities.[8]

In this sense, in implicit and explicit political and social discourse, a collective that opposes production and consumption ideology in whatever way is marked out as a trapped race: work must be done to liberate them from economic irrationality. The different ethnic orientations to a particular economic paradigm must be homogenized. At this level, the disciplinary work involves mitigating racial characteristics, as against enhancing them.

Mitigating the harshness of such disciplinary work is more gratifying as a source of positive qualifications, as knowledge if accessed would empower individuals. Here, attention is directed towards the loss of culture through modernization and the related loss of self — a racial self. Accordingly, race is in this sense to be protected. Protection involves disciplinary work by individuals.

Each individual is part of a collective but each individual must be on constant guard against losing his or her place in the collective. The accomplishment of work in this direction begins with the reference to the detail of language. All races in Singapore have an associated official mother tongue, such as "Chinese" which is used synonymously with "Mandarin", Malay, or Tamil. English is, in this respect, not a mother-tongue language. This meaning of "mother tongue" is inextricably linked to a place of origin. Regardless of whether a person first learnt to speak another language, or the person speaks and identifies with the languages he/she knows, that person is open to being judged with reference to her/his facility in a Beijing dialect of Mandarin, or a standardized Malay that is somewhat removed from everyday life Malay, or a similar standardized Tamil, which are supposed to correspond to her/his mother tongue as "Chinese", "Malay" or "Indian" respectively.

As with the official accomplishment of "race", it is difficult for the average Singaporean to escape the fact of her/his mother tongue. Every schooling child must offer the mother tongue language in school. This formulation in the school programme affects home life considerably. Every family in Singapore who has a school-going child is thus forced to some extent to pay attention to the reality of a state-defined mother tongue.

The meaning of the mother tongue is not just language. Language is the vehicle by which one knows one's roots, one's culture — that is, language measures a person's closeness to her/his race. In an important sense, language is like the notion of racial blood. Just as racial blood can be watered down by "interracial" marriages, language can be watered down by not learning it and thus being able to speak only other languages.

In this respect, the English language is a dominant language. This dominance is seen to be necessitated by economic considerations — in the same sense in which I have just noted, that is, the economy in turn being explicated as separate from racial considerations. But if the language of English is not counterbalanced by a mother tongue language, then the person has lost his or her racial self — the person has become "Westernized". The mother tongue, then, trains a person to be of her or his race:

> The chief function of the disciplinary power is to train ... in order to levy and select all the more. It does not link forces together in order to reduce them; it seeks to bind them together in such a way as to multiply and use them. Instead of bending all its subjects into a single uniform mass, it ... makes individuals ... which functions as a calculated but permanent economy (Foucault 1979, p. 170).

This individualization is effectively achieved in that while race places one in an exclusive group, each person in a race group has varying degrees of race-ness. A Chinese, a Malay and an Indian are differentiated by the fact of "origin" in the sense already described. The same Chinese, Malay and Indian can also be observed along a continuum of Chinese-ness, Malay-ness and Indian-ness. This is measured by his or her facility in her or his mother tongue language. In this respect, race is almost always available for hierarchical observation. These are the key instruments by which successful disciplinary power is reproduced (Foucault 1979, p. 170).

Thus, a person can be asked about, if not asked to speak in, the mother tongue in a myriad of settings. The school is the most obvious. Children who are "Chinese", "Malay" or "Indian" must study the official mother tongue. Consequently, children who are studying Mandarin, Malay or Tamil but are not perceived to be Chinese, Malay or Indian can be painfully excluded by both the "race" group whose mother tongue language they study, and the "race" group whom they are supposed to singularly belong. The policing is spread out from the state, the Ministry of Education, the teachers and so forth, down to the students.

In the school setting, furthermore, there are trained mother tongue language teachers to supervise the learning of the language. The supervision includes continuous assessments that culminate in three term-end examinations, instituted since 1969. Outside school, at any time, one can be confronted by the lack of communicative competence in one's mother tongue language — in a taxi, by one's neighbour, when out shopping, when applying for a flat. At any time during a day, a person can encounter another who feels he/she has the right to question your facility in your mother tongue language, and praise, exhort or shame you as the case may be. As one then sixteen-year-old schoolgirl put it:

> My neighbours, once we were just talking about this second language. He asked me what was mine and I said Malay. Then he said, "But you can speak Tamil at home, can't you?". And then I said, "No". And I felt so ashamed and he asked me, "You ought to be ashamed of yourself if you can't speak your mother tongue." And then I felt quite bitter towards my parents for giving me Malay when I was an Indian (as quoted in PuruShotam 1988, p. 217).

If race encloses mother tongue languages, then it furthers the reproduction of spaces for different peoples. As I have noted elsewhere, acceptance of Mandarin as the proprietary language of ethnic Chinese excludes access to it by both the "owners" of the language and those who share a sense that it is not "their" language. At the same time, however, economic opportunities via Mandarin are increasing considerably, not just because of the move towards capitalism in China today, but even within Singapore. Bilingualism has become an important aspect of employability. Not surprisingly, given the dominance of the Chinese in Singapore, not all English–mother tongue language combinations are equal. It is English-Mandarin that is the most functional combination of all (PuruShotam 1989, p. 512).

Conclusion: Antidote to Disciplined Difference

Until I was twenty-one years of age, I had never been to India. Yet my country and my people had categorized me as "Indian". It was a categorization that I did not think much about as I was growing up. There are several reasons why I did not: the discipline of race then was not as effective as it is today. I had no cultural resources to term myself by an enclosing race name and a mother tongue to be measured by. Indeed, my mother's cultural resources were those that precisely avoided tight definitions of ethnicity, language and value systems. For instance, recognizing that I was a child of a larger world than my family, she sent me to an English medium school, learned and passed on "bazaar" Malay as a necessary means of conversation in multicultural Singapore, provided us with some knowledge of Tamil, albeit insisting on the rule of Telegu at home as our "family" tongue. We were also taken to a variety of temples (Hindu, Chinese, Buddhist) and churches (Protestant and Catholic), places which were useful for teaching us values, including stories of her favourite deity Lord Krishna, and visits to the grotesque plaster-of-Paris hell of Chinese mythology, the Haw Par Villa.

Today, to teach my child the same multicultural values I have had to refuse to let him learn Tamil: it is a mark of enclosure in the "Indian" "race". I have had to agree not to let him learn Mandarin as he became a museum piece in his pre-school for his initial enthusiasm and quick learning of it. I have had to avoid sending him to schools run according to the Ministry of Education's specifications, in which "race" and "mother tongue" are essential elements. I use my other cultural resources to avoid the frames: some of them are special to myself and my family, like my husband's American citizenship, and my sociological interest in ethnicity. I am not necessarily unique. Disciplining differences is a real aspect of life in Singapore, but passive acceptance of it, regardless of the commonly held image of Singaporeans — an image, again, of "The Other" without recourse to their own narratives — is not. There are myriad ways of resisting the discipline — turning it on itself in ways that come back to crack the frames that try to tailor discourse to the state's formulation of it. That too derives from the history of race naming and the consequences of received knowledge that some of us are struggling, seriously, against. I must conclude by noting that there is another face to this discipline: anti-discipline,[9] that needs to be worked out too.

Notes

1. I have examined this in a separate unpublished paper, written in 1976, and titled "The Lady Malay: An Exploration of a Stereotype from the Perspectives of the Stereotyped". At that time there was no language of post-colonialism. I chose the topic after a gut level reaction to an "expatriate" professor from then West Germany, who taught us Development Sociology. In a discussion on the economic history of the region, he referred to the Malays' lack of economic initiative, somewhat in the frames of the infamous need-to-achieve thesis of McClelland that was

in favour then. According to this, some groups of people lacked the N-Ach, as he called it, that blocked their route to development. When I challenged him to his perspective on the Malays, I was asked to examine the issue in my term paper. After writing the paper I presented it at a seminar at which my teachers were present: the main reaction was one of disbelief that, seen from the perspective of the Malays, entering the so-called modern economy would have been akin to ambitiously pursuing downward mobility. I found that no attention was given to my data or my methodology: these I could well have defended. There was only reference to the sub-text that "we all know that the Malays were less economically motivated; even lazy."

2. The first of these was conducted in 1871. Thereafter, decennial censuses were taken until 1931. This flow was apparently disrupted by the war and the Japanese Occupation of Singapore (1942–45). In 1947, two years after the Japanese surrendered to the British, another census was conducted. Their last census of 1957 is not considered here as its categorization and analysis was left for an independent Singapore to do.

3. Except in 1947, when "few women were used, only men were employed as census enumerators."

4. "Return of the population of the Straits Settlements, 2nd April 1871", in *Straits Settlements Census Reports and Returns 1871*, p. 7.

5. Ibid., p. 7.

6. Ibid.

7. See Vlieland (1932, p. 83). Vlieland's assessment mirrored his predecessors' almost word for word. Thus, Nathan wrote: "With regard to the Southern Indians far less trouble was experienced as the bulk of Tamils, Telegus and Malayalis, being employed on estates under European or other responsible management were enumerated by the managers and correctly returned" (1921, p. 86).

8. See, for instance, Mariam Mohd. Ali (1993).

9. See de Certeau (1984).

References

Anderson, Benedict. *Imagined Communities*. London: Verso and NLB, 1985.

de Certeau, Michel. *The Practice of Everyday Life*. Berkeley: University of California Press, 1984.

del Tufo, M. V. *Malaya, Comprising the Federation of Malaya and the Colony of Singapore: A Report on the 1947 Census of Population*. London: Crown Agents for the Government of Malaya and Singapore, 1949.

Foucault, Michel. *Discipline and Punish: The Birth of the Prison*. New York: Vintage Books, 1979.

Innes, J. R. *Report on the Census of the Straits Settlements Taken on the 1st March 1901*. Singapore: Government Printing Office, 1901.

Mariam Mohd. Ali. "Islamic Resurgence in a Mother-Daughter Dialogue". Paper presented at the American Anthropological Association Meeting, Washington, D.C., November 1993.

Merewether, E. M. *Miscellaneous Numerical Returns and Straits Settlements Population, 1881*. Singapore, 1881.

————. *Report of the Straits Settlements Taken on the 5th April 1891*. Singapore: Government Printing Office, 1892.

Nathan, J. E. *The Census of British Malaya, 1921*. London: Dunstable and Watford, 1992.

PuruShotam, Nirmala. "Language and Linguistic Policies". In *Management of Success: The Moulding of Modern Singapore*, edited by Kernial Singh Sandhu and Paul Wheatley. Singapore: Institute of Southeast Asian Studies, 1989.

————. *Negotiating Language. Constructing Race. Disciplining Difference in Singapore*. Berlin and London: Mouton de Gruyter, 1998.

Said, Edward W. *Orientalism*. New York: Vintage Books, 1979.

Vlieland, C. A. *British Malaya (the Colony of the Straits Settlements and the Malay States Under British Protection, namely the Federated States of Perak, Selangor, Negri Sembilan and Pahang and the States of Johore, Kedah, Kelantan, Trengganu, Perlis and Brunei: A Report on the 1931 Census and on Certain Problems of Vital Statistics*. London: Crown Agents for the Colonies, 1932.

chapter four

ETHNIC IDENTITIES AND ERASURE
Chinese Indonesians in Public Culture

ARIEL HERYANTO*

Ethnicity and nationality have been irrevocably problematized in the contemporary social sciences and in the relatively new area of cultural studies. As Joel S. Kahn indicates in his introduction to this volume, a variety of "constructionist" perspectives articulate the problems of these modern subject identities. While adopting some of these "constructionist" insights, I will retain some degree of empiricism in discussing the changing political significance of Chinese ethnicity in Indonesia. Obviously, a constructionist theorist could offer somewhat different insights than those presented here. My limited purpose is to show that ethnicity is already overtly problematic (fragmented, ambiguous, unstable) in the practical experience of post-colonial subjects, to whom the elegantly intellectual problematizing of ethnicity as a concept is unheard of. Even among Indonesia's academic élite, ethnicity is widely accepted (that is "constructed") as existentially "given" and conceptually unproblematic. Yet, something beyond theorists' constructs and constructionists' theories asserts itself in the everyday life of ordinary people.

Class Analysis of Ethnicity

For the first time since the New Order regime assumed power in 1966, the ethnic Chinese in Indonesia have in the 1990s enjoyed a steady increase in respect and legitimacy in public culture. This has occurred without compromising the economic dominance of some wealthy members of the ethnic Chinese community.

Yoon Hwan Shin is one of the first scholars to have taken a close look at this phenomenon (1990). He observes the decline of anti-Chinese sentiment in terms of a politico-economic perspective, that is, as part of a larger process through which the New Order state has engineered the formation of a new, multiracial, capitalist class and hegemony. Yoon notes that not only has discrimination against the Chinese been toned down in public discourse, but that a considerable decline of economic indigenism together with an active ideological campaign for capitalist ethics have worked in tandem to achieve the new class hegemony.

While Yoon's main arguments are tenable and highly instructive, there is a need to explore the issues further. Being concerned primarily with a new development in Indonesian capitalism in terms of class structure, he takes ethnicity as largely given. Yoon demonstrates very well how the Chinese capitalists can now sit comfortably at the apex of the nation's economy, as they share the dominant position with competent indigenous tycoons. However, he says little about whether similar developments are taking place in non-economic areas.[1] Consequently, one needs to reassess the appropriateness of the use of the term "hegemony" in this context to avoid a crude class reductionism.

A series of recent events offers rich material to rethink many of the issues outlined above. These events include the mass rally of workers in Medan in April 1994, the controversial trials of those accused of the murder of the woman labour activist Marsinah, and the bad bank loans in Jakarta. These incidents are relevant here because they have not triggered violent anti-Chinese riots, as one would have expected if they had taken place a decade or so earlier.

The more recent and eventful riots of 27 July 1996 in Jakarta further confirm this observation. Up to the 1980s it would have been difficult to imagine that street violence on such a scale could have taken place in the capital city without singling out the Chinese community as primary targets. The main targets of the angry mob were government and military properties. Surprisingly, no commentator has yet recognized this unprecedented point about the event. In any case, I will not include this more recent incident in the analysis, because unlike the other chosen three cases, no ethnic issue was involved in the circumstances and feelings that gave rise to the 27 July public outrage.

To appreciate the novelty of the current situation, I must first outline what preceded it, namely, the construction or, rather, re-construction of Chinese ethnicity within the dominant discourse during the previous two decades of New Order Indonesia. Of central importance here is the paradox of the Chinese dominance of the economy, and their pariah status in the cultural and political spheres.

Political economy may have offered some insights into our understanding of the logic of this paradox. However, it tells us little of how this paradoxical situation is manifested, narrated and represented in actual texts, images and practices. Political economy is, in any case, theoretically suspect to the extent that it presents an overtly rational and instrumentalist account of neatly interlocking structures. One crucial point generally missing in these accounts of the ethnic Chinese is the forceful narrative of the so-called communist abortive *coup d'état* in 1965–66 in which much emphasis is placed on the alleged complicity of the ethnic Chinese. The official narrative of these events should be regarded as constituting a central component and force in the processes that gave birth to the New Order "Self".

Othering the Ethnic Chinese

The ethnic Chinese are one of the four major "Others" of the New Order Self, the other three being the "West", "Communism", and "Fundamentalist Islam".[2] Othering the ethnic Chinese takes several forms. Firstly, there is the geographical argument. The ethnic Chinese are perceived to have originated from some discrete geographical site outside the boundaries of the nation. As a result, this ethnic group appears to threaten the universal nationalist project of seeking native roots and authentic origins. Theoretically, the Indonesian ethnic Arabs, Indians, or Europeans occupy similar positions, but they have created no comparable threats. There must be other reasons for the Chinese being such a problematic Other.

Secondly, there is the cultural explanation. Unlike the Arabs or Indians, the ethnic Chinese have a long history of being segregated from the majority of the population through the overstatement of differences of religion and cultural tradition. Although this differentiation is a gross caricature, it has proven to be highly functional in propagating the familiar view of why the Chinese have been the least integrated ethnic group in Indonesia.

Thirdly, there is the argument about economic determination. Chinese Indonesians constitute the only ethnic minority that has sustained a dominant position in the nation's economy. Political economy may have argued forcefully that this factor is more fundamental than the first two. However, why this is so has not been adequately addressed.

Fourthly, there is the constructionist consideration. In New Order propaganda, the ethnic Chinese are suspected of being deeply attached or essentially susceptible to communism. A fairly large proportion of Chinese were killed in the extensive purge of communists and their alleged sympathizers in 1965–67, and those who survived continued to be subject to discrimination. The actual death toll is far from clear. In absolute terms, the Chinese casualties may be smaller in comparison to other ethnic groups. However, given the small size of this ethnic group's total population, the loss of lives was felt significant among their surviving ethnic fellows.

The attacks against this ethnic minority may have been driven by two prevailing perceptions. First, despite serious cases of racial discrimination among the élite of the Indonesian Communist Party against individual Chinese comrades, there was a general belief that leftist politics had always been supported by a large portion of Chinese Indonesians. Secondly, because the People's Republic of China was communist, there was a general essentializing identification of this ethnicity with communism. Because the Soekarno government established a close tie with the People's Republic of China and the Indonesian Communist Party, the New Order's allegation of China's implication in the so-called "abortive coup" of the latter made some sense to a large section of the population. Soon after the army took control of the country in 1966, the government enforced a wide range of anti-Chinese measures as part of the wave against communism. These included the banning of all Chinese schools, mass organizations, mass media, use of Chinese characters, personal names and names for firms/shops.

The recent softening of anti-Chinese sentiment cannot be explained solely by referring to changes in the economic structure. Instead, any account must link it to the waning effectiveness of the phantom of communist threat, upon which the nation's previous economic growth and political stability greatly depended. While these two discursive changes — on the Chinese and communists — are closely related, they are nonetheless two separate and distinguishable developments. One is not necessarily subordinate to the other.

What was common to the othering of the Chinese, on the one hand, and communists, on the other, was that in both cases what was involved was the massive physical destruction of the victims. Furthermore, the sinister proportion of this extermination can be gauged more clearly if we consider the way the attacks against the Chinese and communists also took place in a realm beyond any legal, administrative or political logic, so to speak. The stigma of being Chinese and hence ideologically "unclean", or that of being Chinese and hence having been "involved in the 1965 communist coup" were declared contagious and hereditary. The state-sponsored witch-hunt and terror victimized the primary suspects as well as many others having real or suspected associations by birth, marriage, or organizational links with the accused.

Throughout most of New Order history, the government managed to silence, intimidate and discredit all sorts of dissidents by labelling them communists, or communist sympathizers. The 1996 crackdown on pro-democracy movements, with nation-wide anti-communist propaganda, was only a most recent example. Government officials have not only accused Budiman Sudjatmika, head of Partai Demokrasi Rakyat (PDR, or People's Democratic Party) of reviving communism but, to enhance their credibility, they have also accused his father of having been associated in the past with the Indonesian Communist Party. In the days that followed, the press revealed that Sudjatmika's father had in fact been the opposite, namely, a long-time anti-communist. Although such reckless and often refractory labelling practices may not always convince the general population, the frequent deployment of overt violence that accompanied them succeeded in generating a general acquiescence for many years.

Nationalism: Towards an Authentic Native

One very familiar practice of Othering the ethnic Chinese takes the form of calling them non-*pribumi*, or "non-native". The label is a colonial legacy that post-colonial dominant groups decided to impose upon silent Others in order to assert an identity of Self (the so-called *pribumi*, or "native") in a binary opposition.[3] After years of such disciplining, the Indonesian Chinese, especially the younger generations among them, learned to internalize and reproduce these labels.

In theory, the modern nation is anything but an affinity constituted exclusively or primarily by ethnicities, descent, or geographic ties. In the words of Ben Anderson, "the nation was conceived in language, not in blood, and ... one could be 'invented into' the imagined community" (1983, p. 133); hence, the universal practice of "naturalization". Paradoxically, all nations have a universal tendency to construct some sort of authentic origins "in blood", in something seemingly natural, native, or primordial.[4]

Nation-ness, and hence the distinction between Indonesian and non-Indonesian, are only a step away from the ethnic dichotomy of *pribumi* and non-*pribumi*. Nothing illustrates this better than the New Order's grandiose national park, the Taman Mini Indonesia Indah, "Beautiful Mini Indonesia Park".[5] In the park, visitors find a replica of Indonesian archipelagic territory, and twenty-seven pavilions representing the so-called traditional and authentic cultures of the twenty-seven provinces of the nation. Here, however, we find nothing representing the lives of fellow-nationals of Arab, Indian, Chinese, or European ethnicity. Nor is there anything representing the many Javanese young people found in the heart of Yogyakarta, the capital city of Javanese high culture, typically wearing blue jeans, riding Japanese motor-bikes, or queuing for McDonald's hamburgers.[6]

In other multi-ethnic nations, like the neighbouring countries of Singapore or Malaysia, television occasionally becomes a popular window to display token ethnic harmony. Although the New Order regime invested a great amount of resources in projecting similar images of ethnic diversity and harmony, only the so-called *pribumi* ethnic groups are accounted for. Although the Constitution stipulates the principle of equality before the law, Chinese Indonesians are categorized in official and semi-official state administration as less, or other than, "genuine" Indonesians. Worse still, they are occasionally perceived to contaminate the Indonesian authentic self.

Citizens of Chinese descent must carry identification cards with distinct numbers.[7] Extra paper-work and fees are required of them in any legal dealings with the public service. All schools and colleges impose a certain maximum quota for Chinese Indonesians seeking admission. Professions other than commerce are only minimally open to them, if at all. Visitors entering Indonesia will be informed on the customs declaration form that any printed materials in Chinese characters fall in the same category of illegal items as pornography, arms and narcotics.[8]

Ethnic segregation in New Order Indonesia results in the "ghettoization of citizen-Chinese", where in the entire six successive terms of Soeharto's presidency (five years each), "there has never been a 'Chinese' cabinet minister, though such ministers were a regular feature ... [of the preceding regimes] ... Nor will one find any generals or senior civil servants of obvious Chinese ancestry."[9]

The Political Economy of Chinese Ethnicity

The extent to which the New Order Self is premised on the active and conscious othering of the Chinese indicates how indispensable this ethnic Other is for the reproduction of the native Self. If the Chinese were simply unwanted, this minority could have been marginalized, destroyed, or simply ignored. The fact that the "Chinese problem" persists in an extended period of impressive economic-growth suggests that it may not in fact be a problem at all.

In the New Order, Chinese businessmen appear to have always been economically dominant, relative to the rest of the population.

While since 1965 their political and cultural status has declined dramatically, their economic influence has expanded as never before![10]

Political economists have correctly noted that the New Order officials prefer to boost the national economy in partnership with Chinese and foreign businessmen alike. They have no prospect in the foreseeable future of forming an independent force in the nation's political dynamics. Their economic dominance and political/cultural deprivation are not mutually contradictory.

In fact, the paradox has reproduced itself over a long period of time. Chinese economic domination reinforces the long-standing antagonism of the native population. Periodic anti-Chinese riots have been reported, narrated, analysed and remembered as something natural and spontaneous, as a populist search for justice. While security officers usually act to restore order, in the final analysis the violence serves the interests of the regime. It reproduces the Chinese dependence on state protection, and defers, if not undercuts, the potential emergence of a domestic bourgeoisie. The violence discredits popular native efforts to express grievances, and deflects anger away from both the state and sensitive foreign investors. The security apparatus can always play the role of hero.

Following periodic anti-Chinese riots, commentators usually blame the victims for having provoked the angry mass by dominating the national economy and displaying luxurious lifestyles.[11] In some areas, Chinese males are summoned by the local police chief or military commander to be told of their alleged guilt in causing the social unrest and material loss.[12]

Under Erasure
Given the importance of ethnic tension in reproducing the New Order's economic growth and political stability, the government's decision to promote the ineffective programme of ethnic assimilation makes sense. The dominant position of the Chinese in the nation's economy has been widely perceived to be a national problem. This has been explained predominantly in psychologically or culturally essentialist terms; hence, the popular myths of the Chinese superior work ethic, industriousness, thrift or perseverance. While not vicious traits when taken on their own, to treat them as cultural/psychological

attributes unique to the Chinese and to assume that together they exhaust the meaning of Chineseness means that the Indonesian Chinese have been literally stuck with a very narrow range of human characteristics, making it difficult to both imagine and image them in any other way. As such, the Chinese have been branded asocial and unpatriotic, and blamed for supposedly pursuing selfish interests and for remaining aloof from much of national life.

In response to this "Chinese problem", the New Order government endorses a semi-private and military-backed "Program Pembauran", or "Assimilation Programme". The basis of the programme is the presumption that Chinese ethnic identities and their essential character are incompatible with the national personality, and have caused problems for national integration and unity. Recurring anti-Chinese riots are presented as evidence to support the argument. The Assimilation Programme prescribes the total dissolution of any marks and identities of Chineseness, and urges this problematic ethnic group to immerse itself in officially constructed local cultures, which are the only legitimate ethnic cultures.

Intermarriage is highly praised, at least in rhetorical terms. Giving up both Chinese personal names and Chinese business names was strongly urged. Converting to Islam, the religion of the native majority, understandably is another sanctioned way of assimilation.

Once the Assimilation Programme was instituted as the official solution to the "Chinese problem", the *pribumi* and non-*pribumi* dichotomy was reaffirmed as given. Eradicating Chinese characters (in both senses), traditional practices and cultural artifacts is seen as ethically unproblematic. The problems with the Assimilation Programme are largely seen as technical, psychological and requiring time.

However, contradictions in the Assimilation Programmes soon became glaringly evident. While Chinese males are highly praised for intermarriage, such intermarriage does not turn a Chinese groom into an equal fellow-citizen. Chinese males marrying native women still have to carry special identification cards and are subject to various other administrative discriminations. Their children are still classed as non-*pribumi*, regardless of how purely native their mothers are. The pariah status continues indefinitely along the male line, just as does the stigma of having been "involved in the 1965 communist coup".

While changing Chinese names is strongly encouraged, access to public service nevertheless requires that the Chinese declare their former, and now stigmatized, names. Adopting non-Chinese-sounding names does not allow the ethnic population to disappear into the native crowd in state documents and files. Changing names is enforced not really to eradicate racial discrimination. Rather, it celebrates the conquest of a threat that the conquerors had initially fashioned. Badminton world champions of Chinese descent are known by their Indonesian names. But criminals of the same ethnic background appear in the mass media under their Chinese names.[13]

Chinese conversion to Islam is often seen as a noble act of assimilation and nationalism. Understandably, there has been a serious attempt to repress any historical evidence suggesting the pioneering work of the ethnic Chinese in spreading Islam in the archipelago. The simple dichotomy between native and non-native must be purged of ambiguity. For similar reasons, until very recently, the rise of indigenous tycoons has been as much under-reported as has the existence of the Chinese poor.

Chinese identities are never totally to be wiped out. They are carefully and continually reproduced, but always under erasure. In fact, the negation is a necessary element of the making of this ethnic Other. The New Order regime cannot possibly want the Assimilation Programme that it co-sponsors to attain its declared aims. Achieving these aims must instead be forever deferred. To dissolve Chinese identities in an effective programme of "assimilation" means to give up the division of labour by race, upon which the status quo depends so much. The recent growth of multiracial social alliances may indeed signal serious changes to the status quo. No regime lasts forever.

Early Signs of Change in the 1990s
Things began to change rapidly in the 1990s. Chinese Prime Minister Li Peng visited Indonesia in 1990, following a series of exchange visits by officials from the two governments. Soon afterwards, the Chinese-Indonesian Institute for Economic, Social and Cultural Co-operation was founded. While the bans on the use of the Chinese

language and Chinese characters have not been repealed, the Indo-nesian Government is now sponsoring the publication of a Chinese–Indonesian dictionary.[14] In 1996, a prominent linguist wrote a column not only welcoming the "Booming Courses on Speaking Mandarin" in Jakarta, but also at the same time complaining about the peda-gogical quality of many of these courses.

Of course, Li Peng and his government have nothing to do with most Chinese Indonesians. The many meetings between the two governments mean little to the general population in both Indo-nesia and China. However, for reasons which cannot be attributed to the *rapprochement* between these two countries, racial tension has also softened over an extended period and on a scale unprecedented in New Order Indonesia. These changes can be seen at two different levels.

Firstly, more and more prominent Chinese figure as celebrities in the media and popular culture. A substantial number of them have entered the People's Consultative Assembly, the world of fashion, poetry reading, entertainment programmes, and talk shows. More and more successful Chinese businessmen (nearly all men!) are invited to be guest speakers in highly prestigious forums on non-economic matters. In all of these, the ethnic Chinese are simply catching up with the rest of the newly emerging, successful, multi-racial middle class.

But, secondly and more significantly, one can now see a pro-gressive reinsertion of cultural constructs of overtly Chinese images in public space. Since 13 September 1993 a new magazine *Sinar* (Light) has entered the market with what has come to be a markedly Chinese look. Backed by the President's brother-in-law, the weekly primarily targets the Chinese business communities and the ethnic Chinese population more generally.

More often than not, the front cover of *Sinar* presents a close-up of a prominent Chinese personality. Items in the magazine are not only predominantly related to events involving Chinese Indone-sians, or the more intellectual discussion of Chinese traditions in general, but familiar Chinese terms also make a regular appearance in *Sinar* headings, even where Indonesian equivalents exist.[15] Al-though it is unclear how the general population actually feels about the publication, there has been no strong reaction from the public to this novel act. They seem to take it for granted. But a note of qualification is necessary at this point.

The above is not meant to suggest that anti-Chinese sentiment and policies are now gone once and for all. What we see is a juxtaposition of many and often contradictory statements in public culture about the ethnic Chinese. Anti-Chinese sentiment may still be alive and well, just like racism elsewhere, but it no longer asserts itself in public as it did in the past. Occasional government policies sound anti-Chinese, as Arief Budiman observes (1994), but they target only a few of the extremely well-off, and these policies seem like a fleeting phenomenon. Anti-Chinese slogans have disappeared from the regular mass demonstrations' yells and banners, as well as from angry students' publications. Such sentiment have recently survived only in small circles, private gossip, or anonymous pamphlets.

A year before Li Peng visited Indonesia, the Soeharto government still banned the staging of a play in the North Sumatran city of Medan on the pretext that the romance story originated from a Chinese legend, Sam Pek Eng Tay. Commenting on the incident, Mely G. Tan added that one reason for the ban was that the play contained a Chinese dragon dance (1991, p. 118). In 1978, the Minister of Home Affairs instructed the Governor of Central Java to ban the dragon dance in public.[16] As late as 1990, the provincial government reiterated the ban.[17] In both instances, no one questioned or protested against the ban.

In 1993, both the Central Government and the Governor of Central Java reminded the public of the existing ban on the celebration of Chinese New Year in public places, like *vihara* (Buddhist temples), and on the performance of the dragon dance. The Governor even went as far as to ban the sale of a certain Chinese cake, traditionally consumed at New Year. In 1993, critical responses to the restrictions began to appear in the mass media (see Indrakusuma 1993; Subianto 1993). On the following Chinese New Year, the largest Indonesian daily, *Kompas*, published advertisements conveying good wishes for the Chinese holiday season. This provoked no one.

One of Indonesia's most popular novels, a highly-rated television show, and a highly acclaimed play produced at Jakarta's most prestigious arts centre were all based on another Chinese legend, "The Lady White Snake". The dragon dance played an important part in all of these versions of the narrative. The chief appeal of this narrative may be purely apolitical: its familiar plot-line and its special audio-visual effects as presented on screen and stage. Significantly, however, the core theme that runs through it is a defence of individuals victimized by official norms and hostile treatment due to their descent!

Televised film series based on Chinese legends have not only been present, but the number and frequency of their screen appearances have increased significantly. Chinese legends in comics and novels have also taken considerable space in all major bookshops. Sympathetic Sino-Indonesian characters now appear in fiction. In August 1994, the Coordinating Minister for Political and Security Affairs, Lt. General (Retired) Soesilo Soedarman announced a new decree allowing hotels and travel agents to publish leaflets and brochures in Chinese characters. A month later in Jakarta, the Hebei Beijing Opera Troupe presented the first stage performance from China to a New Order Indonesian audience. The pioneering work of the Chinese in the spread of Islam in Indonesia became a topic of seminar discussions in Jakarta in 1993, a cover story in the highly-respected Islamic daily *Republika* (20 March 1994), and the theme for a new film to be produced jointly by the Indonesian Government and its counterpart from the People's Republic of China (*Bernas*, 14 August 1993, p. 6). By early 1996, the debut of Islamic proselytizers of Chinese ethnic background came to prominence, so much so that a news-magazine presented a cover story on the phenomenon (GATRA 1996).

It is difficult to explain these changes and appreciate their significance solely by reference to political and economic factors. Neither the seemingly strong government, nor vigorous capitalism, let alone the Assimilation Programme, can be easily accorded that determining position. For a further investigation of the phenomenon, special attention must be paid to the three most controversial events that took place in the country during the 1990s: the murder of Marsinah in East Java, the case of the bad bank loans in Jakarta, and the large demonstration by industrial workers in the city of

Medan in North Sumatra. The three incidents captured national attention for many different reasons. For our purpose, suffice it to note that all three events point to the waning effectiveness of the stigmatizing discourse of Chinese and communist threats.[18]

Marsinah was a young female worker who was killed for her activism in a local workers' movement demanding better working conditions and wages as stipulated by government regulation. She worked in a factory owned by a Chinese family. It would not have been surprising if the local population quickly took revenge on a racial basis, as exemplified by a number of incidents in the recent past where Chinese families have been accused of mistreating their native house-maids.

In the case of Marsinah, the local authorities in fact propagated such a version of the events, accusing the Chinese factory manager of having raped and later killed her in his own house. The insinuation did not provoke any mass protest. In the court room, the Chinese employer showed wounds on his body. He testified that he had been kidnapped by military officers, and for nearly three weeks had been severely tortured in the military headquarters before being forced to sign a prepared confession. Upon hearing this, his workers in the court-room yelled out their support for his courage in speaking out against the official version of the events, and against the continuing intimidation against him, his family and his lawyers.[19]

In mid-April 1994, hundreds of thousands of industrial workers in the North Sumatran city of Medan went on strike and organized a mass rally. They demanded better wages and working conditions, freedom to organize an independent union, reinstatement of dismissed fellow workers, and an investigation into the death of a fellow worker. Violence, mainly in the suburban industrial zones and in the commercial district in the heart of the city, followed. The military detained about eighty workers, and accused leading figures of the recently established, but officially unrecognized, labour union that they had masterminded the violent demonstration. Union activists, on the other hand, claimed that the violence was instigated by state *agents provocateurs*.[20]

In the mass media, both in Indonesia and overseas, the incident was commonly portrayed as an anti-Chinese riot. Although a few argued otherwise, government and non-government commentators were preoccupied with analyses of deep racial tensions that supposedly underlay the Medan incident. Leaving the question of intention aside, the focus of public debate shifted from a serious industrial dispute, if not class conflict, to historicizing ethnic and cultural tensions.

All of this occurred as an increasing volume of evidence from journalistic reports indicated something quite different. The event is striking in its lack of racism and anti-Chinese violence. True, a Chinese businessman was killed, and a fairly large number of properties were damaged. However, two things run counter to the racial interpretation. One concerns the identity of the perpetrators of the violence, and the other the victims themselves.

Concerning the agents, it remains less than certain that the Medan workers were responsible for the murder of the Chinese businessman. The degree of their responsibility for the damage of properties needs further scrutiny. Racial issues did not appear in the workers' petition, yells, banners or posters. When an anonymous pamphlet calling for anti-Chinese action suddenly circulated later in the crowd, the protesting workers were reportedly less than enthusiastic in their response. The targeting of certain Chinese was in all likelihood more a consequence of their class position than their race/ethnicity.

More importantly, this mass protest involved less violence, and caused fewer casualties and material loss than have comparable anti-Chinese riots in previous New Order history. Significantly, the victims in the Medan riot were mainly members of the big business community, while the angry protesters were exclusively workers. The rest of the ethnic population was reportedly left alone. In contrast, in most preceding anti-Chinese riots, including major ones in 1980 throughout Java, violence was perpetrated by people of various professions, economic status and age. They attacked the Chinese population regardless of their profession, economic status, age, or sex.[21]

Repeatedly, the military leadership accused the Medan demonstrators of using communist tactics. The security officers went further. Before detaining Mochtar Pakpahan, head of the opposition labour union, they accused him in the mass media of being responsible for the riot in Medan, and of having a father who was associated with the communist party twenty years earlier. The communist accusation seemed to have intimidated or impressed no one.

The case of the Rp. 1.3 billion (US$650 million) bad bank loan from the state-owned Indonesian Development Bank provoked the urban and educated sections of the population across the nation primarily because of the amount involved and those implicated in the crime: a Chinese millionaire and top state officials. In the media coverage and in the court-room, public condemnation against the Chinese businessman had a racist flavour to varying extents. However, no anti-Chinese riot ensued.

True, in June 1994 a number of strongly worded anti-Chinese pamphlets were in circulation. In one of these anonymous pamphlets, a reward of Rp. 250,000 (US$100) was offered for a Chinese head. Fear swept most major cities in Java. Yet, paradoxically, the presence of these pamphlets may prove that, if anything, the appeal of anti-Chinese rhetoric has been dramatically in decline. In the past, no anti-Chinese riot needed a pamphlet to mobilize an angry mass.

Conclusion

In the foregoing discussion of the significant changes that have taken place in the way the ethnic Chinese are represented in contemporary Indonesia, I have attempted to go beyond the simple question of whether Chineseness as some sort of "thing" frozen in time and space has survived or disappeared. This whole way of conceiving ethnic Chinese identity either in the present or in the past is somehow misleading since Chineseness is not — and has never been — a quantitative substance or immutable essence that can be said to be either present or absent.

It may well be that to an important degree the new interest in Chineseness by the Indonesian public can be compared, or related, to the growing interest shown by the urban middle classes in the consumption pursuits of artefacts, ethnic cuisines, architectural styles, fashions and countless other "commodity-signs" and lifestyle markers typically found in such "post-modern" spaces as shopping malls, theme parks (for example, the "Beautiful Mini Indonesia Park"), and the like. Whatever the case may be, what is certain is that these discursive changes to Chinese ethnicity in the Indonesian context have taken place because Indonesians in the 1990s have become different subjects who construct and reconstruct, read and re-read, these elements anew. Ethnicity, like all things, is always a set of dynamic relationships of real semiotic beings. It is never a "thing".

What remains unclear is how long the softening of this racial/cultural tension will continue, and how much further it can go. Less certain is the effect this novel phenomenon will have on the social transition from the present to the post-Soeharto period, and also perhaps to the post-New Order regime. Given the importance of sustained racial/cultural tension in the construction and protracted reproduction of the New Order regime, we have good reason to pay special attention to these questions. In addition, given the general tendency of many scholars to concentrate their analyses on the antagonism of Jakarta-based élites, especially between top bureaucratic and military leaderships, a broader view that takes into account different public discursive practices is called for.[22]

Notes

* The writer is grateful to Joel S. Kahn, Stanley Y.A. Prasetyo, Keith Foulcher and Vedi Hadiz for their comments and corrections on an earlier draft of this essay.

1. On one occasion he writes that the ideological crusade has "been remarkably successful" in the economy, but to "a lesser degree" in society (1991, p. 128).

2. These are not new constructs. Nor are they original inventions of the New Order regime. Rather than tracing their historical origins, I will focus narrowly on present events. Historical connections will be provided only as minimally necessary.

3. For convenience, no inverted commas are used in subsequent references to the New Order Self and its Others.

4. Of course, there is nothing unique about that, as the following two quotes show. The first is from Raymond Williams and the second from Bruce King (both cited in Brennan 1990, pp. 45, 53):

> Nation as a term is radically connected with "native". We are born into relationships which are typically settled in a place. This form of primary and "placeable" bonding is of quite fundamental human and natural importance. Yet the jump from that to anything like modern-state is entirely artificial.

> Nationalism is an urban movement which identifies with the rural areas as a source of authenticity, finding in the "folk" the attitudes, beliefs, customs and language to create a sense of national unity among people who have other loyalties. Nationalism aims at … rejection of cosmopolitan upper classes, intellectuals and others likely to be influenced by foreign ideas.

5. On the profile and political significance of Taman Mini Indonesia Indah, see John Pemberton's deconstructive analysis (1994).
6. For a comparison with neighbouring Malaysia, see Kahn (1992).
7. In 1995, the government announced a decision to introduce a new computerized system of identification cards whereby any discriminating markers that appeared on the identification cards of citizens belonging to the ethnic Chinese group would be abolished. At the same time, however, the government said that separate files on this ethnic minority would be kept stored within the new system's database (*KOMPAS* 1995). The actual enforcement of the decree had not taken place at the time of writing.
8. This is probably the only case in modern history where a major world language is officially proscribed by a strong government in a relatively long and stable political climate and has not generated protests. The only other comparable ban, this time during a period of political turmoil, was that of Catalan under Francisco Franco's fascism. From 1939 to 1945 books in Catalan were removed from public access, and many of them were burned. "Any public use of Catalan was proscribed; it was not permitted in any form in public or private schools. Secret police also attempted to penetrate private life …" (Laitin 1989, p. 302).

   The more common practice in several countries is temporary or restricted linguistic bans. For example, in Jakarta the use of English in advertisements has been banned, especially in 1993 and 1995 (see Jakarta-Jakarta 1993; *Jakarta Post*, 1995; *Forum Keadilan*, 1995). Something similar took place in Vietnam (Schwarz 1996). In 1994, the French Government attempted to impose a new regulation to restrict the use of all foreign languages. This was met with strong objections (*Tempo*, 1994).
9. The words are Ben Anderson's (1990, p. 115), originally written in 1983. They still hold true.
10. According to Sjahrir, a supporter of economic indigenism, eighteen of the twenty-five richest Indonesian conglomerates are of ethnic Chinese origin (*Tempo*, 21 May 1994, p. 46). Three of the top ten richest Chinese businessmen in Asia are Indonesian nationals (*Jawa Pos*, 5 June 1994, p. 1). The most famous one, Liem Sioe Liong, "ranked among the forty richest men in the world" (Vatikiotis 1993, p. 50).

11. In a similar way, in Indonesia one often hears commentators publicly blaming victims of rape for having aroused the rapists' desire by speaking or behaving immorally, or wearing inappropriate clothing.
12. For an illustration, see a report in *Review of Indonesian and Malayan Affairs* (1981), p. 100.
13. Similarly, in reporting certain criminal cases, the mass media often emphasize the fact that some of the suspects may be homosexuals, although this has no relevance to the matter at hand.
14. Hong Kong and Taiwan kungfu movies have always flooded Indonesia. However, they have not received any serious attention either in national political discourse or among cultural studies scholars.
15. For instance, Hokkie for Zodiac, or Kua Mia for the Consultation section on miscellaneous matters.
16. *Sinar Harapan*, 5 August 1978, p. 2.
17. *Kedaulatan Rakyat*, 28 August 1990, p. 12.
18. As mentioned earlier, there was another attempt by the government to revive the effectiveness of the "communist threat" rhetoric following the 1996 Jakarta riot, but without much avail.
19. For more details on the case, see the fact-finding report prepared by the Indonesian Legal Aid Institute (1994). In June 1994, the State Court found him guilty and sentenced him to seventeen years in prison. A year later, having been under continued pressure from international protests, the Supreme Court acquitted him, and declared him innocent.
20. More on this can be found in the Amnesty International report (1994).
21. It is therefore ironic that many commentators attribute the relatively minor violence in Medan to the presumably cruder character of North Sumatran racial relations compared to their Javanese counterparts.
22. For a recent example of the common tendency to privilege the Jakarta-based élite, and consequently produce a pessimistic analysis of social change in contemporary Indonesia, see Robison (1993).

References

Amnesty International. "Indonesia: Labour Activists Under Fire". *AI Index* ASA 21/10/94, May 1994.

Anderson, Ben. *Imagined Communities: Reflections on the Origins and Spread of Nationalism*. London: Verso, 1983.

———. "Old State, New Society: Indonesia's New Order in Comparative Historical Perspective". In *Language and Power*, edited by Ben Anderson, pp. 94–120. Ithaca: Cornell University Press, 1990.

Bourchier, David. "Totalitarianism and 'National Personality': Recent Controversy about the Philosophical Basis of the Indonesian State". Unpublished paper, 1993.

Brennan, Timothy. "The National Longing for Form". In *Nation and Narration*, edited by Homi K. Bhabha, pp. 44–70. London: Routledge, 1990.

Budiman, Arief. "Suharto's Revised New Order". *Far Eastern Economic Review*, 22 December 1994, p. 21.

Forum Keadilan. "Menertibkan pahlawan di Jalur Bisnis". Vol. 4, no. 14 (23 October 1995): 72.

Forum Keadilan. "Mereka yang Tersangka dan Terjerat". Vol. 5, no. 10 (26 August 1996): 17–18.

Gatra. "Boom Da'i Keturunan Cina". 17 February 1996, pp. 21–30.

Indonesian Legal Aid Institute. "A Preliminary Report on the Murder of Marsinah". Jakarta, 1994.

Indrakusuma, Danny. "Imlek dan Larangan Menjual Kue Ranjang". *Surya*, 25 January 1993.

Jakarta-Jakarta. "Jangan Berbahasa Inggris". Vol. 364 (26 June – 2 July 1993): 79.

Jakarta Post. "Local firms given until August to alter names". 8 July 1995, p. 3.

Kahn, Joel S. "Class, Ethnicity and Diversity: Some Remarks on Malay Culture in Malaysia". In *Fragmented Vision: Culture and Politics in Contemporary Malaysia*, edited by Joel S. Kahn and Francis Loh. Sydney: Allen and Unwin, 1992.

Kompas. "KTP Baru tak Cantumkan WNI Asli atau Keturunan". 23 August 1995, p. 8.

Kridalaksana, Harimurti. "Merebaknya Kursus Bahasa Mandarin". *Kompas*, 13 July 1996, pp. 4–5.

Laitin, David D. "Linguistic Revival: Politics and Culture in Catalonia". *Comparative Studies in Society and History* 31 (1989): 297–317.

Pemberton, John. "Recollections from 'Beautiful Indonesia': Somewhere Beyond the Postmodern". *Public Culture* 6, no. 2 (1994): 241–62.

Robison, Richard. "Indonesia: Tensions in State and Regime". In *Southeast Asia in the 1990s: Authoritarianism, Democracy, Capitalism*, edited by Kevin Hewison, Richard Robison, Garry Rodan, pp. 41–74. Sydney: Allen & Unwin, 1993.

Schwarz, Adam. "Bonfire of the Vanities". *Far Eastern Economic Review*, 7 March 1996, pp. 14–15.

Subianto, Benny. "Tahun Baru Imlek: Boleh atau Tidak?" *Jakarta-Jakarta* 444, 30 January–5 February 1993, pp. 24–25.

Tan, Mely G. "The Social and Cultural Dimensions of the Role of Ethnic Chinese in Indonesian Society". *Indonesia*, special issue, pp. 113–25. Ithaca: Cornell Southeast Asia Program, 1991.

Vatikiotis, Michael R.J. *Indonesian Politics Under Suharto*. London: Routledge, 1993.

Yoon Hwan Shin. "The Role of Elites in Creating Capitalist Hegemony in Post-Oil Boom Indonesia". *Indonesia*, special issue, pp. 127–43. Ithaca: Cornell Southeast Asia Program, 1991.

chapter five

GLOBALIZATION AND CULTURAL NATIONALISM IN MODERN THAILAND

CRAIG J. REYNOLDS*

Introduction

Early in December 1993, a convoy of forty-six vehicles, containing fifty journalists and others, crossed the Thailand-Myanmar border as the first officially organized overland motor caravan from Thailand to China. Similar journeys are envisioned to take travellers to parts of northern Laos and to Beijing. Organizers of the motor caravan included the Tourism Authority of Thailand, with sponsorship from the Petroleum Authority of Thailand, and Thai Airways. The co-operation of the Myanmar Ministry of Hotels and Tourism, the China National Tourism Administration, and the Travel and Tourism Admin-istration of Yunnan Province was also required to ensure the success of the expedition. At Kengtung in Myanmar's Shan State, an outdoor cultural show was performed to entertain the tourists.

In Jinghong, the capital of the Sishuangbanna region in Yunnan, live many Tai Lue people, whose culture resembles that of the Thai. The Tai Lue "kingdom" vanished after the Chinese communist victory in 1949, and the territory became an autonomous prefecture. Through it, from north to south, runs the Mekong River on its long journey to the Gulf of Thailand. One of the Thai journalists on the caravan commented that the traditional Tai songs and dances seemed to have been heavily influenced by the Chinese Cultural Revolution, and the folk dances "were more akin to Russian ballet than any Thai folk dance this writer has ever seen." The journalist pointed out somewhat ruefully that the Chinese have succeeded well in "assimilating" the Tai people of Sipsong Panna (Anussorn 1994). The punctuation marks around "assimilated" in the original dispatch suggest that Tai Lue multiculturalism might have brought to the journalist's mind what Chinese "assimilation" has meant to Tibetan culture, namely, the displacement of local culture. For the Thai Lue living in Yunnan, the admixture of Russian motifs to the native cultural matrix raises a question about the integrity and durability of Tai Lue culture.

I want to use this brief account of the first officially organized caravan tour from Thailand to China as a point of departure for a discussion of globalization and cultural nationalism in modern Thailand. For, despite the feel of newness and adventure in this account, older instincts were at work in the dispatch of a motor caravan through the Shan states into southern China. The gaze from Bangkok to the north — for reasons of business, politics, or recreation — is of long historical formation and constitutes a process of reclamation rather than of fresh discovery (Reynolds 1996a, p. 119). Not least of the deep structural factors at work was the instinct of the Thai states in the nineteenth century to invade the Shan State of Kengtung when the geopolitics of southern China-northern Southeast Asia deemed it advantageous for them to do so (Melchers 1986).

As Thailand's economic boom has pushed Bangkok-based business to the far corners of the country over the past decade, it has become increasingly difficult to speak of any part of the country as remote. Conventional infrastructure, such as roads, bridges, and rail links, as well as telecommunications via satellite dishes, cable television, and mobile telephones, have transformed villages and provincial towns into places where a certain cosmopolitanism flourishes. While there are asymmetries to the cultural flows across borders, and the ownership of the technology that makes possible these flows rests in the hands of a few, it cannot be denied that the centre–periphery framework that used to function in cultural analysis is less and less applicable to the globalizing process.

The forces driving this development are complex and derive, in the Thai case, from business expansion, tourism, and government development strategies (Hewison 1992). The Sino-Thai merchant culture that was instrumental in founding the Bangkok kingdom more than two hundred years ago still dominates today and is responsible for the expansion of Bangkok business to neighbouring regions.

When we speak of the porosity of borders, which is a distinctive feature of globalizing trends, the long-standing security interests of the Thai military must be taken into account. The Thai military has good reason to be vigilant on the borders, for it has economic interests there. Lucrative extraction of resources from less developed neighbours such as Myanmar and Cambodia by means of military-built infrastructure has brought wealth to tiny border locales. In the Golden Triangle, the most wanted drug dealer in northern Southeast Asia, Khun Sa, has been cultivating international respectability by moving some of his capital into gem cutting rather than the production of heroin (Naowarat 1993).

Apart from the lucrative extraction of resources that has transformed humble hamlets into prospering markets for international products, the policies of the ASEAN countries to stimulate decentralization and to push development towards the periphery has led to a proliferation of economic quadrangles, squares, and circles (Wrangel 1993). The Golden Triangle over which Khun Sa once presided is to become the Golden Quadrangle, fulfilling the dream policy of former Thai Prime Minister Chatichai Choonhavan to turn the battlefields of Indochina into market-places. These macro-economic strategies have the blessing of national governments, but they may at the same time erode national loyalties. The new geometries of regional development raise the possibility that people who flourish in the border zones may not only develop economically but also culturally and politically "away" from the citizenship into which they were born (Cornish 1994). The loyalties on which independent central governments have relied since the end of World War II are changing.

The disintegrative and potentially disruptive consequences of these complex transformations in political and economic terms have long been recognized. The cultural dimensions as well as the tele-communications technology that serves as the vehicle for cultural flows are less well understood, although novel interdisciplinary fields, exemplified by the journal *Public Culture*, are evolving to study the emergent global forms of cosmopolitanism. In a race to keep up with what is happening, academic pursuit of the transformations has brought about a new vocabulary of analysis to account for the cultural processes under way. The "global ecumene", a region where cultural interaction and exchange takes place, is one such term (Hannerz 1989). Arjun Appadurai's much-quoted ethnoscapes, mediascapes, technoscapes, finanscapes, and ideoscapes are another set of terms that strive to make sense of the emergent global cosmopolitanism (Appadurai 1990).

This vocabulary subverts an older terminology of "center–periphery" asymmetries. Asymmetries structured by political and economic imbalances clearly still exist, but advanced media technology also has the capacity to empower local cultural producers. I read in at least some of the prognoses being made for the post-nationalist period the sense not only that there exist powerful new technologies of "invention" and "imagining," but also that the consequences of the transformations are integrative as well as disintegrative. Small language communities may be able to retain their linguistic identity and thus cohere, because desk-top publishing can supply, relatively inexpensively, the literacy needs of speakers.

On this point, protagonists in the Thai debate on globalization can choose to side with optimists, who see opportunity and maybe even liberation in what is happening, while pessimists have plenty of evidence to call attention to the damaging environmental, social, and cultural consequences of globalization. Developers who want to build golf courses on rice fields ally themselves with the multi-national tourist industry, for example. In terms of advertising and cable news networks, the metropolitan capitalist countries (USA, Britain, Germany, and increasingly Japan) possess "global languages" that are challenging Thai life-styles and habits of consumption. International "Madison Avenue-style" advertising techniques have steadily encroached on local practices since the 1970s when big U.S.-based agencies arrived to take over the market. Many people associate the commercialization of sex and the commodification of charismatic monks with globalization and fear that cultural standards are being undermined (Fairclough 1994, p. 22; Jitraphorn 1993, p. 24). A survey of Thai teenagers has shown that they feel an emphasis on using sex appeal in advertising is damaging to Thai culture (Chalinee 1994, pp. 58, 61, 200, 203).

I would not want to trivialize these consequences, but it is important to realize that globalization is proving to be, as Foucault said of power/knowledge, "productive." As with other parts of Southeast Asia, the media, for example, are used by ordinary people in ingenious ways (Hamilton 1992, p. 85). Video, a media form that the state has found difficult to control, spews out images that can serve all sorts of purposes, to enchant as much as to subvert (Hamilton 1993a, 1993b). Another way of saying this more specifically with reference to the contemporary Thai social formation is that globalization is not inherently constructive or destructive. Local activists for improvement in human rights can turn to Amnesty International, just as environmentalists campaigning to protect the natural environment benefit from the international environmental movement (such as Greenpeace, World Wildlife Fund) (Jitraphorn 1993, p. 25). And globalization can be integrative and identity-forming on a personal level as well — in the domain of sexuality, for example. "Gayness" as a masculine model for Thai male homosexuality has emerged only since the early 1980s, not as a breach of an indigenous sex/ gender dichotomy, but as a male identity that "renders explicit what was previously implicit and transforms into an identity what was previously a behaviour" (Jackson n.d.[a]). In this respect, gay male sexual identity has deeper cultural roots than its counterparts in the rest of formerly colonized Southeast Asia where it is a more overtly politicized identity.

In 1994, the "Year to Campaign for Thai Culture", it is worth pausing to consider the dialectic that takes place between past and present when globalization becomes a matter of public debate. I refer to the interactive process of a dialectic here, because with globalization comes anxiety about the survival prospects of indigenous culture. Such anxiety may be as old as human culture itself but has certainly been expressed most acutely and forcefully in the modern era, especially in the colonial and post-colonial periods. Underlying this anxiety, which seems itself to be characteristic of the globalizing process, is an instinctive worry about the authenticity of self, culture, community, and nation. As cultural flows import more and more material from "out there", whether "out there" be Hong Kong, Tokyo, Taiwan, or San Francisco, new regional and ethnic identities are being forged. But the question of what is *really* Thai is of growing concern to culture managers and even ordinary folk. At the same time, the modern techniques of cultural production enable the culture managers to fashion a virtual reality of Thai culture past and present that can be visited and, when converted to electronic bytes, exported.

Historical Precedent

Projecting globalization into the past in a search for the roots of Bangkok's astonishing cosmopolitanism may have its rewards. Cosmopolitanism here means encouraging an orientation to engage with the other, an activity that of necessity establishes a tension between the local and the global (Featherstone 1990, p. 9).

The Bangkok state was founded in 1782 as an ethnically plural entity, certainly more plural at its core than the contemporary Vietnamese court at Hue or the Burmese royal base at Mandalay (Kasian 1994, p. 59). Mon, Lao, and Karen war captives and refugees were settled as labourers and rice cultivators when the Siamese court moved south at the end of the eighteenth century. Later, in the wake of Siamese expeditions to re-establish control over tributary states in the Malay peninsula, Muslims were uprooted from the south and resettled around Bangkok and the old centre at Ayutthaya. The Marxist historian Jit Poumisak used the term *kwat torn*, which conveys the sense of cattle being herded, to describe the dispossession and resettlement of peoples. An eloquent account of the dispossession of the Phuan people from northern Laos, who were resettled in central Siam, has paid homage to the sturdy determination of this resettled people who have come to terms with but have not forgotten their deracinated history (Breazeale and Snit 1988).

The relevant point to make here about the dispossession and resettlement of these peoples is that while Siamese administrative mechanisms encouraged assimilation and identification as Siamese, the policies, at least in the nineteenth century, did not subjugate the minority cultures to the point where they were extinguished. After many decades, the Phuan people now living in the Central Plains still speak Phuan. A kind of hybridization was possible, and was even tolerated and encouraged, for those who wished to retain a semblance of the culture of their ancestors. Central Siam in the nineteenth century was accustomed to a polyethnic population long before the term "multiculturalism" was invented. I would suggest that memory of this polyethnic past and awareness of polyethnic community, preserved in something as innocent as the endless conversations one hears in Thai about loan-words and etymologies that relate to this past, predisposes people to be cosmopolitan.

The massive numbers of Chinese who migrated to Siam, beginning in the eighteenth century via the junk trade, are a special case. Their semi-assimilation, by which they preserved a sense of lineage and affiliation with overseas Chinese elsewhere in the diaspora, has been a key to Thailand's post-World War II economic expansion. Despite racist policies of the state directed against the Chinese during the reign of the sixth Bangkok king, Vajiravudh (r. 1910–25), and during the military regime of Field Marshal Plaek Phibunsongkhram beginning in late 1938, these affiliations were not lost, a fact that lies buried in the history of the much-vaunted assimilationist policies that pushed and pulled the Chinese to speak Thai, dress Thai, and pledge their loyalty to the king and Buddhism (Kasian 1992; Skinner 1957). Given the importance of the overseas Chinese in the economies of Hong Kong, Singapore, Taiwan, Malaysia, Indonesia, these affiliations within the Asian Chinese diaspora have facilitated the expansion of Bangkok-based business in the region.

One example of the link between Chinese cultural heritage and business is the selling of indigenous business acumen by means of manuals drawing on episodes and maxims from the *Romance of the Three Kingdoms* (*Sanguo yanyi*) (Reynolds 1996b). This famous Chinese story cycle was translated into Thai at the beginning of the Bangkok period and has become a key text in the evolution of Sino-Thai culture. Over the past decade, publishers have capitalized on the *Romance*'s popularity by harnessing episodes in a new genre of business manuals, *How to do business successfully by reading Romance of the Three Kingdoms*. The title of one of these manuals was translated from Chinese as *Wisdom of the East*. This marketing of a presumed "native" Sino-Thai business mentality works successfully because authors and publishers can assume that readers of the *Romance* will be sufficiently savvy about the themes of strategic deception, cunning, and how to neutralize a rival in the cut and thrust of gaining competitive advantage. It is possible to assume that readers will have this knowledge because *Romance of the Three Kingdoms* has been accepted not only into the Thai literary canon but is very much a part of political culture generally. In the 1980s, Sino-Thai culture experienced an efflorescence, particularly in Bangkok. Globalization has, so to speak, unmasked the limitations of assimilationist policies by which "the Chinese" were supposed to disappear into "the Thai."

As Bangkok-based business led by the Sino-Thai élite expands into northern Southeast Asia and identifies markets in the socialist states, old proprietary interests in lands containing Tai peoples have been awakened. In some of these lands, such as in Laos for instance, the Bangkok court had strategic and economic interests from the early nineteenth century. For one thing, nationalist myth-making in the 1920s and 1930s had placed Siamese-Thai origins in the kingdom of Nanchao in southern China. Many Sino-Thai have reconnected with relatives in the People's Republic of China (PRC) following resumption of diplomatic relations in the 1970s, so the rediscovery of the pan-Tai world in northern Southeast Asia has had important cultural as well as economic dimensions. The Tai brothers and sisters (*phinorngkan*) in Laos, Burma, Vietnam, and southern China are different in important ways from the Siamese-Tai of the central plains of today's Thailand. There is now substantial Thai research interest in these differences on the part of anthropologists, historians, and archaeologists who discuss their findings in magazines and highly publicized seminars. The cultural and economic dimensions of the expanding Bangkok social formation suggest that the motivations for Thai "interest" in these regions are complex: to build on affiliations, which would be good for business, by identifying similarities; and, by identifying differences, to enlarge the definition of Thai-ness. A flexible approach to what defines Thai-ness that avoids essentializing differences and emphasizes a continually evolving Thai identity has been a feature of Thai cosmopolitanism since the mid-1970s.

Beyond the region, where Thai curiosity and willingness to engage with Tai peoples comes naturally because of linguistic and cultural affinities and leads to a kind of ethnochauvinism, a history of interaction with America since the end of World War II has shaped Thai consumer tastes as well as the political culture generally. Although Thailand was a bastion of loyalty as the Americans prosecuted the Cold War in Southeast Asia, the country remained relatively open to foreigners, and particularly open to Americans. The Peace Corps sent hundreds of young Americans to Thai provincial and district schools, and large numbers of Thai civil servants, business people, and educators received their college education and advanced degrees from American institutions. Young Thais returning from their American education in the late 1960s and early 1970s brought back experiences in the anti-war movement that played a part in the overthrow of the military dictatorship in October 1973. This is not to "explain" the activism that led to the 1973 event as something imported from Berkeley or Columbia University, but to acknowledge the internationalization of Bangkok urban cultural politics. The idea of periodizing Thai literature by labelling these years "the American era" seems calculated to touch sensitivities about autonomy, but the fact is that this periodization has not been set aside by Thai intellectuals (Anderson and Mendiones 1985). Strategic and economic ties between the United States and Thailand have begun to fray in recent years, but with large numbers of American-educated Thais still in positions of responsibility in all sectors of the bureaucracy, business, and public life, it will be some time before the political culture breaks free from its American connections.

It may be a tautology to argue that the quick reception of modern communication in Thailand has facilitated Thai cosmopolitanism, because the reason for that receptivity may lie in an openness and receptivity to the world generally. But it is a fact that, compared with other countries in mainland Southeast Asia, Thailand more readily accepted the printing press, cinema, radio, FM radio, and colour and cable television. Long historical habits of developing the theatrics of power as well as a rich repertoire in the performing arts help explain the predisposition for modern technologies of representation, but the canniness and ambition to control these technologies is not well understood. In the present historical moment, this history of rapid appropriation of technologies of communication has proven decisive in establishing economic dominance in the region, because the televisual age privileges cultural producers, be they individuals, companies, or government departments, who can take advantage of these technologies.

Finally, in explaining Thai cosmopolitanism I would point to the way knowledge was traditionally coded and transmitted before the mid-nineteenth century when Western knowledge paradigms began to exert their pull on the Siamese élite. Traditional manuals on such matters as astrology, medicine, and grammar had a capacity to absorb new material while appearing to remain unchanged. It has been said of the manuals on Thai invulnerability that they are characterized by fragmentation, repetition, and "unsystematicness." These features meant that the alien characteristics of foreign cultural elements were easily stripped away and appeared non-threatening, and certainly not strange. In terms of architectural styles, for example, the admixture of many different artistic traditions — Khmer, Mon, Burmese, Lao, Chinese, Western — meant that a new cultural motif was accepted into a building's design without in any way appearing to be odd or out of place. A Thai colleague has told how he passed a Bangkok monastery on his way to school every day, never noticing that the gates were adapted from the European gothic cathedral. It was only when he had travelled to the West that he realized the style's origins. Thenceforth, the gothic portals on the Thai Buddhist monastery did indeed strike him as odd.

Public Intellectuals and Globalization

The Thai name given to the globalization process is the Pali-derived calque *lokanuwat*, although not all words that name epochs and international styles are translated into the language. Many remain loan-words with distinctive spellings and diacritics that mark them off as alien forms. But *lokanuwat* is now a buzzword in Thai, having made its way into the language at the end of the 1980s at a time when "internationalization" and "NIC" became emblems of Thailand's emerging role in regional and world economies. Like the word for "dynamism" (*phonlawat*) that also became popular at this time, globalization is a boom word.

Credit for coining the translation has been given to Chai-Anan Samudavanija, a political scientist at Chulalongkorn University who has been an active public intellectual since his return in the early 1970s from graduate studies in America. In publications directed at the general public, Chai-Anan waxes lyrical about the transformations taking place, proclaiming that in the age of globalization "knowledge will no longer serve power but will be a power unto itself, autonomous" (Chai-Anan 1994, p. 71). This kind of futuristic and visionary outlook is typical of those public intellectuals who are confident of the capacity of telecommunications to be a liberating rather than a repressive influence in social, political, and economic life.

In the early 1990s, Chai-Anan held the position of senior academic advisor in the Chaiyong Limthongkul Foundation, an educational and philanthropic enterprise headed by Sondhi Limthongkul, the owner of Manager Group, a media conglomerate. Through its Thailand-Australia Foundation, Manager Group has established a base in Australia, at the Asia & Pacific Studies Centre at the University of Central Queensland (Mackay Campus), where it intends to develop management training courses and cultural exchange. As one of the pioneers in the introduction of advanced telecommunications technology to Thai print media, Sondhi might be taken as a globalizer par excellence. Many of Thailand's leading public intellectuals have been lured to write for the Manager Group's publications, and Chai-Anan himself has a regular column in the Thai-language *Manager*. Attributing the loan-translation of *lokanuwat* to Chai-Anan personally runs counter to linguistic principles about how language changes (that is, not at the instigation of individual speakers), but the attribution underscores my thesis about the perceived role of public intellectuals in interpreting what is happening to the country.

Given the Thai propensity for word play, it is not surprising that writers take advantage of the *lokanuwat* currency by exploiting the word's resonances with similar-sounding coinages, *lokawibat*, for example, which means "global catastrophe," or *lokawiwat*, which has the tamer meaning of "global change". In October 1994, the Royal Institute of Thailand stepped into the debate and insisted that the term *lokaphiwat* be used on the grounds that *lokanuwat* carried a connotation of "wordliness", which is not at all what "globalization" should mean in the Thai language. By alliterative punning on *lokanuwat*, which sounds awkward to the Thai ear and is thus the cause of much humour, a single punchy word can call into question the benefits being touted for a globalized Thailand as well as the ethics of the globalizers. A couple of collections of short stories, for example, play on the greed (*lophanuwat*) and unbridled consumerism (*phokanuwat*) that turns rice fields into golf courses and bush land into monoculture eucalyptus farms for the Japanese woodchip industry (Suchat 1994a; 1994b). The first part of the latter term literally means "eat" as well as "consume" or "use up" and conveys the sense that human beings are engulfing the whole world with their voracious appetites for resources. The moralizing message directed at the more rapacious and unscrupulous globalizers is clear.

In the noisy and bruising world of Thai political culture, the debate about the pros and cons of globalization has become more tense and urgent as the ecosystem has deteriorated and as development has radically altered social relations. Some of the arguments are familiar to comparable debates in other countries. Multinational enterprises and foreign investment are held accountable for over-development and damage to the environment. Urbanization and industrialization have drawn people from the countryside, disrupting family and community life in the process. It is of interest that some of these points were made in early 1994 in an article in *Muang Boran*, an archaeology and heritage magazine, because there is a clear connection between heritage management and globalization, as will be discussed below. The article's Thai title, rendered rather weakly in the magazine as "Effects of Globalization on Thai Society", but best translated as "From 'Globalization' to 'Global Catastrophe' in Thai Society", is a punning indictment of the catastrophic consequences (*lokawibat*) of unbridled development hailed as globalization (*Muang Boran* 1994). A social scientist at Chiangmai University has said categorically, "Globalization has already taken place, and it is a very powerful force" (Jitraphorn 1993, p. 25).

Many, but by no means all, of the public intellectuals engaged in these debates have a history of leftist radicalism or activism. Some debaters come from the NGO (non-government organizations) movement where many veteran activitists from the tumultuous 1970s have found a place for themselves in the practical politics of grassroots development. They are advocates for the disenfranchised and the rural and urban poor. Among their number are former Marxists who fled Bangkok in the crackdown that accompanied the return of military power on 6 October 1976 and who then made their way to overseas universities where they acquired advanced degrees. Upon returning from abroad they took up teaching positions in the university system and began to write for the popular press. While Marxism as such no longer exerts a hold on the way development issues are framed, today's public intellectuals who lived through the 1970s, even as youngsters, developed analytical, organizational, and oratorical skills that they have brought to bear on current problems. The politics of culture, dependency theory, and economic determinism were vigorously debated in the 1970s, and with some modifications two decades hence, they are still worthy of scrutiny and argument. With this characteristic flair for a phrase, Kasian Tejapira has termed the protagonists of current debates "globalizers" versus "communitarians" (Kasian n.d.[a]).

One such debate about globalization took place at Thammasat University at the end of 1993, when a historian, a freelance journalist, and a committed globalizer met to exchange views. The historian, Thawit Sukhapanich, performed the etymological duties required on these occasions and pointed out that the Thai term means literally "to adapt to the world" (*patibat tam lok*) (*WT* 1994, pp. 106–7). It was necessary to spend time defining the term, he said, because although many Thai speakers use it, few know what it means. Of the three kinds of speakers Thawit identified in his unscientific survey, one group now grasps the opportunities and processes, especially in terms of telecommunications; the second group criticizes and resists globalization; and the third group, by far the largest and the one in which Thawit counted himself, is more or less confused, wondering what all the fuss is about.

Thawit, the historian, understandably took a long view and pointed out that Thais have been globalizing for centuries, from Ayutthayan times when there were sizeable Portuguese, Dutch, and Japanese settlements in the port-city, to the present, thus proving that Thai culture has long been capable of adapting to what the Western world had to offer in terms of values, knowledge, and abilities. The gist of Thawit's argument was that the Thai language was somewhat deficient in the vocabulary of globalization because there has never been a time when Thai society was not globalizing. There was never a period before globalization, so there was no need for a term to describe what came naturally to the society (p. 108).

The second speaker, the freelance journalist Thianchai Wongchaisuwan, referred to Braudel and Wallerstein as thinkers who had pioneered the world-system theory that helps modern people understand the changes now taking place. Thianchai preferred "global evolution" (*lokawiwat*) for his gloss on globalization and admitted that modernization theory has failed to deliver the benefits it promised. Deforestation and AIDS (acquired immune defiency syndrome) are global phenomena that have penetrated everywhere. And Thianchai warned that retreating into Eastern spiritualism was simply gross ignorance of the problems at hand.

Somchai Phakkhaphakwiwat gave possibly the most spirited presentation at the seminar. A lecturer in political science at Thammasat University who has done graduate work in Spain and studied both Spanish and Italian, he is a living advertisement for globalization. He is a specialist on the stock market, writes a weekly column, and presents a two-minute television programme on world financial trends. He has been an adviser to Sondhi Limthongkul, whose Manager Group has successfully exploited the talents of many intellectuals in its publications. To conquer the problems of doing business in traffic-clogged Bangkok, Somchai has fitted out his van with electronic communications and entertainment equipment (computer, mobile telephone, cassette recorder, fax machine). To relax in the van he sings by himself with karaoke accompaniment. Somchai's facility with languages, telecommunications, and international finance indicates why he might have an irrespressibly optimistic view of opportunities for Thai globalizers. Consequently,

Thai culture is being internationalized, and global culture is being domesticated (*WT* 1994, p. 121). A more eloquent proselytizer for globalization, for whom the phenomenon is an ideology and way of life, could not be found.

Thirayut Bunmi is another public intellectual, "a social thinker" (*nak khit khong sangkhom*) as he puts it, who in his publications is striving to explain the meaning of the present globalizing epoch (Thirayut 1993). A student leader in the mass mobilization that brought down the military government in October 1973, Thirayut was an adviser to the Socialist Party of Thailand and co-ordinator of the Democratic People's group until the military coup in early October 1976. At that time he fled to the jungle with many other young intellectuals and for four years served in Nan province, one of the secure bases of the insurgency, as Secretary for the Co-ordinating Committee of Patriotic and Democratic Peoples. There followed a period of graduate study in the Netherlands until his return to Bangkok in 1985. Since then he has been an active speaker and prolific author, his past as a Marxist intellectual being evident in his pamphlets and articles.

In his most recent books Thirayut has spelled out what he thinks *lokanuwat* means for Thai society. He ranks Thailand as a moderate-to-high "outward-oriented" society. Predictably enough, the societies at the top of his list are the "Little Dragons" of Asia — Singapore, South Korea, Hong Kong (Thirayut 1994, p. 52). Although he is wary of globalization, Thirayut is at the same time willing to see opportunities in the process, in the sense that the global culture penetrating Thai society is bringing ideas, doctrines, strategies, and movements that can be helpful to NGO workers and others fighting for the underdog. As the communications revolution breaks down national boundaries and links societies together, global culture introduces universal (*sakon*) standards in such matters as human rights, democratic institutions (elected parliaments, for example), conservation and environmentalism (Thirayut 1994, p. 40).

Popular culture is also seen to be "standardized," "universalized," and "homogenized" (*an nung an diawkan*). In fact, multinational enterprises find that they have to develop sophisticated advertising campaigns to present their products in a way that will appeal to local (Thai) consumers (Chalinee 1994, ch. 6). In this context, local agency can be seen to have the power to bend and twist standards set elsewhere. The top executive of a Thai conglomerate who boldly says "We want Thai people to eat mayonnaise" has his work cut out for him as far as marketing this most alien of products (Friedland 1989). Thirayut acknowledges that in reaction to the way global culture penetrates Thai society, local culture will assert itself to establish its uniqueness (*ekkalak*) (Thirayut 1994, p. 40). Although he recognizes the damaging consequences of globalization for Thailand, Thirayut is, on the whole, a pragmatic optimist, looking for Thailand's economic development to give it the capacity to contend with the undesirable and hazardous effects of unplanned growth.

Criticisms of a homogenizing global culture usually take the form of a polemic, because increasingly the cultural forms are Asian (from Hong Kong or Japan, for example). Be that as it may, the polemic against the imposition of global culture from elsewhere touches a nerve in the sensibilities of Thai people in all classes. I believe the polemical reaction derives from earlier experiences when the Siamese élite was caught in the dilemmas of being a semi-colony, retaining sovereign powers yet limited in the changes it could advance. Earlier this century, the exemplar and procreator of high culture, King Rama VI (r. 1910–25), embroiled himself in the politics of defining Thai-ness at a time when the legitimacy of the absolute monarchy was being questioned. In order to protect the institution from republican challenges, the monarchy cloaked itself with Thai-ness by representing itself as a cultural artifact epitomizing what *thai* really meant, "free". Thai-ness became essentialized, palpable, something that could be codified in law and bureaucratic regulation. The legacy of this entanglement of culture and politics survives today. Imitation of something designated as non-Thai was thereby construed as a political crime.

The Cult of Imitation
The common theme in the pessimistic assessments of globalization among Thai public intellectuals of a homogenized universal culture raises the political issue of whether that universal culture will

overwhelm and dominate local agency. Bio- and social diversity are diminishing, thus limiting the capacity of human society to confront in a creative way the vast and rapid changes taking place.

This line of argument was articulated forcefully in a speech at Mahidol University in February 1994 by the Chiangmai-based historian, Nidhi Aeusrivongse, who writes regularly for *Art and Culture*, a glossy monthly magazine known for its provocative and nationalistic editorializing. *Art and Culture* was one of the publications that campaigned in 1988 for the return to Thailand of the Cambodian lintel that had been spirited away through the antique-dealer network to the Chicago Art Institute (Keyes 1993, p. 284). In the speech, Nidhi expressed alarm at the sway and influence of global culture, which he identified as European, and which had three characteristics: its hegemony, which means that no country or community of people can escape its influence; the dissolution of borders, which means that local agencies have lost control over decisions that are now made elsewhere; and virtually instantaneous communications (Nidhi 1994, p. 92).

The polarization of "the local" (*thorng thin*) and "the global" (*saphawa lokanuwat*), implicit in the point about the dissolution of borders, was crystalized towards the end of the speech in the following comment.

> In the age of globalization there is more danger in imitating European models [*kanlork tamra farang*] than we have ever realised (Nidhi 1994, p. 94).

Such a formulation of the problem does not point to who is responsible for the threat to Thai society, the European (*farang*) or, as Nidhi also says, "the hegemony of capitalist society". Here and elsewhere in the debate about globalization, the power of the multinational enterprises to affect local conditions independent of local agency has been overstated (*MB* 1994, p. 7). In any case, the issue of imitation — "copying foreign models" — is an old one in Thai cultural debates about whether foreign products, be they consumer products, political systems, health regulatons, or even sexual identities are suitable to be copied. The concern being expressed today is reminiscent of similar concerns expressed at the beginning of this century. The difference in circumstances, in the terms of Nidhi's argument, is that local Thai agency is losing the power to choose, because the range of choices offered is decided in board-rooms in Hong Kong, Tokyo, London, and New York.

Eighty years ago, not long after the Siamese had lost parts of their empire to France and Britain, the sixth Bangkok monarch argued defensively about the power of Western institutions and ideas in shaping cultural and political life. "The Cult of Imitation" was written in 1915 by King Vajiravudh and first published in the newspaper *Phim thai* of April that year (Copeland 1994, ch. 3). Later, in April of the same year, a longer series appeared in the Thai newspaper, *Mud on our Wheels*, which was originally published in English. The series dealt more extensively with the potential damage to the social fabric and the political institutions of foreign models. For these and other essays, the king used a pen-name, Asvabahu, one of the epithets of the Buddha ("a vehicle for men as a horse is a vehicle") that emphasized the role of the king as a teacher, and indeed the tone of these essays is didactic and moralizing (Vella 1978, p. 320). Adopting a pen-name also allowed the king to speak of the monarch in the third person, a rhetorical device that had many advantages in light of the polemic he was developing.

It is important to recall the historical moment when "The Cult of Imitation" was put forward by this most important public intel-lectual of the 1910s. An attempted coup in 1912 had resulted in the arrest of ninety-one persons, some of whom were imprisoned for a dozen years. Apart from personal dissatisfaction with the king and jealousy at his attempts to train a junior cadet corps of Wild Tigers, the more politically astute of the conspirators were critical of the monarchy as an "unprogressive and dying institution". The Young Turk movement, the democratic revolution in Portugal, and Japan's constitutional monarchy were "foreign models" that motivated at least some of the officers (Vella 1978, pp. 53–60). The Bolshevik triumph a few years hence did not give him any comfort either. Not least of these foreign models, because of proximity and the large number of Chinese immigrants in Siam, was the Kuomintang victory and the establishment of a republic in China in 1911–12. Vajiravudh in "The Cult of Imitation" referred scathingly to Sun Yat-sen's wearing of a "frock coat", seeing in this mere item of clothing a sign of a deviant and dangerous European political ideology (Vajiravudh 1951, p. 2). To dress as a European was to dress slavishly, and therefore to follow inappropriate and disloyal political doctrines. It was a tumultuous time, and the inexperienced king was seeking to bring affairs of state under his control after being shaken by the coup attempt. The irony of the argument in "The Cult of Imitation" was that this king had spent his school years in England, had acted on the stage there, and was the first and most bicultural king of the dynasty.

"The Cult of Imitation" was a diatribe against slavish copying of the West. The target seemed to be the visible signs of Westernization, such as clothes, manners, and customs. But by the end of the essay the political consequence of this slavish copying, the destruction of the monarchy, was clear. He mocked those who thought that even a shabby Western garment would be sufficient to ingratiate themselves with Europeans. The god-like powers of this imitation were such that people who fell under their spell were contemputous of their own abilities and mindlessly followed the lead of the West. Basically, the message was that self-reliance and autonomy were the values of "civilization" (*siwilai*) that should be cherished by all Siamese (Vajiravudh 1951, p. 6).

In making this argument, the king perpetuated the equation of Thai with *thai*, that is, free. His father, Chulalongkorn, had abolished debt slavery and his uncle, Prince Damrong Rajanubhab, in his histories had made the reform of labour relations into a doctrine of progress in the narrative of the Siamese-Tai people. So when Vajiravudh accused those who were worshipping "the cult of imitation" of being slaves he was trying to shame them by touching the sensitive nerve of Siam's semi-colonial status, which the dynasty itself had negotiated.

As explained earlier, this polemic against imitation cannot be read without acknowledging the political and social circumstances in which it was produced. But it is possible, indeed necessary, to read the polemic not only as a case for preserving the monarchy but also as an insight into the psyche of the early twentieth-century élite. In this regard, the pessimism and caution expressed by Nidhi

Aeusrivongse, the historian and public intellectual, have much in common with the sixth Bangkok king.

There is a major difference in the two epochs, however, which must be recognized. The danger to the author of 1915 was that he might lose absolute authority. Seventeen years later his successor did. The danger of which the author of 1994 warns is not that sovereignty will be lost, but rather its late twentieth century equivalent, Thai-ness, what makes "us" different. What is common to the two discourses is an "us" and "them" mentality. The hegemonic aspect of globalization has reawakened concern about the viability of the "us". It is to sketch the particular historical formation of the Siamese-Tai "us" in the present epoch that I now turn to conclude the discussion.

Cultural Nationalism and Authenticity

In the globalizing epoch of post-nationalism, when telecommunications are breaking down older forms of loyalty to national communities, it is culture, rather than sovereignty, that is increasingly one of the irreducible "givens" that identifies and differentiates a community. It is not surprising that diasporas — Indian, Chinese, Vietnamese — are now the topic of intensive scholarly work. They are archetypal post-nationalist communities, collectivities that share language, history, and ethnicity but not geo-body (Thongchai 1994). With the modern techniques of representation, fragments of culture can be pried away from their native environs. These cultural fragments can then travel by means of satellite communications.

The process by which "Thai-ness" was formed in twentieth-century élite consciousness is well known (Reynolds 1993). At several specific moments, this "Thai-ness" was made concrete and bureaucratized, its main features being disseminated through the media, the schools, and other institutions. These moments included the late 1930s, when the military regime, which was militantly anti-royalist, needed to Thai-ify itself, and the period following the coup of 6 October 1976 when the prestige of state institutions, including the monarchy, were seriously damaged by the violent methods used to reinstate military rule. Throughout the early 1980s the character of Thai identity (*ekkalak thai*) continued to be an occasional topic in public seminars (Sanga and Athorn 1981). The extensive Tai diaspora in northern Southeast Asia has become of great interest to Bangkok-based intellectuals and culture managers, because the Tai peoples scattered throughout the region offer an answer to the dilemma of how it is possible to remain Thai/Tai in the globalizing age.

The tourist industry, in collaboration with the government tourism authority, is a willing agent in the development and marketing of Thai-ness. In 1985, at the beginning of the economic boom the Tourism Authority of Thailand conducted market research on how Thailand was perceived in overseas markets. An international advertising agency was hired to promote and aggressively sell Thailand's image abroad. From 1986, there followed a series of campaigns unabashedly playing on the Orientalist clichés about the exotic East: "Brilliant Thailand" (1986); "Visit Thailand Year" (1987); "Exotic Thailand — Golden Places, Smiling Faces" to promote "Thailand Arts and Crafts Year" (1989); "I Love Thailand" (1990); "Exotic Thailand — See More of the Country, See More of the People" (1991) (Chalinee 1994, pp. 177–9). The international tourism campaigns are often coupled with domestic cultural themes, so that a kind of feedback mechanism operates which confirms that local identity is shaped in part by how the country is being sold to foreigners. What has been commodified for the international tourist may be consumed by the Thai national, whether that something is a self-image or a handicraft.

Heritage is a particularly interesting way that national or community identity can be forged and reshaped in the globalizing epoch, because heritage is quintessentially local, with the material for its fabrication and validation belonging to "this place". Yet it is more and more the case that the value and prestige of heritage sites increase as they are validated by the international heritage bureaucracy, particularly UNESCO through its International Council of Monuments and Sites (ICOMOS). World Heritage listing is much sought after for the international status and authenticity it gives to a particular site, no less than for the commercial gains through tourism. With tourism, one of the chief vehicles of globalization, the irony is that as the tourism industry develops standardized comforts for the international tourist, "the past and its forms ... are iconicised as the only reliable sources of national identity" (Peleggi 1994, p. 67). The investment in heritage sites is such that they have become national icons on display for the citizenry to visit and admire. But so extensive is the renovation of some of them that their authenticity is often called into question. They are, in fact, sites at which authenticity has been "staged" (Cohen 1988, pp. 374–75).

One such site in Thailand, which has conveyed important meanings to the Thai citizenry about benevolent government throughout the twentieth century, is the Sukhothai Historical Park in north-central Thailand, created in the 1980s with UNESCO assistance (Byrne 1993, pp. 186–93; Peleggi 1994, p. 80–92; Peleggi, 1996). The restoration of the monuments in the park was criticized by one Thai historian for "newly created environments stemming from historical fictions and myths ... a park rich in fantastic structures and recreational sites reflecting no trace or shadow of the urban setting and planning of the past" (Peleggi 1994, p. 85). In response to this criticism, the Fine Arts Department, which was overseeing the restoration, made important changes to the development plan, but the site was so highly charged with symbolism and tourist potential that it was impossible to resist inventing more tradition. A Loy Kratong festival is now held, bringing record numbers of Thai visitors to the Park in November. The historical legend of the festival is a fabrication, incurring the wrath of an archaeologist and ethnohistorian, Srisakra Vallibhotama, who has been a persistent critic of such heritage projects (Peleggi 1994, p. 58). Archaeology is a key science in documenting the national community's history on a particular piece of geography. Archaeologists take sides either to defend projects of this kind or to contest the authenticity of the final result as a misrepresentation of the past.

Once it is accepted that traditions can be rediscovered and even created, it is very difficult for state culture managers to control the process of fabricating tradition. The nation-state has begun to lose its hold on the interpretation of the past (Peleggi 1994, p. 67). In this regard, heritage is an example of globalization having a "liberating" effect, for it has the capacity to pluralize the past. Private or semi-private interests can refurbish sites and present them for consumption by tourists, citizens, and young people, yet these sites may not have the sanction of education authorities or restoration specialists in the Fine Arts Department.

In the dialectic by which the globalizing process facilitates and sometimes forces local identity to establish itself, it is not surprising to find an "us" and "them" mentality. In Thailand, this is expressed in different ways by different speakers and constituencies. As the debate among public intellectuals illustrates, there may be anxiety about the consequences, or there may be an expression of confidence that Thais are "natural" globalizers able to make the necessary adaptations. Media people generally fall into this latter category and are astute in their understanding of what is happening. One communications lecturer, Bunrak Bunyakhetmala who has been described as the Marshall McLuhan of Thailand, believes that the telecommunications revolution will bring into existence an "ersatz Thai" (*thai thiam*) culture, a transnational culture that might even be exported. This ersatz culture will coexist with "authentic Thai" (*thai thae*) culture, which is composed of the drama, music, and literature that has been handed down from the past (Bunrak 1994, p. 442). This was the way he distinguished the two kinds of culture in an interview in English, taking pains to use the Thai terms and explain them. Kasian Tejapira puts the issue slightly differently in arguing for the liberation of identity from nationality, a kind of fragmented subjectivity or split personality (Kasian n.d.[b]).

When writing in Thai on transnational communications, he made a slightly different point, knowing that many public intellectuals, academics among them, are concerned about the important issue of local identity. He said,

> It is not possible to explain the phenomenon of "inside" (*phai nai*) without making reference to what is produced on the "outside" (*phai nork*). This would seem to be the "crisis" in Thai studies everywhere (Bunrak 1994, p. 104).

That is to say, Thai identity is relational and can only be visible against what is non-Thai. Thai studies, concentrating on Thai culture, history, politics, languages, and so forth, are manifestly concerned with what is inside the society, although as the overland caravan to Yunnan with which I began this essay illustrates, what is defined as "inside" is rapidly expanding over the borders to the north.

The Siamese Thai gaze to the north and the current fashion to study the Sinified Tai in southern China and the rest of northern Southeast Asia must be understood as a kind of ethnic nostalgia, a reclamation of identity that resides in the yet-to-be-globalized Tai minority peoples in the region. Central Thai interest on the part of government culture managers as well as of public intellectuals trained as archaeologists and anthropologists in the Sinified Tai peoples of Yunnan in China or the Vietnamized Tai peoples in Vietnam is a sign that diversity within the borders of Thailand is diminishing. Or perhaps one should say "perceived" to be diminishing because of the homogenizing potential of globalization.

The gaze to the north is itself a globalizing phenomenon, because the popular and academic writing on the culture of the Tai peoples in neighbouring countries emphasizes affinity and thus draws these people into a Siamese Thai orbit. It is now being claimed, for example, that the Zhuang people of Kwangsi province, with some 12–13 million speakers, are the "oldest" Tai group, their culture being a kind of relic of what Tai/Thai culture used to be before the more "advanced" civilizations of India and China affected it (Srisakr and Pranee 1993). The public intellectuals who write for the glossy monthly *Art and Culture* have been determinedly studying the Zhuang to document their contribution to Southeast Asian culture, and this has led to the revival of interest in the Dongson culture, significantly called "bronze drum culture" in Thai writing to avoid using a toponym from Vietnam (Aphisit 1994; *SW* 1994).

Apart from the investigation of Tai/Thai origins in the rest of Southeast Asia, other kinds of reactions to the globalizing trends illustrate how local culture is being attended to, even engineered. Public intellectuals have returned to the issue of culture, both on the national level and at the grassroots. Beginning in the early 1980s, for example, development workers, religious leaders (Christian as well as Buddhist), and health professionals involved in the work of NGOs began to campaign for the strengthening of village societies in order to help rural people contend with the more damaging effects of overdevelopment. The ideology that lies behind this campaign has been called "the community culture school of thought" by an economic historian, Chatthip Nartsupha, who himself has been an active public intellectual for the past two decades (Chatthip 1991a; Chatthip 1991b).

As Chatthip advocated in the early 1990s, this particular re-action to globalization is characterized not by its collaboration with the globalizers but by resistance to them. Just as the Thai Buddhist monk-philosopher Buddhadasa sought to find the core of Buddhism by a radical critique of the Buddhist canon, so the "community culture" movement seeks to establish the core of Thai-ness by a radical critique of urban culture. Citing the ideas of the eminent haematologist Prawet Wasi, who won the Magsaysay Award in 1981 for his work with NGOs and who has been a leader in AIDS prevention, Chatthip argued that the community culture ideology was anti-state (Chatthip 1991a, pp. 124–25). It promoted local com-munity values, and it believed that development must take into account the spiritual and environmental dimensions of human experience. Others who support the movement stress its mutuality, empathy, and egalitarianism (Jitraphorn 1993, p. 25). Chatthip used the term "anarchistic" to describe the movement's thrust. This odd term refers to the self-help, mutuality, and autonomy of village life which constitute "the fundamental discourse that has existed from the beginning". Moreover, in Chatthip's words, the values being advocated "are characteristics of Thai consciousness, which, from ancient times, has been inseparable from Thai communities" (Chatthip 1991a, p. 136). There is an explicit attempt in this formulation to distill the essentials of Thai-ness, albeit at the village level. In fact, the values advocated by the community culture school of thought, according to Chatthip, bear a striking resemblance to what King Vajiravudh said in 1915.

Finally, there is the issue of local agency and how it is con-ceptualized and mobilized by activists and cultural conservationists alike. Coincidental with the discussion of "internationalization" and "globalization" in the late 1980s, the term *phum panya* made its appearance. Roughly translated as "native/local wisdom", the term for "native" is the Indic *phum* (Pali, *bhumi*), the same term that appears in the Malay discourse of Malaysia-for-the-Malays, *bumiputra*. The business manuals that assume reader familiarity with *The Romance of the Three Kingdoms* trade on the cultural pride that "we" (in Asia) are more savvy than "them" (in the West). It is this notion of "native wisdom" that has been exploited in the business manual entitled *Wisdom of the East: A Manual for Utilizing People* (Foeng Moeng Long 1991).

This idea of "native wisdom" is remarkably similar to the concept called "local genius", so close that they appear to be translations of each other. "Local genius" was advocated by H. G. Quaritch Wales, an Englishman who published his own books and whom academics read thirty years ago but never took very seriously (Wales 1951; 1957). The concept enjoyed some vogue with Western historians of Southeast Asia after World War II as they attempted to displace colonial history with "autonomous" history (Sears 1993).

The difference between "native wisdom" and "local genius" is that the former is increasingly a weapon in the hands of both globalizers and their critics. "Native wisdom" is a powerful marketing tool, as transnational advertising agencies localize their advertising campaigns to sell their products. But at the same time, the notion of "native wisdom" lies behind the community culture ideology advocated by the NGO workers struggling to help villagers resist capitalists and state planners. In the words of one of these workers, "popular [native] wisdom is a whole body of knowledge presented holistically and representing the villagers' art of living" (Seri 1992, p. 140). "Native wisdom" thus expresses the irreducible "something" that stands for local agency. Significantly, the term for "wisdom" is one of the stalwart words for "intellect" in the Buddhist lexicon. The Thai Buddhist philosopher Buddhadasa used the term "native wisdom" to characterize the Thai faculty of reason that is as equally capable of contributing to the processes of globalization as the Western faculty of reason (Jackson n.d.[b]).

Conclusion

Globalization has many manifestations in Thailand, and many advocates and critics. Like other discursive formations such as "modernity" and "democracy" that make complex connections between institutions and consciousness, origins of globalization seem to lie somewhere else, "over there" in Europe or America. But as with these other discursive formations, globalization is both contested and appropriated by different constituencies to serve different purposes. In the Thai case, "the global" is being used by capitalists to export "the local", whether "the local" is a Thai consumer product or the national culture, even as it is used by environmentalists to confront the developers. That is to say, globalization is not only a historical process bound up with capitalism and telecommunications technology but also a way of looking at the world which sees opportunities as well as perils in the changes taking place.

The tensions inherent in the dialectical relationship between globalization and local identity are leading to the search for new, authentic selves at the personal, community, and national levels. I regard the expressive forms of this search, the kinds of cultural products, debates, and academic projects that I have discussed here, as evidence of particular ways of thinking about the world, what one might consider to be cosmologies. To investigate these cosmologies further one would have to take them separately and understand them as discursive formations.

Note
* I would like to thank Chris Barker, Joel Kahn, Glen Lewis, Pasuk Phongphaichit, Patrick Jory, Phouangthong Rungswasdisab, Sakkharin Niyomsilpa, Thaveeporn Vasavakul, Tessa Morris-Suzuki, Thomas Kirsch, Maurizio Pelaggi and O. W. Wolters for invaluable comments and references.

References
Anderson, Benedict and Ruchira Mendiones, eds. and trans. *In the Mirror: Literature and Politics in Siam in the American Era*. Bangkok, Editions Duang Kamol, 1985.

Anussorn Thavisin. "Pioneering a New Tourism Frontier". *Bangkok Post Weekly Review*, 7 January 1994.

Aphisit Thirajaruwan. "Chonchat juang khrayat trakun thai thi kao kae lae yingyai thisut [The Zhuang: The Oldest and the Most Numerous Tai]". *Sinlapa Watthanatham* 15, no. 10 (August 1994): 187.

Appadurai, Arjun. "Disjuncture and Difference in the Global Cultural Economy". *Public Culture* 2, no. 2 (Spring 1990): 1–24.

Breazeale, Kennon and Snit Smukarn. *A Culture in Search of Survival: The Phuan of Thailand and Laos*. Monograph Series 31. New Haven: Yale University Southeast Asia Studies, 1988.

Bunrak Bunyakhetmala. *Thanandorn thi si jak rabop lok thung rat thai [The Fourth Estate: From the World System to the Thai State].* Bangkok, Green Frog Press, 1994.

Byrne, Denis. "The Past of Others: Archaeological Heritage Management in Thailand and Australia." Ph.D. dissertation. Canberra: Australian National University, 1993.

Chai-anan Samudavanija. *Kanplianplaeng kap khwamru nai yuk lokkanuwat [Knowledge and Change in the Age of Globalisation].* Bangkok: Manager Publications, 1994.

Chalinee Atthakornkovit. "An Analysis of Marketing Communications Development and Practices in Thailand from 1987 to 1991". M.A. dissertation. University of Canberra, 1994.

Chatthip Nartsupha. "The 'Community Culture' School of Thought". In *Thai Constructions of Knowledge,* edited by Manas Chitakasem and Andrew Turton. London: University of London, School of Oriental and African Studies, 1991a.

————. "Naew khit watthanatham chumchon" [The Community Culture School of Thought]. In *Watthanatham thai kap khabuan kanplianplaeng sangkhom [Thai Culture and Movements for Social Change],* edited by Chatthip Nartsupha. Bangkok: Chulalongkorn University, 1991.

Cohen, Erik. "Authenticity and Commoditization in Tourism". *Annals of Tourism Research* 15 (1988): 371–86.

Copeland, Matthew Phillip. "Contested Nationalism and the 1932 Overthrow of the Absolute Monarchy". Ph.D. dissertation. Canberra: Australian National University, 1994.

Cornish, Andrew. "ASEAN and its Fringe: Neo-Geometrics in Southeast Asia". *ASESS Newsletter* (Centre for East and Southeast Asian Studies, James Cook University of North Queensland), 1 (1994): 12–13.

Fairclough, Gordon. "Sacred and Profane: Monk Embroiled in Sex and Plagiarism Scandal". *Far Eastern Economic Review,* 3 March 1994, pp. 22–23.

Featherstone, M. *Global Culture: Nationalism, Globalization and Modernity. Theory, Culture and Society* 7, no. 2–3. Special Issue, *Global Culture.* London, Sage Publications, 1990.

Foeng Moeng Long. *Phum panya tawanork khamphi kan chai khon [Wisdom of the East: A Manual for Utilizing People].* Translated by Adun Ratanamankasem. Edited by Thorngthaem Natjamnong. Bangkok: Dorkya Press 1991.

Friedland, Jonathan. "A Finger in Every Pie". *Far Eastern Economic Review,* 28 December 1989, pp. 42–44.

Hamilton, Annette. "The Mediascape of Modern Southeast Asia". *Screen* 33, no. 1 (1992): 81–92.

Hamilton, Annette. "Rumours, Foul Calumnies and the Safety of the State: Mass Media and National Identity in Thailand". In *National Identity and its Defenders: Thailand, 1939–1989*, edited by Craig J. Reynolds. Chiangmai: Silkworm Books, 1993a.

——. "Video Crackdown, or The Sacrificial Pirate: Censorship and Cultural Consequences in Thailand". *Public Culture* 5 (1993b): 515–31.

Hannerz, U. "Notes on the Global Ecumene". *Public Culture*, no. 2 (1989): 66–75.

Hewison, Kevin. "Thailand: On Becoming a NIC". *Pacific Review* 5, no. 4 (1992): 328–37.

Jackson, Peter A. "Kathoey > < Gay > < Man: The Historical Emergence of Gay Male Identity in Thailand". In *Sites of Desire/Economies of Pleasure: Sexualities in Asia and the Pacific*, edited by Lenore Manderson and Margaret Jolly. Chicago: University of Chicago Press, n.d.(a).

——. "Epilogue". *Buddhadasa: A Buddhist Thinker for the Modern World*. 2nd rev. ed. Bangkok: Siam Society, n.d.(b).

Jitraphorn Wanatsaphong. "Samphat chalatchai ramitanon watthanatham chumchon nai krasae lokkanuwat [Interview with Chalatchai Ramitanon: The Community Culture Movement in the Age of Globalisation]". *Sayamrat Weekly*, 17–23 October 1993, pp. 23–25.

Kasian Tejapira. "Pigtail: A Pre-History of Chineseness in Siam". *SOJOURN* 7, no. 1 (1992): 95–122.

——. *Lae lort lai mangkorn [Looking through the Dragon Design]*. Bangkok: Khopfai Publishing, 1994.

——. "'Globalisers' vs. 'Communitarians': The Current Intellectual Scene in Thailand". Unpublished paper, n.d.(a).

——. "The Postmodernization of Thainess." Unpublished paper, n.d.(b).

Keyes, Charles F. "The Case of the Purloined Lintel: The Politics of a Khmer Shrine as a Thai National Treasure". In Reynolds (1993).

Muang Boran (MB). "Jak 'lokanuwat' thung 'lokawibat' nai sangkhom thai [Thai Society: From 'Globalisation' to 'Global Catastrophe]. *Muang Boran* 20, no. 1 (1994): 6–12.

Melchers, K. William. "The Thai Invasion of Kengtung During the Reign of King Rama III". In *Anuson Walter Vella*, edited by Ronald D. Renard. Honolulu: University of Hawaii Press, and Centre for Asian and Pacific Studies, 1986.

Naowarat Suksamran. "Selling Political Dreams." *Bangkok Post*, 18 July 1993.

Nidhi Aeusrivongse. Watthanatham yuk lokkanwat [Culture in the Globalising Epoch]. *Sinlapa watthanatham [Art and Culture]*, no. 6 (1994): 92–94.

Peleggi, Maurizio. "National Heritage and Nationalist Narrative in Contemporary Thailand: An Essay on Culture and Politics." M.A. (Asian Studies) dissertation. Canberra: Australian National University, 1994.

――――. "National Heritage and Global Tourism in Thailand". *Annals of Tourism Research* 23, no. 2 (1996): 432–48.

Reynolds, Craig J., ed. *National Identity and its Defenders: Thailand, 1939–1989*. Chiang Mai: Silkworm Books, 1993.

――――. "Thailand". In *Australia in Asia: Communities of Thought*, edited by Anthony Milner and Mary Quilty. Melbourne: Oxford University Press, 1996a.

――――. "Tycoons and Warlords". In *Tycoons and Warlords*. St Leonards, NSW: Allen and Unwin, 1996b.

――――. "Tycoons and Warlords: Modern Thai Social Formations and Chinese Historical Romance". In *Sojourners and Settlers: Histories of Southeast Asia and the Chinese, A Volume in Honour of Jennifer Cushman*, edited by Anthony Reid. Allen & Unwin, forthcoming.

Sanga Luchaphatthanaphorn and Athorn Techathada, eds. *Wikkaruttakan thang ekkalak banthuk khorng khon run mai [Identity Crisis: A Report from the Younger Generation]*. Bangkok: Pajarayasan, 1981.

Sears, Laurie. "The Contingency of Autonomous History". In *Autonomous Histories, Particular Truths: Essays in Honour of John Smail*, edited by Laurie Sears. Monograph no. 11. Madison: University of Wisconsin, Center for Southeast Asian Studies, 1993.

Seri Pongphit. "Popular Wisdom and the Search for Identity in Northeast Thailand". In *Proceedings to Present the Results of Projects Funded under the Toyota Foundation's International Grant Program*, pp. 138–42. Tokyo: The Tokyo Foundation, 1992.

Skinner, G. William. *Chinese Society in Thailand: An Analytical History*. Ithaca: Cornell University Press, 1957.

Srisakr Vallibhotama and Pranee Wongthes. *Zhuang: The Oldest Tai* [in Thai]. Bangkok: Silpakorn University, 1993.

Suchat Sawatsi, ed. *Lophanuwat [Greed]*. Bangkok: Changwannakam, 1994a.

――――. *Phokhanuwat [Consumerism]*. Bangkok: Changwannakam, 1994b.

Sinlapa Watthanatham (SW). Editorial in *Sinlapa watthanatham* 15, no. 10 (1994): 14–16.

Thirayut Bunmi. *Jut plian haeng yuk samai [A Pivotal Moment]*. 2nd printing. Bangkok: Winyuchon Publication House, 1993.

――――. *Sangkhom khem kaeng [A Vigorous Society]*. Bangkok: Mingmit Press, 1994.

Thongchai Winichakul. *Siam Mapped: The History of the Geo-Body of a Nation*. Honolulu: University of Hawaii Press, 1994.

Vajiravudh, King. "Latthi aoyang" [The Cult of Imitation]. In *Pramuan phraratchaniphon nai phrabat somdet phramongkut klao jao yu hua [Collected Essays of King Mongkutklao]*. Cremation volume for Major General Phraya Anirutthewa. Bangkok, 1951.

Vella, Walter F. *Chaiyo! King Vajiravudh and the Development of Thai Nationalism*. Honolulu: University Press of Hawaii, 1978.

Wales, H. G. Q. *The Making of Greater India: A Study in South-East Asian Culture Change*. London: Quaritch, 1951.

———. *Prehistory and Religion in South-East Asia*. London: Quaritch, 1957.

Warasan Thammasat (WT). "Lokanuwat lokantaranuwat lokawiwat". *Warasan thammasat* 20, no. 1 (1994): 101–24.

Wrangel, Marc. "A Geometry Lesson". *Manager*, October 1993, pp. 34–38.

chapter six

GENDER AND THE GLOBALIZATION OF ISLAMIC DISCOURSES
A Case Study

RACHEL A. D. BLOUL

This chapter explores some aspects of the globalization of Muslim/ Islamic discourses. Certainly, there is nothing new in the concept of an international Muslim space (indeed, the enduring links between various Muslim societies have been well documented; Abaza 1991, Nagata 1984, Weyland 1990). Contemporary developments (notably communication technology), however, have added on a new dimension to these global cultural flows, in particular as they give expression to Muslim cultural politics in the form of resistance to Western imperialism whether economic, political or cultural (Rais 1985; Lee 1993).

This is not to say that there is one global Muslim, or even Islamist,[1] movement. While it is important to distinguish here between Muslim and Islamist discourses, with Islamist referring to specific Muslim politico-religious militant trends generally defined as radical Islamism (Etienne 1987), neither of these epithets is meant to refer to a homogeneous trend. On the contrary, there is a proliferation of global Muslim and Islamist discourses (whether traditional, modernist, secular, radical, feminist,[2] and so on; see Hamdani 1993; Salla 1991) competing over the interpretations of the Islamic message and the definitions of Muslim practices.

No theme is more argued over than that of gender. Yet, however different the many Muslim and Islamist positions and discourses are from each other, the arguments on what has been for now more than a century called "The Woman Question" (Hatem 1988; Kandiyoti 1991; Moghadam 1993, 1994b; Nader 1989; Najmabadi 1991, 1994; Yeganeh 1993; Yuval-Davis and Anthias 1989) have become increasingly reified and strikingly similar from one Muslim country to another.

The aim of this chapter is to focus on the articulation of gender themes in *Islamist* discourses, and then to examine *Muslim* women's responses to this as demonstrated at a conference in Penang, Malaysia, which was attended by Muslim (some of them Islamist) women of diverse nationalities representing a wide variety of positions *vis-à-vis* Islam and the "Woman Question". What was striking in the Penang conference was the familiarity, and the universalistic quality of the various arguments about the status of women even though those arguments were articulated from a variety of Islamic and national/ cultural points of view. Yet, the gender themes in Muslim, and especially Islamist, discourses do not construct the narrow-minded patriarchal monologues on women that Western critiques often perceive. In fact, the articulation of these themes leads often to contradictions both at the level of the arguments presented, and at the level of their effects in everyday practices. These contradictions thus contrast with the universalistic quality of the arguments. This equivocal universalism is a result of the way in which gender themes are articulated as a core issue of Muslim and Islamist discourses, and of how the "Woman Question" is conceptualized as a central trope for Muslim and Islamist social/religious/political projects.

A similar argument can be made on the question of Muslim cultures. The debate on Muslim cultures, the diversity of which is often opposed to the universality of Islamic revelation, is also the site of many contradictions, especially in Islamist (as opposed to simply Muslim) discourses. On the one hand, there are a number of global Islamic discourses (within Muslim or Islamist frameworks as defined above), and on the other, there are their local interpretations when the universal message of Islam is made to work in the context of national objectives. Again, within this proliferating heterogeneity of Islamic positions, the "Woman Question" functions as a central focus of organization for both Muslim and cultural (collective) identities.[3]

Thus, the case is made here that this "universalistic quality" of the discussion of "women in Islam" is not simply an effect of Western imperialism and orientalism, but is also built into the construction of Islam, by Muslims, as the one "true" universalism. The first section argues how this universalistic quality is built into Islamist global political strategies of Muslim identity(ies) for the Ummah. Secondly, it will be shown, as demonstrated by the Penang conference, that the centrality of the "Woman Question" for collective identities (Muslim and/or Islamist) and the globalized quality of the arguments about gender transform the discussion of specific realities into ideological disputes. This prevents the meaningful discussion of gender issues across various perspectives. Instead, differences are artificially overcome through ambiguous assertions which allow for the displacement of the debate to some ulterior moment.

Islamist Discourse On Gender

The discussion will first focus on the widely spread gender themes of globalized Islamist discourses. The discussion of Islamist literature on women will be illustrated with examples from various articles (including news items, editorials and in-depth articles) published in *Kayhan International*,[4] during the period from December 1993 to September 1994. In addition, the main theoretical implications of these articles will be further substantiated by reference to a bevy of Islamist written works from various parts of the world.

Kayhan International is an Iranian, Teheran-based newspaper, written in English, whose targetted readership is the international Islamist élite. It collects international Muslim news and has a daily section dedicated to Islamist struggles around the world, in addition to in-depths analyses of Islamic doctrinal points and critical commentaries on social questions. The themes, arguments and style are typical of sophisticated Islamist literature the world over, though with a distinct Iranian outlook on some questions of international politics. Needless to say, the "Woman Question" is one to which it dedicates a lot of space, and *on this theme the Shi'ite specificity more or less disappears to give way to the familiar arguments about proper Muslim womanhood.* This Islamist discourse in *Kayhan International* can be characterized as androcentric insofar as it represents the point of view of the male Iranian hierarchy.

The treatment of the gender theme in *Kayhan International* is one example of an Islamist strategy for consensus which uses the "Woman Question" to articulate a rhetoric of universal Muslim identity to oppose a demonized West. As has been noted before (Hélie-Lucas 1993; Moghadam, 1993, 1994a), whatever the political and historical contexts of Islamist discourses, they always present Islam as a religious and cultural identity, as

> threatened by colonialism, imperialism, capitalism, socialism, foreign ideologies or other dominant religions (Hélie-Lucas 1993, p. 5).

Moreover:

> The Islamist movement's concern with religious and cultural identity is invariably translated into a focus on gender and the position of women (Moghadam 1993, p. 244).

It is argued here that the Islamist gender strategies which link the position and role of women to the rhetoric of Islamic identity is by no means unambiguous. On the contrary, it contains many seeds for potential contradictions and paradoxical effects, all of which can be, and have been, used by Muslim, and Islamist women, in their own strategies for agency.

Four main themes can be distinguished in the Islamist discourse on gender. Firstly, there are affirmations of *the nature and place of women according to the universal truth of Islam.* These are based on the major assumption that Islam is the Word of God, that it is based on the true understanding of an eternal human nature and that its proposed way of life is henceforth valid for all times and societies.

> Islam being an intuitive religion, has observed the real needs of mankind (*Kayhan International*, 10 March 1994, p. 10).

Among the real needs of mankind (as opposed to the false, that is, socially created, needs that are contingent and not to be indulged in by believers) are the need to procreate, and sexual needs that are to be satisfied within the Islamic institution of the family. Prescribed relationships within the Islamic family are based on the true understanding of human nature, which is not the same for men and women. Thus, women are described as having more rights in Islam relative to those offered by Western institutions (Doi 1983, Abd al-Ati n.d.). The rights of women in Islam respect the true nature of women (for example, their need for motherhood, their feminine delicacy of feeling, their womanly dignity, and so on) and therefore offer true liberation, true fulfilment, especially compared to the "empty rights" that Western women have acquired after long struggles. When the Islamic family, as described in the sacred texts, allows male control, polygyny, and early marriage for women, it is said to be also according to the true nature of women. Thus, early marriage in Iran is justified because

> female human beings can constitutionally become competent to marry when nine years old (*while male human beings are slower to mature*) (*Kayhan International*, 10 March 1994, p. 14).

The gender discourse on the sanctity of the family extends to an Islamic conception of the rights of children, which is truer and therefore better than the Western ones (hence the opposition to the international agreement on children's rights):

> Certain elements of the children's rights convention are not consistent with the progressive laws of Islam... (Another) glaring flaw of the convention is the blanket use of the word 'child' without taking into consideration the finer points of male or female and their physical and psychological frame[5] ... Islamic laws in keeping with the physical and mental frames of both the male and female are not unscientific and rigid like those of most non-Islamic societies, where as a result, social ills are widespread and children subjected to all undue pressure (*Kayhan International*, 17 January 1994, p. 14).

For example, Muslim perceptions of the World Population Conference (Cairo, 1994) link the notion of a Western plot aiming to eradicate

Muslim populations with concepts of cultural assault against the sanctity of the Muslim family aiming (through the advocacy of abortion and free fornication, that is, heterosexuality outside wedlock and homosexuality) to corrupt and destroy the moral fibre of Muslim nations:

> The conference's action plan includes issues which contradict Islamic (principles)... These issues violate the Islamic Sharia.... The Cairo Conference calls for the annihilation of weakened peoples, and in particular Muslims.... The plan is not aimed at developing the impoverished world, but it is a racist plan for the welfare of the controlling white element... (it) aims at spreading fornication, destroying marriage and the family unit and condoning abortion.... They want our society to become barren like theirs (*Kayhan International*, 15 August 1994, p. 14).

The sanctity of the family (and women's place within it) is thus linked to the second theme, which is the *sensitivity to cultural assault*. The "Westernized painted whores" of Iranian news, the "Westoxified women" of the Egyptian Muslim Brotherhood's catchwords, the "gharbzadeh", are all victims of Western consumerism and cultural traitors through whom the West is able to bring destructive Western degenerate habits to the core institution of the Muslim family (Najamabadi 1991, 1994; Moghadam 1993; Hélie-Lucas 1993). The "Westoxified women" become the embodiment of all the ills of Muslim societies. Thus, the question of women becomes

> central to the revival of Muslim identity and the reconstruction of the Islamic moral and social order (Moghadam 1993, p. 245).

Women are urged to embrace a Muslim model of womanhood which represents cultural authenticity (Nader 1989; Najmabadi 1994). Consequently, the "Woman Question" and its relation to concerns over public morality becomes both the first step in socio-political and religious reforms and the symbol of successful reformation, from Algeria to Iran.

A third theme, of the sensitivity to Western prejudice, concurrently appears, so that the call to *hijab* as resistance to "Westoxification" and return to Islamic purity is also affirming *Islamic superiority in giving women more rights and true equality.* The *hijab* gives women "freedom from human wolves":

> In Islam, the liberation of women is far superior, noble and dignified than in these so-called permissive societies. The hypocrite West is quick to condemn Islamic laws which protect women from degradation... A truly liberated woman always dresses decently and modestly... The Hijab itself gives an aura of freedom to womankind, facilitating their movements in public, and protecting them from provocation and wanton greed of human wolves. Thus, in an Islamic society, women enjoy a far more dignified status than that of their sisters in the West (*Kayhan International*, 9 December 1993, p. 14).

A fourth theme is linked to this concept of freedom through following Islamic precepts respecting the true nature of women, that is, *a discourse of rights* (see also A'la Mawdudi 1980; Khan 1991; Olayiwola 1993). It stresses the right of women to self-fulfilment and self-realization of their human potential (that is, the right to work, to participate in public life, to develop one's talents). These rights are better understood and provided for in Islam than in the West, especially as they are granted in a way which respect women's true nature (that is, without detracting from women's first responsibility and emotional commitment to "her" family).

> In Islam, a woman has the right to participate in public affairs, own property, marry the man of her choice and if the case has gone beyond reconciliation, to divorce her husband (ibid.)

Thus, *Kayhan International* gives pride of place to initiatives enhancing women's participation in public life, in cultural activities (interviews with women film-makers, women writers and so on), in sports — a female participation distinguished by its "keeping with Islamic tradition". Here are some article captions:

> MP decries Western propaganda against women's rights in Iran (5 July 1994).
>
> Women enjoy more freedom under present setup (22 January 1994).
>
> *Hijab* no hindrance to women's social activities (20 December 1993).

President Rafsanjani: wrong traditions responsible for women's social problems (11 May 1994).

President says: Women should be encouraged to join physical education (14 February 1994).

Iranian women conquer country's highest mountain (1 September 1994, on 16 Iranian students "covered in keeping with Islamic tradition" who "climbed to the top of the country's highest mountain for the first time").

This is linked to an underlying critique of "*wrong cultural traditions*" and *a reformist discourse* of the true understanding of Islam: Western critiques, besides being hypocritical, are confusing the effects of "wrong traditions" with the "true nature of Islam".

There are already many seeds for potential contradictions and paradoxical effects in the above. For example, the potential contradictions between the right to realize one's potential and the necessity to follow Islamic restrictions, though resolved at an intellectual level in the positing of a "true human eternal nature" revealed in Islam, lead in practice to paradoxical initiatives. Such paradoxes abound particularly in the case of women's status when prescriptive restrictions, such as forbidding certain professions and studies, or incompatible "rights" (such as the age of marriage for girls) coexist with more empowering initiatives, such as providing the context for more political representation of women in the *majlis* (though the proportion of women is still minimal), increased participation in public life, and so on.

In addition, it is worth noting how the "Woman's Question" is a public affair vitally concerning men. Muslim men actively participate, indeed often dominate the debate on women's rights which is rightly perceived as a matter for the politics of collective identity. There is nothing new in this. More than a century ago, ideas on the promotion of women's rights and the improvement of women's education and situation were at first adopted by enlightened men who saw in "the debasement of Muslim women" one of the reasons for the degeneration of Muslim countries. The argument, with its distinctive Victorian undertones, rested on the importance of the educative and civilizing functions of women as mothers and spouses.

It was part of a more general renaissance (Nadra) movement of Muslim culture with the Egyptian Qasim Amin 1865–1908 as a leading figure (Hoffman-Ladd 1987). This was a socio-political and humanitarian project of "(limited) freedom and progress" and its early proponents did not see it as undermining religion and the "Muslim way of life" in any way. But it was, in the words of Mai Ghoussoub (1987) a "male affair", as indeed is the contemporary Islamist pre-occupation with gender, and the central role given to the "Women's Question" in the renewal of Muslim societies. But is it?

So far we have seen how the four main ways in which gender is imbricated in universalizing Islamist discourses (more rights according to the true nature of women, sensitivity to Western cultural assault but uneasy perception of true global Islam versus erring Muslim cultures, sensitivity to Western prejudices and a discourse of subjective self-realization, and women's place in the politics of collective identity as men's business) are a potentially fruitful source of contradictions and paradoxical effects. But what is the nature of women's participation in, and reactions to, such discourses?

Islam and Women: Women's Perspectives

Muslim women's reactions to the discourses exemplified by *Kayhan International* are varied. As previously noted, there are at least two sorts of feminist positions for women (modernist and secular versus Islamist and militant, and also militant Islamist). In addition, many women do not articulate a feminist position, staying within the traditional cultural logic of what Kandiyoti (1988) calls patriarchal bargains,[6] which may or may not take modern Islamist form. The following section will focus on women's perspectives as delineated in the 1993 "Women and Islam" Conference in Penang. First, a brief description of the conference's proceedings will be presented. An attempt is then made to evaluate women's discourses in relation to the four themes in the articulation of gender within Islamist discourses delineated above. Possible directions are then indicated for the understanding of Muslim women's strategies for agency within the context of the globalization of Muslim/Islamist discourses and their potential contradictions.

The Penang Conference

Though the conference gathered predominantly Malay Muslim women activists, a number of Malaysian women present were Buddhist, Hindu or Christian. There were also a minority of Muslim women guests from other Muslim countries, in particular from the Middle East and North Africa, from Pakistan and Bangladesh, and from other Southeast Asian countries.

What was striking in the aims and unfolding of the conference was not only its "global resonance", but also the universalistic quality of the discussions, even when they dealt with particular empirical case studies. These observations were confirmed by other participants who also mentioned how both the form and content of the issues and discussions echoed similar discussions in Bangladesh, Indonesia, Pakistan, Egypt and Tunisia, although these observations contradict the accounts of Malay-Muslim specificity found in the anthropological and sociological literature (Ong 1990; Mutalib 1990). This is not to deny the specificity of local conditions, but to show the centrality of the "Woman's Question" and Islamist discursive strategies, and the ideological dominance of certain global themes make a meaningful political discussion of Muslim women's status impossible, even in situations specifically set up to offer a wide variety of Muslim women the possibility of discussing such issues. In short, the conference showed how Muslim women's participation in, and reactions to, the construction of Islam as a heterogeneous universalism unified by its thematic treatment of gender and set up in opposition to Western universalism, illustrated the effects of the latent contradictions between the various ways in which gender themes are articulated in Muslim and Islamist discourses.

The stated aims of the conference contained some distinctly emancipatory overtones. It aimed:[7]

1. to promote open discussions on the meaning and interpretation of the Q'uran, as well as other Islamic texts, on the question of gender and gender relations from both historical and contemporary perspectives.
2. to understand the basis of authority, power, dominance and influence in Islamic social, cultural and political contexts;

3. to bring together concerned women, Muslims and non-Muslims, Malaysians and non-Malaysians, to take part in discussions involving mutual and universal aspirations; and

4. to review and assess Malaysian Syariah laws (in comparison with other Muslim societies), with a view to promoting positive reforms.

The programme itself included speakers from various countries, some of whom were Muslim feminist academics of international standing (Leila Ahmed, Riffat Hassan), others, Islamist political activists, yet others, Muslim feminist political activists (Selma Sobhan, a Bangladeshi representative of the international women's organization, Women Living Under Muslim Laws, hereafter referred to as WLUML).

The first session was given to an exploration of Islamic texts, first the Q'uran, and then the Hadith and the Syariah, with the overt intention of questioning the hegemonic patriarchal interpretations of such texts. The other sessions concentrated on the experience of Muslim women in various Muslim countries. The intent was one of contrast and comparison between various Muslim countries' customs and their variations in Syariah applications (a strategy made popular by WLUML). Finally, a plenary session was held to summarize the findings and to pass various resolutions.

Fifty-eight women (including the author) participated in the conference in various capacities. Twenty women wore what they called the *tudong* (covering both hair and neck in the fashion of a wimple) and loose garments which left only the face and hands uncovered. Overall, their dress was similar to that worn by young women in Egypt, Algeria and no doubt elsewhere in the Muslim world, the kind of dress which has become the signifier of Islamist movements on countless magazine covers. Only one woman wore a Western summer dress. She was the Tunisian speaker, whose dress was the subject of many negative comments (one participant went as far as to publicly declare that, considering the way she dressed, she could not possibly be granted any credibility when talking about Islam). Most of the women present were either professionals, or belonging to the élite, or both. Most were university-educated.

There were various opening ceremonies, most notable for the level of political patronage and/or networking that they entailed: a woman federal minister and two of the organizers commanded the audience on the importance of initiatives such as the Conference, which they firmly placed within the context of "nation-building". The Conference was deemed part of an effort in "nation-building" because of its underlying project of "educating the masses", which, in this instance, was seen to entertain many ignorant and false assumptions about Islam. Already some of the global themes can be seen to emerge ("wrong cultural traditions", reformist discourse, and the rhetoric of collective identity).

A religious specialist (Riffat Hassan) gave the first theoretical paper. This in itself was quite subversive as, not withstanding a few historical figures, Muslim women on the whole have been barred from studying their faith. She examined the Q'uran and the Ahadith (collection of Hadith, or reported sayings of the Prophet) on women, with particular attention on those verses most frequently quoted to justify women's subordinate status. She set out to prove, by means of linguistic/philological interpretations and socio-historical contextualizations, that even those verses, properly understood in the spirit rather than the letter of the Revelation, were in fact in favour of women's equality. Other Islamic texts (that is, the Hadith and the Syariah), she asserted, were fallible, based on human interpretation (and quite given to contradict the spirit of the Q'uran). She argued that Muslim cultures were based on such fallible and misogynistic Hadith interpretations rather than on the true spirit of the Q'uran, the only Sacred Text. This is an increasingly popular argument among Muslim feminists (for example, in Malaysia, see Wadud-Muhsin 1992) although it is very challenging to the majority of Muslims who believe that both Hadith and Syariah share the sacred character of the Q'uran. Variations of this type of argument, however, are increasingly frequent in Muslim feminist thought (Mernissi 1991; Ahmed 1992).

The other theoretical paper pursued the theme that Muslim/ Islamist discourses which do not acknowledge in theory, and do not structure in fact, equal rights for women, are part of a class discourse of ignorance, and not properly Islamic at all. Muslim understanding of modernization as Westernization, *qua* moral decadence, symbolized by, and condemned through, "emancipated" (that is, Westernized) upper-class Muslim women were criticized. So were Muslim men's emotional and political investments in the control of Muslim women as their (males', that is) last stand against colonizers and/or "the West". In other words, the paper gave a sophisticated critique of the Islamist discourse on "Westoxification" as being male-biased, and outlined a familiar academic argument on the links between the state, nationalism and the control of women because of their function as reproducers and as symbolic bearers of cultural values (Moghadam 1994a, 1994b; Najamabadi 1991; Yeganeh 1993).

The reactions of the audience to both papers were mixed. A few were both restless and silent. Some used obscure linguistic points to argue over the proper translation of ancient Arabic, which practically no one knew. The rejection of the Hadith made quite a number of women uncomfortable, but they did not have the cultural resources to question it. Most of the women who enthusiastically joined the discussion at this stage were obviously the very pro-feminist modernist Muslim ones. One Malay woman in particular, well-known for her Muslim feminist activism, made a number of daring interventions in the direction of *ijtihad* (reinterpretation) that were not followed up by anyone. Many of these women also liberally subscribed to a pluralist position, emphasizing that many interpretations of Islamic texts had been in existence and therefore probably would be in the future. They did not object to this, but wanted to propose a space for democratic discussion where various religious positions were possible and acceptable.

The rest of the conference was devoted to case studies of women's situations in various Muslim countries. The Tunisian speaker, coming from a Muslim country reputed to be the most liberal in personal status codes,[8] talked about the gap between laws that "looked good on paper," and their lack of application in everyday life. She did not involve her audience at all, except for the two Muslim feminist activists who had delivered the previous daring papers. This pattern of involvement/non-involvement became more marked as the conference followed its course. The practical details of the various case studies were commented upon by some conference members, but their political and ideological implications as to equal rights for women in Islam were left to be discussed by a few committed academic activists who were made to look more and more isolated. They were also made to increasingly give the impression that they belonged to a Westernized élite, in particular because of the use of specific rhetorical devices. For example, women in *tudong* interspersed Arabic words in their speech, frequently pronounced the Arabic invocation of God and other various linguistic markers to demonstrate their Islamic legitimacy. This is not a Malay specificity. Indeed, these rhetorical devices as a means to mark one's Muslim legitimacy, and the lack of such in one's opponents, can be found in much Islamist literature. (For example, it is a favourite way of discounting arguments without really engaging with them for many reviewers in the *Muslim World Books Review*, published in Leicester, United Kingdom, by the Islamic Foundation). The same women also used Malay words frequently (when English was the lingua franca) whether by default, or as a strategy, I do not know. All in all, they gave off an impression of the Malay-Muslim legitimacy which is described in the ethnographic and sociological literature on Malaysia as combining Malay ethnicity and Muslim legitimacy in a programme of nation-building (Lee 1990).

It was noted that the Malay academic who organized the conference, and made important personal and political investment in it (according to other Malay Muslim academics participating), became more and more silent and/or non-committal with time. The only moment that something like a general discussion took place was when the topic of veiling raised after a historian's (Leila Ahmed) paper questioned the Islamic nature of this practice by demonstrating its origin in the cultural practices of the Middle East before Islam. The (veiled) commentator struggled painfully to give a summary of the argument (which she did not attempt to assess), then renounced it, contenting herself with thanking the author for giving such interesting information. The ensuing discussion was illuminating both for being for once general, and having absolutely no effect, as not a single woman was moved from her original position by the argument of the other side. Interestingly, however, a few women, after defending their veil as "Islamic", but being unable to compete at the level of ancient Arabic, historical and Q'uranic interpretation, proclaimed that they were not wearing "a veil", but "the *tudong*" which they presented as a traditional Malay custom. This issue will be discussed below.

Finally, during the plenary session, when resolutions were to be passed, there was a reversal. The very vocal minority of committed feminists was to all purposes shouted down, and the previously rather silent minority of women with *tudong* spoke with great emphasis, with all the previously noted rhetorical devices (Arabic and Malay words, references to Islamic and national/traditional Malay allegiances). Most propositions were toned down effectively. For example, one woman had proposed condemning polygamy. After some discussion, it seemed that many women favoured this proposition. But when it came to writing down the final propositions, the discussion was reopened by opponents using "Islamic" and class arguments (such as poor middle-aged women would be repudiated by husbands seeking younger wives and left without resources[9]). As a result, this proposition was rejected. In fact, no consensus was reached on any "proposition" and "resolution" and the Conference closed with some very vague and ambiguous "recommendations", which allowed for the displacement of the same debate towards future discussions. Here are the recommendations:

1. a need for dialogue among women of different faiths (the women "of other faiths" participating in this conference hardly spoke);
2. a need for research on theoretical interpretations of religious texts;
3. a need for the creation of an Islamic Research Institute for Muslim women;
4. a need for improvement in the implementation of the Syariah, though no particular reform was proposed. The Syariah's status as sacred text was *not* disclaimed, and the problems needing "improvement" were attributed to "bad administration".

Thinking about the Conference and Women's Strategies for Agency

My understanding of what happened in the Conference is directly linked to my understanding of how Muslims' self-perception and self-construction anywhere are influenced by the various Muslim/ Islamist global flows that make up a fluid, multidimensional Muslim universe.

A feeling of *déja vu* haunted me for the whole conference and led me to anxiously interrogate myself (was I orientalizing?). Where were the "Malay specificity", the "localized interpretations"? Indeed, the arguments on "Westoxification" (and how "Occidentalizing" were those?), on the place of women in the regeneration of Muslim culture and moral universe, the rhetoric of identity, were the same ones that I — and many other participants as they also recognized, in answer to my queries — have often encountered elsewhere in the Muslim world. In this instance, women, in particular Malaysian women, were positioning themselves in relation to the same universalizing arguments concerning the proper status and functions of women in Muslim societies, and specifically the modes of their participation in the regeneration of Muslim (here also, Malay) cultures.

There were at least two distinct trends. Firstly, there was a Muslim feminist orientation that argued that, properly understood, the Q'uran favours women's equality and women's rights. This particular effort at *ijtihad* did not make any reference to a true, eternal and specifically female nature. Women situating themselves in this trend used every resource at their disposal (Q'uranic exegesis, histori-cal analysis, sociological/anthropological critiques of Muslim cultures and societies). They were very careful to remain within a Muslim framework: Leila Ahmed, Riffat Hassan, Selma Sobhan, the three representations of Sisters in Islam from Kuala Lumpur, all argued along these lines. They carefully allowed for a pluralistic, global Islamic space which could accommodate diverging arguments, in-cluding some Islamist positions, thus trying to draw "democratically" the Islamist representatives into a discussion with them. They also resisted any association with cultural contamination by the West. Yet, they encountered very little success in their attempts to "engage in a dialogue". Indeed, it is not clear whether their positions and arguments were distinguished from the secular ones of the Tunisian speaker who was the only proponent of the position that the "Woman's Question" is a social problem to be debated outside the terrain of Islam. And certainly, the final recommendations showed that this particular trend in Muslim feminism, however vocal, was a minority position.

Secondly, an Islamist orientation accepted without presenting any argument the *a priori* of a specific female nature for which the *hijab* is the best protection. This second position was less clearly articulated. For example, women following this particular trend argued for the "veil" as, first, an Islamic injunction, and then, when unable to contest a Q'uranic/Arabic exegesis showing that it is not so, and unable to respond to the historical analysis of the veil as a Middle Eastern custom of non-Islamic origin, shifted their argument to the veil as *tudong* being a Malay custom. This, of course, is not true either. Traditional Malays wear the *selendang*, a scarf used primarily as an accessory and a good deal less strict that the wimple-like *tudong* (Virginia Hooker, personal communication). In fact, what these young women were wearing does not have a proper Malay linguistic referrent, much less a "traditional" one: *tudong* means lid/covering. This wimple can also be referred to as a mini-*telekung* (Omar 1993; Karim 1992). The *telekung* is a prayer veil which, as its name indicates, is put on by Muslim women specifically when praying. Thus, it seems that *tudong* or mini-*telekung* economically conflate the local appropriation of global trends (what they are wearing is the sort of wimple-like headcovering worn the world over by radical Islamic women) with the invention of tradition required for nation-building (the numerous references to nation-building and affirmations of Malay nationalism were an indication of the importance of this strategy of collective identity).

Yet, this second group was by no means devoid of proto-feminist consciousness, if by this one understands an awareness of an undeserved lower status for women. A number of women arguing from this position were political activists — professional women actively engaged in political and social activities within the Islamist currents. For example, Hajah Ilani binti Dato Haj Isahak, an Islamist member of the Kelantan State Parliament, declared that:

> ...under Islamic governance, women may be winners and not losers if they are wise enough to demand and strive for justice whenever inaccurate implementation of Islam leads to injustice. If we Kelantanese Muslim women preserve and increase our assertiveness we might be

instrumental in achieving the objective of a humane just society which is...egalitarian.

Another Islamist women celebrated the educational, work and financial achievements of professional Muslim Malay women in Singapore.

These women were thus quite aware of their rights and were determined to obtain them. They thought they would have a better chance of reaching their goals within an Islamist framework which they understand as stressing a social reconstruction away from the abuses and errors of the "wrong cultural traditions". Insofar as they seemed to think that women's problems were due to these "wrong cultural traditions" which they also saw to be a consequence of male abuses of power, their position was rather similar to that of feminist Muslims. Thus, they had their own proto-feminist interpretation of Islamist discourses which stressed males' failing due to an insufficient concern with Islamic teachings. But their solution, logically enough, was to advocate the intensification of Islamicization efforts. In so doing, and in their acceptance of a given female nature, they diverged from the feminist Muslim position, though they did show a specific female, even proto-feminist and certainly egalitarian, interpretation of the various themes on gender in Islamist discourses, an interpretation which argued for the reforming of Muslim men as a complement to the reforming of Muslim women.

Such a normative response, which reasserts Islamic principles, can be shared by many Islamist militants, both males and females, and has the merit of economy. It affirms the superiority of true Islam over the West by denigrating Western "degeneracy" in the name of Islamic norms, not Muslim realities. And it offers a solution to the same Muslim realities by showing the proper Islamic path. Muslim women choosing this answer fulfill many contradictory imperatives: they cannot be accused of cultural treachery, they gain a respectable public voice and identity (a way, as *Kayhan International* argues, to self-realization and participation in public life), and they can criticize some cultural customs (and implicitly the men who uphold them) in the name of true Islamic values. In other words, they can, as Kandiyoti (1988) writes, bargain with Muslim patriarchies and the implicit paradoxes within Islamist discursive strategies. The Islamist women's bargaining response seems to have many advantages, and as the Penang conference demonstrates, many advocates. But it also has many problems.

Firstly, the strength of women's bargaining position depends quite heavily on a religious discourse of male normative obligations (for example, not to take a second spouse if he thinks he cannot behave justly and equally *vis-à-vis* both). This severely limits the possibilities for women's individual and collective empowerment.

Secondly, it is also a strategy that must refuse, as the Conference showed, the pluralist alliance offered by the Muslim feminists arguing for *ijtihad* and democratic tolerance of various interpretations. This is because it does not allow the questioning of "the truth of human/feminine nature according to Islam" which asserts Islamist political strategies of representation using the "Woman's Question" in attempts to promote a universal Muslim identity.

Thirdly, this refusal blocks the meaningful discussion of specific gender issues as differences and contradictions are obscured by rhetorics. This reinforces the similarities and repetitiveness of the discussions on the status of Muslim women across countries and cultures. Discursive resolution is prevented in favour of an ambiguous displacement, such as the inconclusive recognition of "needs" in the Penang conference recommendations.

Obviously, it is difficult to precisely evaluate how much the difficulties in publicly (politically) discussing how the heterogeneity of Muslim women's situations across Muslim and Islamist perspectives bear upon Muslim women's lives. But the Penang conference, as in so many other similar forums, makes it difficult to imagine that the ideological effects of the Islamist discourses of a universal Muslim identity, based on "the truth of human/feminine nature according to Islam" will promote women's collective empowerment when such effects prevent the public recognition of unresolved issues.

Notes

1. In this chapter, "Muslim", as an adjective, describes whatever pertains to Muslim realities in the world, while "Islamic" refers to religious models and issues in Islam, and "Islamist" to specific politico-religious

militant trends that seek to "purify" Muslim thoughts and practices, especially from contamination by the West. The various quotes, however, may use the words Muslim and Islamic differently. Similarly, I respect the various spellings of Sharia, Syariah and so on, given in the original Muslim texts.

2. There are at least two types of feminist Muslim discourses: a modernist feminist discourse that advocates a secular approach to the Muslim women question, and a radical feminist discourse that advocates *ijtihad* as a return to, and reinterpretation of, Q'uranic sources that will respect the spirit rather than the letter of the Q'uranic revelation. The former is, of course, presented as in favour of women's rights while the latter is often perceived as steeped in traditional cultures deeply hostile to women.

3. See Hélie-Lucas (1993) and Moghadam (1993, 1994b) on the articulation of the "Woman's Question" in Islamist rhetorics of identity.

4. My thanks to the Center for Middle Eastern and Central Asian Studies, The Australian National University, for the use of their library.

5. I take this to be an implicit justification of the early (9 years old) age at which girls, in Iran, can now be married.

6. "Patriarchal bargains" characterize women's accommodations with "classic patriarchal systems", "characteristic of South and East Asia as well as the Muslim Middle East" (Kandiyoti 1988, p. 274). Such patrilineal systems organize the appropriation of women's labour and progeny, but senior women as mothers of sons can access a substantial degree of authority, a fact which "encourage a thorough internalization of this form of patriarchy by women themselves" (ibid, p. 279). Yet "male authority has a very material base, while male responsibility is normatively controlled", a fact which in the period of socio-economic change work against women as the old normative order slips away without offering empowering alternatives for women. Women's responses then often take the form of pressuring men "to live up to their normative obligations". To manage this, women will refuse "to compromise the basis for their claims by stepping out of line and losing their respectability" (ibid, p. 282). The relevance of such concepts in throwing light on women choosing to join Islamist movements is readily apparent.

7. The following points are quoted directly from the Conference programme.

8. Tunisia, in 1956, through its Personal Status Code (the Matalla) made polygamy illegal, has liberal contraception and abortion laws, has legalized adoption and the status of natural children (that is, children born out of wedlock), and recognizes many rights to women, from

divorce and alimony to the right to work without the consent of their husband.

9. Sources, however, stress the sociological unlikelihood of this happening, as it is not the poor who become polygamous. Poor men wanting another, often younger, wife already do repudiate the older one.

References

Abaza, M. "The Discourse on Islamic Fundamentalism in the Middle-East and South-East Asia: A Critical Perspective". *Sojourn*, no. 2 (1991): 203–39.

Abd al-Ati, H. *Islam in Focus*. Qatar: The Religious Affairs, n.d.

Ahmed, L. *Women and Gender in Islam: Historical Roots of a Modern Debate*. New Haven: Yale University Press, 1992.

A'la Mawdudi, A. *Human Rights in Islam*. Leicester: The Islamic Foundation, 1980.

Doi, A. I. *Women in Shari'ah*. Nigeria: Gaskiya Printing Press, 1983.

Etienne, Biono. *L'islamisme Radical*. Paris: Hachette, 1987.

Ghoussoub, Mai. Feminism — or the Eternal Masculine — in the Arab World. *New Left Review* 161 (1987): 3–18.

Hamdani, A. "Islamic Fundamentalism." *Mediterranean Quarterly* 4, no. 4 (1993): 38–47.

Hatem, M. "Egypt's Middle-Class in Crisis: The Sexual Division of Labor." *Middle-East Journal* 42, no. 3 (1988): 407–22.

Hélie-Lucas, M.-A. "The Preferential Symbol for Islamic Identity: Women in Muslim Personal Laws." *WLUML Dossier* n. 11/12/13 (1993): 5–12.

Hoffman-Ladd, V. "Polemics on the Modesty and Segregation of Women in Contemporary Egypt." *International Journal of Middle Eastern Studies* 19 (1987): 23–50.

Kandiyoti, D. "Bargaining with Patriarchy." *Gender and Society* 2, no. 3 (1988): 274–90.

———. *Women, Islam and the State*. Philadelphia: Temple University Press, 1991.

Karim, W. J. *Women and Culture: Between Malay Adat and Islam*. Boulder: Westview Press, 1992.

Khan, M. A. A Comparative Study of Universal Declaration of Human Rights and Declaration of Human Rights in Islam. *Islam and the Modern Age* (August 1991), pp. 168–93.

Lee, R. L. M. "The State, Religious Nationalism, and Ethnic Rationalization in Malaysia." *Ethnic and Racial Studies* 13 (1990): 317–37.

———. "The Globalization of Religious Markets: International Innovations, Malaysian Consumption." *SOJOURN* 8, no. 1 (1993): 35–61.

Mernissi, F. *Harem Politique. The Veil and the Male Elite: A Feminist Interpretation of Women's Rights in Islam Reading.* Mass: Addison-Wesley Publishing Co., 1991.

Moghadam, V. "Rhetorics and Rights of Identity in Islamist Movements." *Journal of World History* 4, no. 2 (1993): 243–64.

Moghadam, V., ed. *Gender and National Identity: Women and Politics in Muslim Societies.* UNU/WIDER, ZED Bks Ltd and Oxford University Press, 1994a.

———. *Identity Politics and Women: Cultural Reassertions and Feminisms in International Perspectives.* Oxford: Westview Press, 1994b.

Mutalib, H. *Islam and Ethnicity in Malay Politics.* London: Oxford University Press, 1990.

Nader, L. "Orientalism, Occidentalism and the Control of Women." *Cultural Dynamics* 2, no. 3 (1989): 323–55.

Nagata, J. *The Reflowering of Malaysian Islam: Modern Religious Radicals and their Roots.* Vancouver: University of British Columbia Press, 1984.

Najmabadi, A. "Hazards of Modernity and Morality: Women, State and Ideology. In *Women, Islam and the State*, edited by D. Kandiyoti, pp. 48–76. Philadelphia: Temple University Press, 1991.

———. "Power, Morality and the New Muslim Womanhood." In *The Politics of Social Transformation in Afghanistan, Iran and Pakistan*, edited by M. Weiner and A. Banuazizi. New-York: Syracuse University Press, 1994.

Olayiwola, A. O. "Democracy in Islam." *Islamic Quarterly* 37, no. 3 (1993): 190–206.

Omar, R. "State, Islam and Malay Reproduction." Paper presented at the Conference on State, Sexuality and Reproduction in Asia and the Pacific, the Australian National University, 16–18 July 1993.

Ong, A. "State versus Islam: Malay Families, Women's Bodies and the Body Politic in Malaysia". *American Ethnologist* 17, no. 2 (1990): 258–73.

Rais, A. "International Islamic Movements and their Influence upon the Islamic Movement in Indonesia." *Prisma* 35 (1985): 27–48.

Salla, M. A. "Islamic Fundamentalism: Its Consequences for the West." *Islam and the Modern Age* (February 1991), pp. 22–46.

Wadud-Muhsin, A. *Qur'an and Woman.* Kuala Lumpur: Penerbit Fajar Bakti, 1992.

Weyland, P. "International Muslim Networks and Islam in Singapore." *SOJOURN* 5, no. 2 (1990): 219–54.

Yeganeh, N. "Women, Nationalism and Islam in Contemporary Political Discourse in Iran." *Feminist Review* 44 (1993): 3–18.

Yuval-Davis, N. and F. Anthias, eds. *Woman, Nation, State.* Basingstoke: MacMillan, 1989.

chapter seven

MODERN DREAMS
An Enquiry into Power, Cityscape Transformations and Cultural Difference in Contemporary Malaysia

GOH BENG LAN*

Introduction

In recent times, the debates over the reconceptualization of modernity have become so diverse that it is futile to pin modernity to any one specific definition. Nonetheless, a central concern in the many works on modernity is the construction and reconstruction of cultural identity (see, for example, Lash and Friedman 1992).

While much in these debates has focused on the experiences of the industrialized Western countries, the rapidly modernizing economies in Asia are unquestionably presenting us with new models of modernity. Indeed, two recent volumes, edited by Kahn and Loh (1992) and Gomes (1994), have endeavoured to develop a theory of modernity in these Asian countries. One area of particular focus is the problem of culture and identity in the Asian experience of modernity.

It has been suggested that the Asian quest for modernity is guided to a large extent by national policies for growth and progress.

It is also apparent that these schemes of modernity do not go un-contested. The volume by Kahn and Loh (1992) has thrown light on just such contestations as they appear in the case of Malaysia. They have demonstrated, among other things, that the Malaysian push for modernization has created a contested terrain where different groups (classes, ethnic groups, and so on) construct different identities to create a constituency to further their own interests, resulting in a highly fragmented cultural and political situation (Kahn and Loh 1992, p. 15).

In this chapter, some of the complexities involved in the articu-lation of capital, cultural identity and modernity in contemporary Malaysia are explored. It will draw on recent theoretical develop-ments which have been described as attempts "to inscribe the project of modernity in urbanism" (Gregory 1994, p. 344; some examples are: Berman 1983; Harvey 1989; Jameson 1991; and Rabinow 1989a, 1989b), in particular, some insights provided by Paul Rabinow who has shown how the modern cityscape is an important identity signifier.[1]

In his study of colonial modernism in Morocco, Rabinow shows how élites expressed their modernist aspirations through architec-ture and city planning in order to demonstrate a position of cultural superiority (1989a, 1989b, 1992). Following Rabinow, the modernist urban skyline has become an important visual and cultural represen-tation of Malaysia's impending "developed" status and a *sine qua non* of international prestige. Using ethnographic and macro investiga-tions into urban development in Georgetown, Penang, from the late 1980s until the present, it will be shown how these changes in the cityscape are inevitably intertwined with the broader picture of identity constructions taking place in Malaysia today.[2]

It will be argued that the built environment, particularly the cityscape, is the place where identity finds concrete expression. In analysing the link between identity and the urban built environ-ment, it will be shown that the processes of identity formation and articulation of cultural difference are much more complex than is generally assumed in the literature on identities.

First, the analysis leads me to disagree with those who consider the social articulation of cultural difference as essentially signifying a marginal or subaltern position which seeks to resist totalization (see, for example, Bhabha 1994). Instead, the study shows how this repertoire of cultural differences can be deployed by the more powerful sections within a community for larger interests.

Secondly, in most writing there is a presumption that the construction of cultural difference (albeit through discursive and contingent processes) is essentially resourced from "the power of [cultural] tradition", which, in other words, is linked to cultural processes (ibid, p. 2). However, the study shows that the processes of identity formation and contestation are also intricately related to other non-cultural processes, in particular the contestation in power relations. In my view, it is not possible to consider the articulations of cultural difference, identity and modernity without also looking under the surface to understand the contestations in power relations in the construction of identity and cultural difference.

The chapter will also examine some of the connections between the Malaysian vision and changes in the cityscape, the perpetual state dilemma in balancing its commitment to the redistribution goals of the New Economic Policy (NEP) and greater economic liberalization, the role of foreign capital in the Malaysian property scene, and a case study of the city of Georgetown in which contestations over urban development exemplify the articulation of capital, cultural identity and modernity in Malaysia.

Visioning the Malaysian Way Forward

It was in February 1991, in the heyday of economic confidence that Malaysia's "Vision 2020" to become an "industrialized" country was launched by Prime Minister Dr Mahathir Mohamad while delivering a speech entitled "Malaysia: The Way Forward". Essentially a modernist vision, it prescribes the following:

> Malaysia should not be developed only in the economic sense. It must be a nation that is fully developed along all the dimensions: economically, politically, socially, spiritually, psychologically and culturally. We must be fully developed in terms of national unity and social cohesion, in terms of social justice, political stability, system of government, quality of life, social and spiritual values, national pride and confidence. (Mahathir Mohamad, "Malaysia: The Way Forward", 1991.)

This period of rapid economic growth which began in the late 1980s has been accompanied by significant transformations in the skyline of the Malaysian city. Spawned by this new prosperity and growing levels of consumption, huge shopping complexes, tower office blocks, luxurious condominiums, resorts, golf and other recreational clubs have come to dominate the urban landscape.

Of course, I am not suggesting that these transformations in the city only occurred from this period. As some Malaysian architects have already pointed out, European modernist building forms were present in Malaya before World War II, usually in the form of public buildings such as schools, administrative offices, courts and railway stations (Chan 1987, p. 16). Rather, my point of departure is the more recent transformations that have occurred in Malaysian cities since the mid to late 1980s.

In my view, city growth in Malaysia prior to the late 1980s was most immediately related to the need to expand Malaysia's heavy-industry and high-technology resources. This was evident in the spending spree on public infrastructure in the early 1980s. Incidentally, this spate of infrastructural growth was also largely dependent on Japanese technology. During this period, the construction of many turnkey projects was undertaken predominantly by Japanese construction companies after Malaysia launched its "Look East" policy (see Chang 1988 and Bowie 1991). In 1982 Malaysia emerged as the country with the largest orders for Japan's construction exports (*Japan Economic Review* 20, no. 1000 [6 April 1982]: 14). Indeed, this spate of construction was to pave the way for the much loftier endeavours to come.

Reaching for the Sky

In the late 1980s, things took a somewhat different turn. What came to mark more recent construction was the fetish for height. The following observation describes this fad:

> This brings us to the national obsession with the tallest, the biggest, the longest and the widest. In these urban centres, we have witnessed the construction of, for instance, the tallest tower, the highest building, the biggest shopping mall, the longest bridge, etc. All these modern constructions are proudly considered by the country's leadership as

physical reminders of the country's tremendous achievements. (*Aliran Monthly* 15, no. 3 [1995]: 5)

The trail in pursuit of these "modern icons" was, however, not without its hiccups. In 1990, local Malaysian authorities and the Foreign Investment Committee (FIC), which regulates foreign investment in Malaysia, conspicuously speeded up their endorsement of applications for the construction of what was supposed to be "Asia's tallest condominium" project in the capital city of Kuala Lumpur. The project, however, failed to materialize, as the Tokyo-based property company behind it became entangled in tax scandals back in Japan and had to abandon it (see Tsuruoka 1990, pp. 51–52).

Not surprisingly, however, other ventures followed, eventually meeting with success and much hype. The construction of the 421-metre tall Kuala Lumpur Tower, which upon completion in 1995 ranked third in the world, albeit being the tallest building in Asia, was reported in the local press as "the tallest structure in the world and capable of providing the state-of-art [sic] telecommunications facilities" (see *Star*, 24 September 1993).

Treading on the heels of the Kuala Lumpur Tower project was the proposed National Science Centre, affirmed to be "the country's first truly intelligent building".[3] It seems that apart from height, buildings are professedly also to have come of age by becoming "intelligent". The intelligent building made its debut in the city of Kuala Lumpur in 1992. This 27-storey building was promoted as an "ultra modern" high-tech building.[4] Subsequently, the Kuala Lumpur City Hall (or the City Council) announced that it would give priority to the development of such "intelligent buildings" to ensure that the city maintained its competitive edge in wooing foreign investors (*Star*, 29 July 1993).

Malaysia's dream of having the tallest building in the world has now come true with the ultimate razzmatazz — the 1,457 feet (88 storeys) Petronas Tower, owned by the national oil corporation, and completed in 1996 (see Glancey 1994, pp. 3–4).[5] The architect commissioned for the project was Cesar Pelli, the internationally acclaimed Argentinian-born and New York-based architect who designed Canary Wharf in London. Petronas Tower has twin commercial peaks of stainless steel and glass-clad construction, linked by a bridge at the 44th floor. Much attention has been given to the Islamic motifs expressed on the external design of the towers. The internal design, comprising floors patterned with superimposed squares and circles, is said to symbolize unity, harmony and strength.

It seems reasonable to suggest that there are factors other than purely economic ones at work in the dramatic transformation of the cityscape in Malaysia. The correlation between height and stature is nowhere more marked than in an advertisement for a high-rise residential project which reads, "At 500 feet above sea level, you can't help but look down on others".[6] Clearly, these debates point to a growing concern to display these modern icons to the world community, as much as the Malaysian public itself.

This rapid urban development also points to significant shifts in capital flows into the property market. It is no coincidence that the period from the mid to late 1980s, the period of the construction boom, was marked by the emergence of foreign capital flows into Malaysia's property sector. To understand this, a brief picture of the property industry in Malaysia is necessary.

Setting the Scene for a Modern Urban Culture: A Perpetual Dilemma of the State

Property booms are not new in Malaysia. In fact, the current one is commonly considered to be the third (*Permodalan Nasional Berhad* 1988/89, p. 41; *Star*, 29 September 1993).[7] Who then are the players in the property sector?

Domestic Chinese capital has long dominated this sector. Indeed, diversifying into property development almost became a ritual for bigger Chinese businesses in the post-independence era (Tan 1982). It has been argued that this tendency became even more pronounced after the introduction of the New Economic Policy (NEP)[8] (see Jesudason 1989; Jomo 1990; and Khoo 1992). Requirements that Chinese firms incorporate Malay partners, together with the government's consistent favouring of foreign over Chinese capital in the manufacturing sector, led many Malaysian Chinese to take a short-term view of their economic activities and venture into property development.

For example, in 1981 Chinese capitalists invested heavily in tourist and hotel complexes, amounting to a total of RM124 million, or 27.4 per cent of total Chinese investments (Jesudason 1989, p. 164). Another trend was the spread of assets and activities outside Malaysia (Seaward 1987, p. 84). An estimated US$12 billion worth of non-Malay capital was said to have left Malaysia between 1976 and 1985 (ibid.).

However, from the 1980s, Malay capital began to emerge as a powerful rival in the property sector. This Malay capital typically took the form of huge public enterprises (now referred to as Non-Financial Public Enterprises, or NFPEs), such as PERNAS and the Urban Development Authority (UDA). PERNAS is said to be one of the most ambitious public enterprises set up to achieve NEP goals (see Khoo 1992, p. 49; Gale 1981; and Jesudason 1989). PERNAS owns a major five-star beach hotel in Penang, and is planning to construct another in the southwestern part of Penang island (*New Straits Times*, 20 July 1992). UDA is a semi-government enterprise set up under the NEP. Its main holding company, Paremba, was sold to the United Malays National Organization's (UMNO's) Fleet Group (Gomez 1990, p. 95). Paremba's dealings in the property sector are well known (ibid., pp. 40, 93–95). Private investment companies owned by the country's dominant political party, UMNO,[9] such as the Fleet Group, also became active in the property sector.

The presence of foreign capital in the late 1980s as a result of the government's economic liberalization, further complicated the situation. Prior to 1986, foreign companies were required to structure their equity so that at least 70 per cent was held by Malaysian investors, with at least 30 per cent *bumiputra* (Malay) equity under the NEP. In response to the severe recession in the mid-1980s, the Malaysian Government introduced a series of deregulatory economic policies aimed at promoting growth. A key feature was the relaxation of foreign equity stipulations under the NEP. Since October 1986, 100 per cent foreign ownership has been permitted under certain conditions.

Although this has mainly resulted in an influx of foreign investments in the manufacturing sector, some of these liberalization measures were explicitly designed to stimulate the property market, by encouraging the flow of foreign capital into the sector.

This scenario of liberalizing foreign investments appears to denote a de-emphasis on the equity distribution goals of the NEP on the part of the government, but the situation is by no means clear-cut. In fact, when foreign capital comes into conflict with the interests of Malay capital, the government reacts by reimposing restrictions. The state of events discussed below suggests an unresolved conflict within the government over its commitment to the redistributive goals of the New Economic Policy and the desire to move towards greater foreign investment to promote growth.

I shall demonstrate how the consequences of this conflict are even more pronounced in the property development sector, where policies have become rather confusing or transitory in nature, being formulated in an almost ad hoc manner due to the shifting outcomes of the conflict.

Foreign Presence

The dependence on foreign capital is known to be a hallmark of Malaysia's recent economic growth. The pervasive pro-growth rhetoric embodied in Mahathir's "Vision 2020" serves as an impetus to the spread of urban development throughout the country, as each state government assiduously drafts development plans in line with the national vision.

In line with this, the creation of the national tourism plan under the Sixth Malaysian Plan (1991–1995) also heightened the flow of capital into the development of tourism-related infrastructure, such as resorts, theme parks and golf courses (see *Sixth Malaysia Plan 1991*, p. 233). Among the incentives for the promotion of tourism in 1988 was the permitting of a 100 per cent foreign equity ownership for new hotel and tourist projects. This incentive still applies, although the foreign-owned company is required to restructure its equity such that at least 49 per cent is held by Malaysians (30 per cent *bumiputra*) after five years from the date of first operation (*Economic Report* 1992/3, p. 325).

Together with this deregulation in foreign investment policies, land legislation in Malaysia also underwent rapid change. Foreign ownership of land, which featured prominently in agriculture, has always been a sensitive nationalist issue. After almost a decade of lobbying by various nationalist groups to prohibit foreign land ownership, the government introduced restrictions in the National Land Code (NLC) in 1985.[10] However, just a year later in 1986, these restrictions, which prevented foreigners from owning landed properties, were repealed. This led to an unprecedented upsurge in foreign acquisition of urban property in Malaysia (*New Straits Times*, 21 September 1989; Seaward 1989, pp. 49–50; Tsuruoka 1990, p. 50; Kamal 1991, p. 51).[11]

This spree of foreign acquisitions of Malaysian property caught high media attention which resulted in political pressure to clamp down on these activities. The scenario in Johor, and to a certain extent Selangor, Malacca and Penang had sparked fears that "Singaporean and Taiwanese investors were devouring a disproportionate share of the [property] market at the expense of *bumiputra* (native Malay) competitors" (Tsuruoka 1991, pp. 44–45; Tsuruoka 1992, pp. 52–53).

With the growing threat of foreign capital eroding the interests of Malay capital, the Foreign Investment Committee (FIC) issued guidelines that all foreign acquisitions of properties required its prior approval.[12] These FIC rulings changed so rapidly in the initial stages that developers, bankers, lawyers and even state governments became confused. It was reported that approvals of foreign purchases of Malaysian property were as low as 4 per cent at the height of the FIC controversy in 1992 (*Star*, 9 September 1993).

In addition, after a five-year liberalization of the NLC, restrictions on foreign ownership were re-introduced in 1992 (via Act A832) which required foreigners to produce prior written approval from the respective state authorities in their acquisition of "agricultural" land in the country, although at the same time the FIC eased its hardline attitude towards foreign purchases of Malaysian property (see *Star*, 12 March 1993; and *New Straits Times*, 9 September 1993). In 1996, the NLC was yet again amended (via Act 941) which, among other things, provided for state authorities to impose their own terms and conditions as well as a levy on all foreign acquisition of properties. This was followed by a federal government announcement that a

RM100,000 levy be imposed on all property transactions (executed on or after 27 October 1995) involving foreigners.

During the conflict over foreign capital investment in the Malaysian property market, new financial mechanisms were instituted to support the property market. In 1989, Property Trust Funds were established in the Kuala Lumpur Stock Exchange (KLSE) for the first time. Property trusts are investment instruments to raise funds through the stock market for investment in the property sector. In 1993, the property sector represented 6.8 per cent of the KLSE market capitalization (*New Straits Times*, 11 August 1993) which stood at RM370 billion in total (*Star*, 18 October 1993). Behind this move was the former Finance Minister, Daim Zainuddin, a successful Malay businessman who owes his initial success to property deals (see Jesudason 1989, p. 107).

Besides being a boost to the property market, these property trusts also opened the gates to "foreign money" (Marchand 1989, pp. 105–6). The first of such trusts, the Arab-Malaysia First Property Trust, set up by the Arab-Malaysian Bank, with Merrill Lynch Capital Markets, Swiss Bank Corporation Investment Banking, and SG Warburg Securities as its underwriters, offered 70 million units, of which half were taken by foreigners (*New Straits Times*, 25 July 1989). In the launch of the second property trust, the First Malaysia Property Trust (FMPT), owned by the Bank of Commerce (70 per cent equity) and Australian interests (30 per cent), foreign institutional buyers were reported to have snapped up more than half of the 630,001 units offered (*New Straits Times*, 18 October 1989). The foreign buyers were said to be from Hong Kong, Singapore, Britain, Japan and North America. FMPT has invested in industrial parks in Penang and Johor Bahru (ibid.).

The Property Trust Funds were also given favourable tax treatment (*New Straits Times*, 7 March 1989). Interestingly, the FIC also agreed not to restrict the size of individual unit-holdings or the percentage level of aggregate unit-holdings by foreigners in these property trusts (ibid).

Having described the background of the national property development scene, I will look at the specific case of Penang.[13]

The Case of Penang

Penang ranks as one of the most urbanized states in Malaysia, with urbanization rates expected to reach 80 per cent by 1995 (Ali Abu Hassan 1994, p. 4). The hub of Penang's development takes place mainly on the small island on which Georgetown is located. There is thus much pressure on land utilization on the island. If we compare Penang to other island cities like Singapore, we find that the central core of Georgetown's skyline has not changed much since British colonial days, with its rows of double-storey shophouses of eclectic Straits Chinese architecture.

This retention of older buildings in Penang is mainly due to the fact that the majority of the buildings located in the urban core are protected under the Rent Control Act, 1966. Rent Control applies to all buildings built before 1 February 1948. The Act was implemented after the war to protect tenants because of the acute shortage of buildings, which resulted in skyrocketing rents. The Act limits the rents of these pre-war buildings and stipulates that landlords must apply to a Rent Tribunal for permission to redevelop their premises. The Act also assists tenants to challenge in the courts any Rent Tribunal decision approving development. Penang state has the highest number of these rent-controlled houses — 12,000 out of the country's total 39,000 (*Star*, 20 August 1993).

Consequently, much of Penang's development occurs on the outer periphery of the urban core. There is, however, a federal move to phase out the law gradually in the next five years (*Star*, 2 June 1993). The Penang state Rent Tribunal was formerly known for its tough stand against redevelopment, but it has relaxed its stance in recent years.

In order to have a better grasp of Penang's development, we first need to consider its economic performance.

Economic Performance

Penang's recent economic performance has been highly impressive. Between 1991 and 1993 its economy grew by 9.7 per cent per anuum — higher than the national average of 8.1 per cent (Ali Abul Hassan 1994, p. 2). The main area of growth has been in the manufacturing sector, which contributes 51 per cent of Penang's gross domestic product (GDP) (ibid). Penang's per capita GDP was RM11,000 in 1993 (equivalent to US$4,400 per capita) (Koh 1994, p. 12), which is 28 per cent higher than the national average (Ali Abul Hassan 1994, p. 2). This figure brings Penang close to the US$5,000 per capita GDP qualification for a "developed country", as defined by the World Bank (Koh 1994, p. 12).

In November 1990, Penang became the first Malaysian state to unveil its own strategic development plan in line with the national "Vision 2020". Called "Penang into the 21st Century", the plan targets improvements in its infrastructural framework to move towards a fully industrialized and developed economy.

One of Penang's "visions" is to promote the state as the regional centre in the nascent Indonesia-Thailand-Malaysia Growth Triangle (known as the "Northern Growth Triangle"). The concept of the Northern Growth Triangle was agreed in principle by the countries involved in July 1993, pending detailed recommendations by the Asian Development Bank (*New Straits Times*, 23 May 1993).

It is evident that Penang is likely to benefit most from this co-operation. Facing a severe labour shortage, the Penang state government has looked to northern Sumatra to provide multinational corporations located in Penang with additional labour (*Star*, 10 February 1993). Currently 22.6 per cent of Penang's work-force comes from either other states in Malaysia or overseas (Kang 1994, p. 3). The Penang Skills Development Centre (PSDC), a co-operative venture between the state and industry established in 1989, already has a vision of establishing Penang and the northern region as the Asia-Pacific manufacturing centre (Boonler Somchit 1994, p. 12).

Tourism has also become a significant industry in Penang. The Penang State Executive Councillor and the chairman of the State Culture and Tourism Committee announced that in 1992 revenue from tourism-related sectors reached RM1.3 million, making it the second highest income earner for the state after the industrial sector (*New Straits Times*, 9 March 1993).

All this economic growth led to an increase in the professional and upper middle classes in Penang, and has created a critical mass of consumers of modern lifestyles. For example, 63 per cent of the total manufacturing work-force consists of skilled workers (Koh 1994,

p. 15). There are an estimated 12,000 scientists and engineers currently working in Penang (ibid, p. 17). (The state has projected a need for a supply of 3,000 engineers and scientists per year.)

Growth of a Modern Cityscape

Up to the mid-1970s, high-rise buildings were associated with low-cost public housing in Penang (see Tan Soo Hai and Hamzah Sendut n.d.). When the tallest public housing project was built between 1968 and the early 1970s, "seventeen and eighteen storey flats were almost unheard of" (Jagatheesan, n.d., p. 205).

However, the situation changed in the 1980s. Owing to changing consumption patterns and a shortage of land, the construction of high-rise buildings, especially on Penang island, began. The change was marked by the completion of two modern icons in the mid-1980s: the 13.5 kilometre-long Penang Bridge (reputed to be "the third longest of its kind in the world" (Penang Development Corporation 1990, p. 47)) and the mammoth 65-storey KOMTAR (Kompleks Tun Abdul Razak) project which features a geodesic dome (claimed to be "the only one of its kind in South-East Asia" (ibid., p. 31)). The opening of these two projects was marked by elaborate celebrations and images of the two monuments have proudly adorned many state government publications.

This period also witnessed an intensification of high-rise construction, epitomized by the condominium, which has come to symbolize modern living in Penang. The condominium concept was introduced in Malaysia during the late 1970s, and endorsed by the government in the Fourth Malaysia Plan as a means of optimizing land usage. But it only gained popularity with the Malaysian public in the mid-1980s with the country's growing affluence (*Property Malaysia*, June–July 1993, p. 17). Most of this condominium development is taking place in the Pulau Tikus area[14] and the northern coastal belt of the island, which have the advantage of a panoptic view of the mainland across the Northern Channel and the Georgetown cityscape.

It is not surprising that Penang's properties also attract foreigners. This is reflected in the numerous hotel transactions as well as foreign joint ventures in residential and commercial development projects.

In 1989, for example, three hotels (two beach and one downtown) were sold to investors from Hong Kong and Singapore (*Property Market Report 1989*, p. A-78). In 1990, Japanese investors bought land in Balik Pulau to develop a golf course (*Property Market Report 1990*, p. A-103) and a Taiwanese investor also bought land in Teluk Kumbar for commercial and residential developments (*Property Market Report 1990*, p. A-121, and my own interview with the developer concerned). In 1991, Taiwanese and Singaporean developers invested in Wisma Tahwa, an office complex in Georgetown (*Property Market Report 1991*, p. A-101). And in 1992, an Indonesian investor opened a new beach hotel (*Property Market Report 1992*, p. A-94).

Amidst this growth, the Penang branch of UMNO has on numerous occasions voiced its concerns that Malays[15] should not be left out of development.[16] This has led to the implementation of various projects to help the Malays catch up with the achievements of the non-Malays. The Penang Regional Development Authority (PERDA), a federal statutory board under the Ministry of Land and Regional Development, was set up in 1983 to help the rural poor in Penang. As the majority of the rural population in Penang are Malays, PERDA's role has been to ensure that rural Malays are not left out of urban growth. PERDA is active in developing housing, commercial, industrial and tourism projects for the Malay population in Penang. The Urban Development Authority (UDA), the semi-government agency under the Ministry of Public Enterprise whose task is to increase Malay participation in property ownership and urban business, is also involved in constructing new Malay townships in Penang.

There is an increasing tendency to perceive land in mere financial terms by various non-profit-making bodies which own land in Penang. For example, the Penang State Islamic Religious Council announced plans to redevelop *wakaf* (endowment) land. *Wakaf* land is land held in trust for welfare or religious purposes (see Fujimoto 1988; Nagata 1979, p. 107). This plan was announced following the discovery that the Penang Malays were sitting on a gold mine — 18 tracts of endowment land located in the prime northeast district (some of which is in Pulau Tikus), which could fetch almost RM62 million (*New Straits Times*, 30 June 1992). The Religious Council has since taken control of all *wakaf* land, and a private company has been set up to oversee its development. This move has generated an as yet unresolved controversy within the Malay community of Penang.

I will now focus on a particular neighbourhood, the fast developing Pulau Tikus area. Apart from the panoramic views from this area, Pulau Tikus also has the advantage of being on the outer phreriphery of the urban core, with less congestion and a significantly fewer number of buildings subject to the Rent Control Act. All these factors have made it a prime target area for developers.

Pulau Tikus — The New Address

Pulau Tikus has always been a middle and upper-middle class residential town. As early as the 1920s, it was a choice resort suburb, a place for the town élite to build their second homes (see Khoo 1993, p. 55). But since the mid-1980s, it has become an increasingly fashionable location for condominiums. Pulau Tikus was the site of the first completed condominium development in Penang island, the Sunrise Tower, in 1980 (*Property Market Report 1980*, p. 52). Along the seafront, adjacent to Pulau Tikus town, is the highly sought-after Gurney Drive. Among the sprouting condominiums and apartments along this shoreline promenade stands the prestigious No. 1 Persiaran Gurney condominiums. The construction of office blocks, shopping complexes, banks and finance companies also signifies a growing preference on the part of business to relocate here.

Using "modern lifestyle" as the main selling point, developers have artfully chosen names bearing romantic, exotic, exclusive and auspicious innuendoes for their projects, such as Bella Vista, Belle Vue, Arcadia, Sri Emas, Desa Mas, Mutiara Villa, Cascadia, Fortune Heights and Naninong.[17]

The practice of *feng shui* has also become increasingly popular in this vogue for modern high-rise living. *Feng shui* literally means "wind and water", and is the practice of Chinese geomancy, which has its origins in ancient folk beliefs (Emmons 1992, p. 39). *Feng shui*:

> stands for the power of the natural environment, the wind and the
> airs of the mountains and hills; the streams and the rain; and more

than that: the composite influence of natural processes.... By placing oneself well in the environment *feng shui* will bring good fortune. (Feuchtwang 1974, p. 2)

At first glance, the practice of *feng shui* may seem contradictory to a modern lifestyle. However, as the recent appearance of numerous books on the subject attests, it is surprisingly popular in Malaysia today. It has also been noted by a geomancer that many of his clients "are either professionals like bankers, accountants, medical doctors, architects or businessmen" and that "more and more English-speaking people are seeking geomancy services" (Gwee 1991, p. 79). While space does not permit detailed discussion of *feng shui*, I consider it a significant example of the dynamics of appropriation of an ancient cultural practice by the new middle classes in contemporary urban Malaysian society.

Another salient feature of condominium and apartment living is security — the reputedly "hi-tech" intercom systems and twenty-four hour security these projects offer. Upon closer investigation, there is more hype than actual surveillance in all this. The "hi-tech" communication systems sometimes do no more than provide a buzz button for comunication. Guards are reported to fall asleep on duty and, due to the labour shortage in Penang, most guards are retirees. However, there are attempts to remedy the situation, such as the proposal by the Malaysian Professional Security Association to set up a Security Training College in Penang (*Star*, 8 June 1993).

There is, therefore, a great demand for development land in the Pulau Tikus area. Among major projects earmarked for Pulau Tikus is the conversion of a former 18.68 hectare Catholic seminary site into a shopping mall, luxury hotel and condominium financed by Japanese, Singaporean and Malaysian capital. There was much controversy over the sale of this site in 1982 to a local developer for a reputed RM36 million. Upon purchase, the company immediately demolished the 1810 seminary building. The Penang Island City Council (henceforth referred to as the City Council) had rezoned the area from religious to residential-cum-commercial use within four months of the transaction, despite protests from residents (*New Straits Times*, 20 December 1988). The original developer went bankrupt in the mid-1980s recession and the land was auctioned off to a Japanese real estate company in 1985 for RM55 million (*Property Market Report 1989*, p. A-78) before being sold to a Hong Kong tycoon and a Japanese department store chain (*Star*, 31 October 1993). The Japanese department store chain subsequently became the sole landowner (see *Star*, 2 September 1994). In 1994, the Japanese landowner entered into a joint venture with a prominent Penang-based developer and Singaporean interests to develop a RM1 billion project to be named "Gurney Park". This project will consist of a shopping mall, a five-star hotel, apartments and a "super-condominium" block, making it "Penang's largest condominium and commercial centre" (ibid.).

The Pulau Tikus area also saw the first privatization of a two-hectare "under-utilized" site owned by the City Council. It is being developed into a comprehensive one-stop centre comprising commercial, residential and recreational developments by the prominent Penang-based developer involved in the Gurney Park project. The site was leased for 99 years for RM18.7 million (*New Straits Times*, 31 October 1993). The City Council expects to collect about RM 7.5 million in annual assessment rates when the project is completed in two years time (*Star*, 31 October 1993).

What has all this redevelopment meant for the existing residents of Pulau Tikus?

Communities in the Pulau Tikus Area

Pulau Tikus has been the locale for a variety of communities: *"Serani"* or Eurasians, Burmese, Indians, Chinese, as well as Malays of South Indian, Arabic and Javanese descent. There are pockets of "urban *kampung*"[18] in Pulau Tikus, but they are slowly being pushed out of existence.

The ongoing reconfiguration of the area into an exclusive domain is occurring not only through the activities of developers, but also through recent endeavours among residents. This is reflected in a conflict over the seemingly innocuous renaming of Scott Road, an exclusive enclave in Pulau Tikus. Scott Road was named after the English businessman, James Scott, a friend of Francis Light, the founder of Penang. Interestingly, Scott married a local Portuguese-Eurasian woman (Augustin n.d., p. 10). In 1990, the City Council changed the name to D.S. Ramanathan Road, after the second mayor of Georgetown.[19] Ever since, new road signs put up by the City Council have been vandalized, whitewashed over and pulled down. This spate of vandalism coincided with strong protests against the renaming from wealthy residents. The reasons for their protests, quoting the chairman of the protest panel set up by the residents were, "Ramanathan is relatively unknown to the people in Scott Road...moreover, areas with a proliferation of British names should be maintained to sustain their uniqueness; like Brown, Park, Rose, Briggs and Wright...[all road names in the area]." (*New Straits Times*, 14 August 1993). The residents reportedly continue to use Scott Road as their postal address.

While this struggle to maintain prestige and difference continues, alongside it another struggle, perhaps one of graver consequence, took place. This struggle was over the history, life and future of a community of Eurasian people who have become reluctant participants in the battle over urban space.[20]

Ethnography — Kampung Serani

Kampung Serani is a 4.8 acre site located in Pulau Tikus. It is an "urban *kampung*" consisting predominantly of Portuguese-Eurasians. Eurasians, as the term implies, are people born of unions between Europeans and Asians. In Penang, if both paternal and maternal ancestries are considered, one can find Portuguese, Dutch, English, Irish, Scottish, French, Italian and German ancestors on one side and, Malays, Chinese, Indians, Siamese and Burmese on the other (*PEA Survey 1987*, p. i).

Chong (1975, p. 127) argues that *Serani*[21] is a term used only in Penang, referring exclusively to Eurasians of Portuguese descent. Nevertheless, the term is also found in Singapore (Blake 1973) and in Malacca (Daus 1989, p. 11). Such an exclusive reference is also doubtful as there remains a high degree of diversity in the origins of these Portuguese-Eurasians (Braga-Blake 1992, p. 37; Daus 1989, p. 70; and Nagata 1979, p. 40).

In fact, the experience of the British colonial period in Penang made it even more difficult for the establishment of exclusive Portuguese descent among the Eurasians. The differentiation of

Portuguese-Eurasians from other Eurasians is made somewhat arbi-
trarily, often with the identification of a single Portuguese past in
the line of descent. However, the main characteristic differentiating
Portuguese-Eurasians from Anglo-Saxon Eurasians is their Roman
Catholic faith (Chan 1983, p. 276; Baxter 1989, p. 7; Chong 1975,
p. 129).

The Battle Site

The site of the *kampung* is earmarked for a commercial and a
condominium project called "Bellisa Row" and "Bellisa Court", respectively. A search I conducted at the Penang Land Office (on 15
October 1992) showed that the title to the land is registered in the
Land Office under the name of the Titular Catholic Bishop of Penang.
The Catholic church had entered into a joint agreement with a
company I shall call "A" to develop the land as early as 1980.

Company A found itself in financial difficulties in the recession
of the mid-1980s and it was only in 1992 that moves to develop the
site of the *kampung* commenced when Company A was taken over
by Indonesian and domestic joint-venture capital in the form of
Company X. Company X bought into Company A in 1991. In the
joint venture, the name of Company A was retained. Company X
was the active partner in pursuing the Kampung Serani project.

Company X had been very active already, with four existing
projects in the Pulau Tikus area and three more elsewhere on the
island. Before any construction work could proceed, the buildings of
Kampung Serani had first to be demolished and the residents moved
out. At this time, the conflict between the residents of the *kampung*
and the church escalated.

History and Heritage

The crux of the conflict lay in the close historical ties between the
Catholic church and the *kampung* community. Historically, Kampung
Serani was known to be the nucleus of the Portuguese-Eurasian
community in Penang.[22] The *kampung* community was said to be
descended from a group of Portuguese-Eurasians who had arrived in
Penang with some Portuguese priests in the early 1800s from the
island of Phuket (Teixeira 1963, p. 327; Khoo 1993, p. 49; Augustine

n.d., p. 10, Lee 1963, p. 46). Their ancestors were supposedly the second group of Eurasians from Phuket led by a priest called Pasqual.

Village life has centred on the Church of the Immaculate Conception, built in 1811[23], which is located at the edge of the *kampung*. The church has been responsible for the administration of the *kampung* land, of which the residents are ground tenants.

Although Kampung Serani has a historical identity as a Portuguese-Eurasian *kampung*, it is not a homogenous community. In spite of a majority of Portuguese-Eurasians as well as an active projection of its image as a Portuguese-Eurasian *kampung*, there are also Eurasians of other European descent living in the *kampung*.

Among the Penang Eurasian community, the Eurasians in Kampung Serani are seen as the "poorer" section. Since the 1960s, there has been a move out of the *kampung* by the more affluent residents into middle-class housing estates on other parts of Penang island.[24]

Until 1992 there were 40 families, with a total of about 150 residents, living in Kampung Serani. The village originally consisted of sixteen houses, two sheds, one casket company and a structure called the "Noah's Ark". So named perhaps because it resembled a ship, Noah's Ark was built over a hundred years ago by the then parish priest. It served as the first school in Pulau Tikus. When I began fieldwork in 1993, there were only three houses and a shed left in the *kampung*. The community was made up of nine extended families.

Throughout this conflict, the residents have claimed that the land is endowment land held in trust by the church. The land where Kampung Serani stood has also been regarded by generations of Eurasians as endowment land, that is, religious charity land held in trust by the church for the poor Catholics. This has been the main contention by the residents, although there is no documentary proof of their claims.

My search at the Penang Land Office revealed that the land was registered by Deed Registration No. 1368 in 1889. The deeds system, with issues of Grants of Title, was administered by the East India Company which had occupied Penang from 1786, at least from 1807. In 1839, the Straits Land Act was passed which provided, among other things, for a land office to issue titles. A series of subsequent enactments provided a more stable deeds system. In July 1887, the Law of Property and Registration of Deeds Ordinances were implemented. Such was the position until the National Land Code 1965 was passed to provide a uniform system based on the Torrens Scheme for the whole of Peninsular Malaysia (Sihombing 1981, p. 4).

The residents had different versions of who had donated the land to the church, but all had the same belief that the land was to be used for the welfare of poor Eurasians. The residents repeatedly claimed that until the 1950s, the church had only allowed Eurasians as residents in the *kampung*. Ironically, the church did not stipulate any conditions to the developer, and left the question of settlement in the developer's hands.

In 1980, there was a series of dialogues and correspondence between the *kampung* residents and the Bishop. In the minutes of one such dialogue, a priest explained the church's former difficult experiences in the resettlement of "squatters" on church land development on the mainland. He said that the church had decided not to deal directly with "squatters" anymore.[25] The residents in turn argued that the church had a moral responsibility to see to their compensation as they were not "squatters", but legal tenants.

The residents wanted relocation within the *kampung* but this was not deemed possible by the developer who did not want low cost flats in the vicinity of a supposedly luxurious condominium project.

In 1984, the *kampung* residents decided to request the assistance of the Penang Eurasian Association (PEA) in their negotiations for compensation. The recession crept in, and all was quiet until the property boom in 1992, when Company X set the ball rolling again. Since then, the PEA has become active as a mediator in the negotiation process.

Elites and Identity Construction
The PEA was set up in 1919, but has undergone major changes in its vision for the Eurasian community. In the 1970s, there was a general indifference towards the Association among the Eurasians

(see Chong 1975, p. 133). This was in part due to the purely recreational role then adopted by the Association (see Nagata 1979, p. 40).[26]

With "élite" Eurasians as its leaders, the PEA has increasingly legitimized its position in recent years as the guardian of Eurasian culture and identity.[27] From the 1980s, there has been an increasing number of university graduates and professionals on the PEA executive committee.

Here, I want to turn briefly to the larger context within which the current process of redefining the Portuguese-Eurasian identity is taking place. I believe this will provide an understanding of the cultural repertoire which was to emerge in the battle over Kampung Serani.

In 1984, the Malaysian Government opened the Amanah Saham Nasional (ASN), a national unit trust scheme, to Portuguese-Eurasians.[28] The ASN is reserved only for Malays and other indigenous groups (*bumiputera*). As such the eligibility of the Portuguese-Eurasians may at first seem puzzling as they have yet to be officially recognized as *bumiputeras*. But this "eligibility" of the Portuguese-Eurasians to privileges reserved only for Malays or other indigenous groups is precisely a repercussion of the current construction and reconstruction of cultural identity in Malaysia.

As mentioned above, in Malaysia today both political and cultural fragmentation is taking place. In particular, the concept of "Malayness" is changing dramatically (see Kahn and Loh 1992). The arbitrary and often ambiguous definitions of "Malayness" among which include claims of indigeneity, religion (Islam), language and cultural practices has been widely discussed (see Kahn 1992). The relaxation of the boundaries of Malayness occurring in Malaysia today is perhaps influencing current Portuguese-Eurasian identity constructions. In particular, recent political developments have led to the "flexibility" now accorded to the definition of Malayness. Membership of UMNO, the dominant political party in the ruling coalition, has always been open only to Malays (or at least this has generally been assumed to be the case).[29] However, this "Malay only" membership policy has changed with political events in the state of Sabah in East Malaysia. Sabah, which is largely populated by indigenous groups, voted an opposition party into government. In 1992, the federal government set up UMNO branches in Sabah and opened UMNO's membership to other indigenous groups apart from the Malays in an attempt to wrest political control of Sabah from the opposition party (see Loh 1992).

Seizing this opportunity, other minorities with more "authentic" claims to indigenous status sought to take advantage of this precedent. In 1993, some Portuguese-Eurasian (*Star*, 25 February 1993) and Baba Chinese (*New Straits Times*, 31 March 1993) community leaders in Malacca urged the government to allow them to join UMNO. They claimed a longer history in Malaysia, in particular that they existed even prior to British colonial rule and asserted that their way of life was similar to that of the Malays.

In claiming indigenous status as *bumiputera*, the Portuguese-Eurasians were seeking to have the same special privileges previously accorded only to Malays. These include being able to invest in the ASN.

It was after these lobbying efforts by the Portuguese-Eurasian community leaders that the ASN was opened to this community. Now, to qualify for the ASN a Eurasian must be able to prove Portuguese descent. Portuguese descent is determined by family names and the Roman Catholic faith, the legitimacy of which is vetted by the Rigador (community leader) in Malacca.

In Penang, the PEA became the channel for processing these applications. There are certainly irregularities in the selection process in that any Catholic Eurasian, whether of Portuguese descent or not, is allowed to invest in the ASN. A Eurasian of the Protestant faith, however, does not qualify.

Although in the past, scholars have noted the sense of "identification limbo" in the Eurasian community, attributing this absence of cohesion to a lack of "common interest and issues" to mobilize the group (see Nagata 1979, p. 40), the situation has changed considerably in recent times. Other scholars, however, have taken issue with the notion of Eurasian "identification limbo". For example, Chong has noted that the Portuguese-Eurasian identity is not a mere construct but that there is a strong sense of identification of the Portuguese-Eurasians with the Pulau Tikus area, not only within the community itself, but also by other ethnic communities in Penang (1975, p. 127).

Parallel to these national developments, PEA leaders have been actively engaged in constructing a Eurasian history and culture centred on a Portuguese-Eurasian identity in spite of the heterogenous nature of the Penang Eurasian community. Although in former times, the Eurasians regarded themselves as the main link between East and West, as the medium through which the West was able to understand the East better, this "neutral" stance has since wavered. The main discourse of current identity construction concerns the reclaiming of the Asian part of their heritage. The PEA leaders claimed that they were closer to Malay than to Portuguese culture. For example, among the reasons stated by one of the community leaders in the request for UMNO membership by the Portuguese-Eurasians in Malacca was that the community was culturally closer to the Malays than the people of modern day Portugal. "Whatever little direct contact we had did not have any major influence on us", he said (*Star*, 25 February 1993).

These leaders, in fact, coined the term Luso-Malay for themselves, to reflect their overt identification with Malayness. It was claimed that the term Luso-Malays was first used by a priest, Rev. M.J. Pinto, because the majority of the early inter-marriages and conversions were between Portuguese males and Malay or Indonesian females (Sta Maria 1982, p. 26). C.M. Turnbull, in his book, *The Straits Settlement 1826–67*, and Isabella Bird, in her novel *The Golden Chersonese and the Way Thither*, have used the term "Malay-Portuguese".

This identification with Malayness does not go unchallenged by other members of the Eurasian community. There are Eurasians in Penang who still consider themselves as different from their Malaccan counterparts. I quote a common comment I heard on this matter from the Portuguese-Eurasians whom I interviewed: "The Malaccan Eurasians were brought up the Malay way. But we in Penang were brought up by the Portuguese way, the European way." The push for UMNO membership has also not been popular, even among the PEA. Most Penang Eurasians are satisfied to be accepted as *bumiputras* as long as they do not have to denounce their Roman Catholic faith. To them their religious identity is still of utmost importance.

Noah's Ark and Cultural Repertoire

The negotiation process over Kampung Serani sparked off a debate over the preservation of Portuguese-Eurasian cultural heritage and identity in the Pulau Tikus area. Articulated both by the PEA and the residents, Noah's Ark, despite its very dilapidated state, became the material symbol of continuity with the past.

It was at this time that another equally aggressive developer in Pulau Tikus, whom I shall call Company C, approached the PEA with the offer of better cash compensation (compared to Company X) for the residents. In addition, they offered to build a club house or a heritage house on the site. Company C is a local developer which has built a modern office complex and has an ongoing apartment project in the Pulau Tikus area. Company C has a partnership with another prominent, and politically well-connected, property development company, Company P. Indeed, the directors of these two companies are siblings. Company P is involved in the City Council privatization project and in the Gurney Park development mentioned earlier.

It was rumoured that the agreement between Company X and the Church would terminate at the end of 1992 should Company X fail to develop the site. When one resident's house was partially bulldozed before there was any agreement over compensation, the PEA organized a protest in front of Noah's Ark calling for its preservation as a Eurasian legacy.

Company X heard of this and counter-offered a 10,000 sq. ft. site for building a Eurasian heritage house to be owned and managed by the PEA on the site. Chaos ensued and the residents accused the PEA of selling them out. To be fair to the PEA, there was a record stating that after having reached an agreement with Company X over the provision of a heritage house, the PEA executive committee did suggest that the plans for the double-storey heritage house be altered to a high-rise building in order to accommodate low-cost flats which the *kampung* residents could purchase and still reside near the church (*PEA Report on Kampung Serani*, p. 10). This suggestion was turned down by Company X.

By this time, there was too much distrust between some of the residents and the PEA. Many of the residents were overcome by despondency and sold out to the developer. The remaining families were taken to court by the Bishop. Left with little choice, they eventually settled out of court. The company had begun construction work in the first phase of the commercial row and the residents, while their court hearings were pending, were living amidst deafening conditions. There were wide discrepancies in the amount of cash compensation received. The residents have since vacated the grounds and today Kampung Serani no longer exists.[30]

However, the former residents remain bitter about what they perceive to be a "betrayal by the PEA", which they accuse of having "hijacked" the agenda. They feel that the PEA leaders, none of whom ever lived in the *kampung*, had no right to any gain. They see the settlement offer of the heritage house to be at their expense, arguing that low-cost flats could have easily housed all of them.

The PEA, on the other hand, claims that as the guardian of Eurasian cultural heritage, it was justified in its claims on the land to "build up" the Eurasian community. A memorandum of understanding was signed between the PEA and the Roman Catholic Bishop for the church to execute a 90-year lease in the PEA's favour for the 10,000 sq.ft. site at Kampung Serani (*Star*, 15 October 1994). Company X is expected to deliver the heritage house within a year (ibid). Among the plans by the PEA for the heritage house are the setting up of a museum to exhibit Eurasian history, culture and the community's contributions in Penang.

Conclusion

I have presented above an overview of the disparate forces impli-cating the state, property developers, the urban middle-classes and community groups in the urban development scene of contempo-rary Malaysia. I have shown the intricate link between the state's aspirations for modernity and cityscape changes. It is obvious that the main tension in the pursuit of modernity lies in the dilemma faced by the Malaysian State in counter-balancing the ethnic-based redistribution commitment of the NEP with the need to encourage rapid growth through hypermobile international capital flows. While it seems that economic factors are currently favoured in Malaysia, the tension remains unresolved and will certainly continue to plague the Malaysian political-economy and cultural developments for some time to come.

Against the backdrop of the national policies of progress and cityscape transformations, I have outlined Penang's property and development boom, and highlighted the role of developers as conceptualizers, organizers and constructors of a modern lifestyle. This in turn is connected to the emerging "cosmopolitan" consumer and modern lifestyle choices of the condominium dwellers.

Caught in this construction mania, the people of Kampung Serani were dragged into the conflict over urban development because the land-owner, the Catholic Church, had gone into a joint development with a private developer. If one looks into the history of the Catholic Church in Malaysia, one finds that it has never really felt "secure" in its position, even less so now, given the process of "Islamization". It is doubtful whether the government will use its powers under the Land Acquisition Act to alienate church land for developmental purposes. The political consequences would be too great. Nonetheless, the mere existence of this legislation is perceived as a threat by the church authorities. This fear was aggravated by what one church authority called the "dilapidated" condition of the "eyesore" buildings in Kampung Serani, in contrast to the prime modern surroundings, which, he alleged, would create a cause for acquisition of the land by the government. While the church may have valid reasons for the redevelopment of its land, their action may be partly due to the increasing pressure to treat land in merely financial terms, influenced by the larger forces of modern development and urban transformations in Penang.

It is also evident that the particularity of place contributes to the forms of cultural and historical contestation in response to the changing landscape. The Pulau Tikus area, with its history as a "nucleus" of the Portuguese-Eurasians, is the site for considerable ethnic attachment. The upsurge in reclaiming heritage and identity was therefore inevitable in the face of its destruction. Nevertheless, it is clear that this "identity and heritage" can be appropriated and reworked by the more powerful and resourceful élite for larger interests.

Thus, while the residents may have lost out to the developers, the same cannot be said of other members of the Eurasian community, who have won a heritage house from the developer to "showpiece" Eurasian culture.

As developers compete among themselves, they also face checks and balances, sometimes to the advantage of powerful sections of community groups. It is here that we see the importance of taking into account the nature of power relations underlying the emerging repertoire of cultural heritage and identity seen in the Kampung Serani case. This, I believe, is not an isolated example, but is also prevalent among other identity struggles in contemporary Malaysia.

Notes

* I am extremely grateful to Lucy Healy, Sharmini Sherrard, Julianne Long and Wendy Mee for their helpful comments on this paper. My thanks also go to Juliet Yee who facilitated my telecommunication with Wendy.

1. I am grateful to Joel S. Kahn for bringing Rabinow's insight on "cityscape as identity signifier" to my attention.

2. This is based on data from fieldwork in Penang collected between March 1993 and February 1994.

3. The official launching of the National Science project was featured in a front-page article in a local daily under the caption "Buildings to go smart" (*Star*, 12 March 1993). The Kuala Lumpur Tower, a RM270 million joint project between Syarikat Telekom Malaysia Berhad (the semi-privatized national telecommunications company) and a German company, features a revolving restaurant, observation platform and a theatre. It was completed in 1995 and officially opened in 1996. (RM = Ringgit Malaysia or Malaysian dollar).

4. This project was built along Jalan Raja Laut by a member of the Cycle and Carriage Group, the Bintang Kemajuan Limited Company (see *Malaysian Business*, 1–15 March 1992, p. 27).

5. The Petronas Tower is some 20 feet higher than the Sears Tower in Chicago, which has held the record for the world's tallest building for the past twenty years (Glancey 1994). It is interesting to note that China's Chingqing Tower, at 1,500 feet, is supposed to surpass this height when it is built in 1997, and the Japanese are proposing a "Millennium Tower" of more than 2,600 feet (ibid.).

6. This advertisement for Gasing Heights in Petaling Jaya, Kuala Lumpur, appeared in the *Star*, 4 July 1993.

7. However, according to a leading property consultant, Malaysia is said to have experienced property booms in 1963–64, 1973–74 and 1981–83, making the current one, which began in 1989, the fourth (Marbeck 1993, p. 62).

8. The objectives of the NEP (1970–90) were: (i) to make the ethnic distribution of the work-force in each sector similar to that of the population as a whole, and (ii) to increase *bumiputera* (Malay) share of corporate-sector ownership from 2.4 per cent in 1970 to 30 per cent in 1990. It has been replaced by the New Development Policy (NDP) commencing in July 1991, in which the 30 per cent corporate equity rule for *bumiputeras* has been relaxed.

9. UMNO is the dominant partner in the ruling alliance in Malaysia. For details of the UMNO split in 1987, see Khoo (1992), and for details of UMNO's Fleet Group's merger into Faber Merlin, a property development company, see Gomez (1990, p. 79–91).

10. Pressures to restrict foreign ownership of land were felt from the 1970s, and these pressures eventually led to restrictions being imposed on the disposal, transfer, and bidding at the sale of "agricultural" and "building" land (for residential and commercial uses) to non-citizens under amendments in the NLC in 1985 (see Senftleben 1978, p. 163). However, upon appeals by the Bankers Association Malaysia, it was amended (via Act 624 in 1985) to allow banks to create charges and liens on these land categories, but prohibited them to bid, in case the land was put up for auction. Restrictions were never imposed on industrial land under the NLC.

11. Official statistics on foreign ownership mainly relate to commercial real estate, usually in cases involving huge acquisitions. In 1988, of the total volume of transactions valued at RM8.14 billion, US$500 million worth of commercial property was bought by foreign investors (*New Straits Times*, 7 April 1989). Figures for the first half of 1989, announced by the Deputy Finance Minister, showed that foreigners only accounted for RM300 million, or 5.7 per cent of the RM5 billion worth of total property transactions. However, the Minister added that he was aware that the statistics did not reflect the actual situation (*New Straits Times*, 23 September 1989). In Penang, foreign ownership of properties was reported to be 14.5 per cent in 1987 (*Property Market Report 1987*, p. A-54).

12. The FIC is made up of high-ranking administrators from the Ministries of Trade and Industry, the Economic Planning Unit, and the Registrar of Companies. It was set up originally in 1974 to monitor foreign acquisitions of Malaysian companies (see Jesudason 1989, p. 79). The series of conditions set out in the FIC rulings include minimum purchase

value per unit, housing types, terms of owner-occupancy, and resale period.

13. Penang is the smallest state by area in Malaysia and is situated to the northwest of Peninsular Malaysia. Its total area is 1,031 sq. km. (or 397.92 sq. miles) (PDC: Statistics Penang Malaysia, n.d.). The city proper is 9.4 sq. miles, or 3116 acres (Courtenay and Van n.d.).

14. All district boundaries in Malaysia are determined under the NLC. Penang island is divided into two administrative districts, the Northeast and the Southwest Districts. Pulau Tikus falls within the Northeast District of Georgetown. Hence, any reference to Pulau Tikus as an area is essentially a social definition and remains debatable.

15. In 1990, out of Penang's total population of 1,150,400, Malays formed 34.5 per cent, Chinese 52.9 per cent, Indians 11.5 per cent and Others 1.1 per cent (PDC: Statistics Penang Malaysia, n.d.).

16. See *New Straits Times*, 23 May 1989; *Star*, 1 February 1993; *New Straits Times*, 2 July 1993; and *New Straits Times*, 11 August 1993.

17. *Emas* or *mas* means "gold"; *Desa* means "villa", and *mutiara* means "pearl". Penang is also referred to as the "Pearl of the Orient". *Naninong* is supposedly an Australian aboriginal name since the architect who designed the project was trained in Australia.

18. *Kampung* is the Malay word for "village". These are essentially enclaves of traditional villages with houses of wood and zinc often found in juxtaposition to a "modern" urban built environment.

19. A Royal Charter by the British Government which elevated Penang from a municipality to city status in 1957 provided for a Mayor to head the Municipal Council (Choo 1979, p. 10). This system was abolished in 1966 (ibid.).

20. Such a scenario is, of course, not uncommon in Penang. A tragic case was the Thien Teik development project where the conflict between ground tenants and the land developer resulted in the death of a woman ground tenant during the process of eviction (see Chan et al., 1983).

21. *Serani* is said to be a term derived from the Arabic word *Nazarene* (Chong 1975, p. 120; Baxter 1988, p. 15).

22. It was estimated that in 1834, there were 4,000 Catholics in Penang, of whom 2,000 were in Georgetown and 500 in Pulau Tikus (Lee 1963, p. 48). According to the 1980 population census, the Eurasian population in Penang numbered 2,501, or 0.3 per cent of the total 954,600 population. The Penang Eurasian population forms 16 per cent of the total Eurasian population of 15,435 in Malaysia (PEA Survey 1987, p. i).

23. Teixeira (1963, p. 327) and Khoo (1993, p. 57) state that it was Padre Juan Pasqual who first built the wooden church in 1811. It was replaced

by a brick church built by a Lusitanian trader from Brazil named Ferrao who was made the Siamese Consul to Penang (Teixeira 1963, p. 327). The present church was constructed in 1899 (Khoo 1993, p. 57), allegedly by a Father Bohet (Lee 1963, p. 48), and was last renovated in the 1970s.

24. According to the 1987 Penang Eurasian Association (PEA) survey, of about 58 per cent of Penang's total Eurasian population, the largest number (19.7 per cent) of Eurasians now live in the southern and western suburbs of the island, followed by the northern suburb of Tanjung Bunga (16.7 per cent), with the rest on the mainland (PEA Survey 1987).

25. *Report on Penang Reflection Group*, 10 December 1980.

26. However, in Malacca, the state with the biggest population of Portuguese-Eurasians, the situation was a little different. There were attempts to work together as a community as early as 1968 with the formation of the Portuguese Cultural Society (Chan 1983, p. 277).

27. The PEA has organized Cristao classes (the Portuguese patois, although Penang Eurasians, unlike their Malaccan counterparts do not speak Cristao), traditional dance classes and more social events among the Eurasians.

28. The ASN was launched in 1981. It was established under the New Economic Policy to promote active distribution of corporate wealth among individuals within the *bumiputera community* (*Malaysia 1990–91 Year Book*, p. 290). Another similar scheme is the Amanah Saham Bumiputera (ASB). Both unit trusts are run by the Permodalan Nasional Berhad or the National Equity Corporation.

29. Recently, however, some groups like the Baba Chinese community in Malacca have provided documentary proof that some of them had joined UMNO more than 25 years ago (see *New Straits Times*, 31 March 1993).

30. The residents have found alternative housing in all parts of Penang, and some have moved to the mainland. A majority of them are still tenants in their new premises.

References

Ali Abul Hassan bin Sulaiman, Tan Sri Dato'. "Penang's Economic Performance and Future Prospects: Challenges, Issues and Developments". Paper presented at the International Conference on Penang 2002 — Into The 21st Century, held at Hotel Equatorial, Penang, 26–27 July 1994.

Augustine, James F. *Bygone Eurasia: The Life Story of the Eurasians of Malaya*. Kuala Lumpur: Rajiv Printers, n.d.

Baxter, Alan N. *A Grammar of Kristang (Malacca Creole Portuguese)*. Pacific Linguistics Series B-No. 95. Canberra: Department of Linguistics, Research School of Pacific Affairs, Australian National University, 1988.

Berman, Marshall. *All That is Solid Melts Into Air: The Experience of Modernity,* sixth impression. New York: Verso, 1983.

Bhabha, Homi K. *The Location of Culture.* London: Routledge, 1994.

Bird, Isabella L. *The Golden Chersonese and the Way Thither.* Kuala Lumpur: Oxford University Press, 1883 (reprinted 1967).

Blake, Myrna L. "Kampung Eurasians". Working Papers, No. 17. Department of Sociology, University of Singapore, 1973.

Boonler Somchit. "Meeting Penang's Needs for More Trained Manpower and Overcoming Skills Shortage — The PSDC Experience". Paper presented at the International Conference on Penang 2002: Into The 21st Century, held at Hotel Equatorial, Penang, 26–27 July 1994.

Bowie, Alasdair. *Crossing the Industrial Divide: State, Society, and the Politics of Economic Transformation in Malaysia.* New York: Columbia University Press, 1991.

Braga-Blake, Myrna, ed. *Singapore Eurasians: Memories and Hopes.* Singapore: Times Editions and The Eurasian Association, 1992.

Chan Chee Khoon, Chin Wey Tze and Loh Kok Wah. *Thean Teik and the Other Side of Development.* Penang: Aliran, 1983.

Chan Chee Yoong, ed. *Post-Merdeka Architecture Malaysia 1957–1987.* Kuala Lumpur: Pertubuhan Arkitek Malaysia, 1987.

Chan Kok Eng. "The Eurasians of Melaka". In *Melaka: The Transformation of a Malay Capital C.1400–1980,* edited by Kernial Singh Sandhu and Paul Wheatley, Vol. 2. Kuala Lumpur: Oxford University Press, 1983.

Chang Yii Tan. "Tilting East — The Construction Problem". In *Mahathir's Economic Policies,* edited by K.S. Jomo. Kuala Lumpur: Insan, 1988.

Chong Yoke Lin, Linda. "The Portuguese-Eurasians (Serani of Penang)". In *Malaysian Ethnic Relations,* edited by S. Gardner. Penang: School of Social Sciences, Universiti Sain Malaysia, 1975.

Choo Eng Guan. "A Study of the Administrative Process of the City Council of George Town". B. Econs. Graduation Exercise, Faculty of Economics and Administration, Universiti Malaya, 1970.

Courtenay, P.P. & Kate K.Y. Van. "Cartographic Frames for Peninsular Malaysia District Statistics, 1947–1982." Malaysia Society of the Asian Studies Association of Australia, n.d.

Daus, Ronald. *Portuguese Eurasian Communities in Southeast Asia.* Singapore: Institute of Southeast Asian Studies, 1989.

Emmons, Charles F. "Hong Kong's Feng Shui: Popular Magic in a Modern Urban Setting". *Journal of Popular Culture* 26, no. 1 (1992): 39–50.

Feutchwang, Stephan D.R. *An Anthropological Analysis of Chinese Geomancy,* first edition. Vientiane, Laos: Vithagna, 1974.

Fujimoto, Helen. *The South Indian Muslim Community and the Evolution of the Jawi Peranakan in Penang up to 1948.* Comparative Study in Multi-Ethnic

Societies, Monograph Series No. 1. Tokyo: Tokyo Gaikokugo Daigaku, 1988.

Gale, Bruce. *Politics and Public Enterprise in Malaysia.* Petaling Jaya, Selangor: Eastern Universities (M) Press, 1981.

Glancey, Jonathan. "Far East Reaches for the Sky". *The Independent,* reproduced in *the Star,* Section 2, 28 July 1994, pp. 3–4.

Gomes, Alberto, ed. *Modernity and Identity: Asian Illustrations.* Bundoora, Victoria, Australia: La Trobe University Press, 1994.

Gomez, Edmund Terence. *Politics in Business: UMNO's Corporate Investments.* Kuala Lumpur: Forum, 1990.

Gregory, Derek. *Geographical Imaginations.* Oxford: Blackwell, 1994.

Gwee Kim Woon, Peter. *FENGSHUI: The Geomancy and Economy of Singapore.* Singapore: Shinglee Publishers, 1991.

Harvey, David. *The Condition of Postmodernity: An Enquiry into the Origins of Cultural Change.* Oxford: Blackwell, 1989.

Jagatheesan, N. "Industrialised Housing — An Appraisal". In *Aspects of Housing in Malaysia,* edited by Tan Soo Hai and Hamzah Sendut. International Development Research Centre, Ontario, Canada and University Science Malaysia, South East Asia Low Cost Housing Study Monograph, n.d.

Jameson, Fredric. *Postmodernism or The Cultural Logic of Late Capitalism.* New York: Verso, 1991.

Jesudason, James V. *Ethnicity and the Economy: The State, Chinese Business, and Multinationals in Malaysia.* Singapore: Oxford University Press, 1989.

Jomo, K.S. *Beyond the New Economic Policy? Malaysia in the Nineties.* Asian Studies Association of Australia, 1990.

Kahn, Joel, S. "Class, Ethnicity and Diversity: Some Remarks on Malay Culture in Malaysia". In *Fragmented Vision: Culture and Politics in Contemporary Malaysia,* edited by Joel S. Kahn and F. Loh, pp. 158–78. Sydney: Allen & Unwin, 1992.

Kahn, Joel, S., and F. Loh, eds. *Fragmented Vision: Culture and Politics in Contemporary Malaysia.* Sydney: Allen & Unwin, 1992.

Kamal Salih. "The Malaysian Economy in the 1990s: Alternative Scenarios". In *The Malaysian Economy Beyond 1990: International and Domestic Perspectives,* edited by Lee Kiong Hock & Shyamala Nagaraj. Kuala Lumpur: Persatuan Ekonomi Malaysia, 1991.

Kang Chin Seng. "Making Penang a Center Of Education — Challenges and Opportunities in the Age Of Knowledge". Paper presented at the International Conference on Penang 2002: Into the 21st Century, held at Hotel Equatorial, Penang, 26–17 July 1994.

Khoo Khay Jin. "The Grand Vision: Mahathir and Modernisation". In *Fragmented Vision: Culture and Politics in Contemporary Malaysia,* edited by J.S. Kahn and F. Loh. Sydney: Allen & Unwin, 1992.

Khoo Su Nin. *Streets of Georgetown Penang: An Illustrated Guide to Penang's City Streets and Historic Attractions.* Penang: Janus Print & Resources, 1993.
Koh Tsu Koon. "Preparing for the Next Major Transformation towards an Advanced Industrialised Economy for Penang". Keynote Address at the International Conference on Penang 2002: Into the 21st Century, held at Hotel Equatorial, Penang, 26–27 July 1994.
Lash, Scott and Jonathan Friedman. *Modernity and Identity.* Oxford: Basil Blackwell, 1992.
Lim, Linda Y.C. and Pang Eng Fong. *Foreign Direct Investment and Industriali- sation in Malaysia, Singapore, Taiwan & Thailand.* Paris: Development Centre of the Organisation for Economic Cooperation and Develop- ment, 1991.
Lee, Felix George, Rev. *The Catholic Church in Malaya.* Singapore: Eastern Universities Press, 1963.
Loh Kok Wah, Francis. "Modernisation, Cultural Revival and Counter- Hegemony: The Kadazans of Sabah in the 1980s". In *Fragmented Vision: Culture and Politics in Contemporary Malaysia,* edited by J.S. Kahn and F. Loh. Sydney: Allen & Unwin, 1992.
Malaysia. *Malaysia 1990–91 Year Book.* Kuala Lumpur: Berita Publishing Sdn., Bhd, 1990.
———. *Sixth Malaysia Plan, 1991–1995.* Kuala Lumpur: Government Printers, 1991.
Malaysia, Ministry of Finance. *Economic Report 1992/93.* Kuala Lumpur: National Printing Department, 1992.
Marbeck, Aloysius B. "Investing in Residential Property". *Property Malaysia,* June–July 1993, pp. 57–63.
Marchand, Christopher. "Blocked Entrance: No easy ways to buy into Malaysia's property boom". *Far Eastern Economic Review,* 14 December 1989, pp. 105–6.
Nagata, Judith. *Malaysian Mosaic: Perspectives from a Poly-Ethnic Society.* Vancouver: University of British Columbia Press, 1979.
Penang Eurasian Association (PEA). "Penang Eurasian Community Population Survey 1987". 1987.
———. "Penang Eurasian Association and the Kampung Serani Issue Report, 20 June 1992". 1992.
Penang Development Corporation. *Statistics Penang Malaysia.* n.d.
———. *Penang: Looking Back, Looking Ahead: 20 Years of Progress.* Penang: Penang Development Corporation, 1990.
Permodalan Nasional Bhd. *Malaysian Corporate Performance, 1988/89 Edition.* Kuala Lumpur: Permodalan Nasional Bhd, 1989.
Property Malaysia. Kuala Lumpur: Housing Developers' Association Malaysia, June–July 1993.

Property Market Report. Kuala Lumpur: Percetakan Nasional Malaysia Bhd, various years.

Rabinow, Paul. *French Modern: Norms and Forms of the Social Environment.* Cambridge, Massachusetts: MIT Press, 1989a.

——. "Governing Morocco: Modernity and Difference". *International Journal of Urban and Regional Research* 13, no. 1 (1989b): 32–46.

——. "Colonialism, Modernity: The French in Morocco". In *Forms of Dominance: On the Architecture and Urbanism of the Colonial Enterprise,* edited by Nezar Alsayyad. Aldershot: Avebury, 1992.

Seaward, Nick. "A question of quantifying investments". *Far Eastern Economic Review,* 3 December 1987, pp. 84–85.

——. "Foreigners on the lookout for bargains". *Far Eastern Economic Review,* 16 March 1989, pp. 49–50.

Senftleben, Wolfgang. *Background to Agricultural Land Policy in Malaysia.* Wiesbaden: Otto Harrassowitz, 1978.

Sihombing, Judith E. *National Land Code: A Commentary.* Kuala Lumpur: Malayan Law Journal Pte. Ltd, 1981.

Sta Maria, Bernard. *My People My Country.* Malacca: The Malacca Portuguese Development Centre Publication, 1982.

Tan Soo Hai and Hamzah Sendut, eds. *Aspects of Housing in Malaysia.* International Development Research Centre, Ontario, Canada, and University Science Malaysia, South East Asia Low Cost Housing Study Monograph, n.d.

Tan Tat Wai. *Income Distribution in West Malaysia.* Kuala Lumpur: Oxford University Press, 1982.

Teixeira Manuel, Fr. *The Portuguese Missions in Malacca and Singapore (1511–1958),* Vol. 3. Singapore: Agencia Geral Do Ultramar, Lisboa, 1963.

Tsuruoka, Doug. "Eager buyers look for more". *Far Eastern Economic Review,* 29 March 1990a, p. 50.

——. "Feet of Clay: Japanese firm denies hitches with KL tower plan". *Far Eastern Economic Review,* 26 July 1990b, pp. 51–52.

——. "A brake gives bumis a break". *Far Eastern Economic Review,* 21 March 1991, pp. 44–45.

——. "Stake in the cake: Malaysian government split over foreign-investment rules". *Far Eastern Economic Review,* 5 March 1992, pp. 52–53.

Turnbull, C.M. *The Straits Settlements 1826–1867.* London: The Athlone Press, 1972.

Newspapers and Periodicals

Aliran Monthly 15, no. 3 (1995).
Japan Economic Review 20, no. 1000 (6 April 1982).
New Straits Times, various issues.
The Star, various issues.

chapter eight

RETURNING TO THE "ORIGIN"
Church and State in the Ethnographies of the "To Pamona"

ALBERT SCHRAUWERS

In 1989, the government of Indonesia expanded its annual Independence Day celebrations in the small church town of Tentena (with a population of 8,000) into a major provincial cultural exhibition, the first annual Lake Poso Festival. Tentena lies at the head of the Poso River, nestled between mountains and lake, and more importantly, along the Trans-Sulawesi highway which links it to Tana Toraja, the second most popular tourist destination in Indonesia after Bali. The Festival, like the Independence Day celebrations out of which it grew, was marked by presentations of *asli* (authentic) arts, songs and dance of Central Sulawesi, including those of Balinese transmigrants. The Festival, however, quickly drew the ire of some in the local church, which objected to the now Protestant To Pamona, the dominant ethnic group in the area, being characterized by resurrected animist rites associated with headhunting. In 1991, the Church Synod, which owned the Festival grounds, asked for their return and announced its own plans to use the site for religiously oriented events. The following year, a monument to Christian Youth was constructed atop a rock outcropping overlooking the Festival site. The government, in turn, expropriated the rice fields 200 metres to the west, and began construction of new Festival buildings at a reported cost of several billion rupiah, this time in the shape of *lobo*, the animist temples of the highlands in the previous century. Each of the major ethnic groups of the highlands was represented by its own building, leading one local wag to dub the complex "Beautiful Sulawesi in Miniature Gardens", in reference to the popular Jakarta cultural theme park where each of Indonesia's twenty-seven provinces is represented by a pavilion in the shape of its indigenous traditional structure. The Church answered with the construction of Banua mPogombo, the Meeting House, an enormous conference centre serving the same function as a *lobo*.

At the root of this impressive construction boom lies a contest of representations. The "Beautiful Sulawesi in Miniature Gardens", like its inspiration in Jakarta, represents a sustained attempt by the state to restore a timeless local tradition within the context of "Beautiful Indonesia" as a whole — a process Pemberton dubs "mini-ization" (1994, p. 12). The aim is to make this local, timeless, "authentic" tradition unthinkable except in the context of its relation to the nation as a whole. To find this authentic tradition, they went back to the "origin". The original Festival grounds lay near Pamona, the legendary village of origin of those now called the To Pamona (people of Pamona). The reconstruction of the *lobo* and the resuscitation of the songs and dances which once took place there — now as high art — defined this group in terms of its *asli* (authentic) traditions. It is, however, a truncated and outdated tradition which homogenizes internal differentiation and includes only easily marketed tourist objects like costumes, handicrafts, songs and dances, while ignoring such important intangibles as religion, kinship structure, means of subsistence, oratory, land laws, or etiquette. Kipp characterizes this underplaying of the social context of regional arts as "ethnic blindness and showcase culture" (1993, p. 108). She notes that the principled "ethnic blindness" of the state and educational system is balanced by the active promotion of regional *kebudayaan* (culture) severed from actual social groups and identified only by province. It is this attempt to recapture and amalgamate To Pamona origins with those of other groups in Central Sulawesi, while ignoring regnant identities, which troubled the Church. The To Pamona are overwhelmingly Protestant, a Christian minority in an Islamic nation.

The irony of the scale of this contest of representations is the very vagueness of the group to which they are said to apply. Ethnic consciousness as "To Pamona" is a relatively new phenomenon, the product of efforts like those described above. There is a general confusion as to whom the designation applies. In part, this confusion stems from government attempts to shift the definition of ethnicity from some "primordial" group to a shared appreciation of the public performance of decontextualized "traditional" songs and dances. In turn, the Church has sought to define To Pamona ethnicity in terms of Christianity, a larger category within which the distinctive cultural features of the group recede. These ironies, and the large sums of money involved, lead to the questions: Why does the New Order government persist in constituting To Pamona identity in terms of a *dead past*? And, if it is a dead past, why is the Church threatened by it?

These questions can only be answered by looking at the history of how the To Pamona have come to be an object of discourse, both locally, and within the anthropological literature. Pamonan ethnicity has its roots in anthropological representations utilized descriptively, and prescriptively, by both the state and religious missions. Rather than add a new twist to old representations, and so both solidify conceptions of this discursive object and, perforce, take sides in the contesting visions of who the To Pamona "really" are, the aim here is to deconstruct the very notion that an "authentic" To Pamona culture can be uncovered (cf. Kahn 1993, pp. 15–20). The To Pamona, like any ethnic group, are internally differentiated. They are not homogeneous, but purposively set apart in larger social arenas by contested cultural markers. These ethnic markers and the internally coherent "cultures" they are said to represent are themselves the product of the universalizing discourses of competing authorities. It should be immediately apparent that the battle over the Festival grounds represents more than a conflict between a "rational" modernizing nationalism and some primordial ethnic sentiment. Rather, we see here the construction and utilization of ethnicity in two variant nationalist discourses being used to further different "nationalist projects". These discourses have their roots in Dutch political and religious culture. This chapter then focuses upon these authorities — Church and State — rather than the reaction of the To Pamona themselves, and examines how a colonial legacy has shaped current representations.

The Reification of the To Pamona

Central Sulawesi is one of Indonesia's twenty-seven provinces. Its scant population of 1,703,000 is divided among no less than five language groups and twenty-five languages (Noorduyn 1991). Ethnic diversity is equally complex, but less easily delimited, and herein lies the problem for ethnographers, whose initial task is to define their ethnographic subject. We, however, must recognize the power differential between cultural categorization and self ascription and ask what political, economic and cultural discourses make such categorization both possible and desirable? Anthropological discourse was often shaped by the practical demands of a larger colonial system, as will be seen in the case of the To Pamona. I would like then to contrast the categorizations by which the To Pamona have come to exist, with the various Dutch colonial groups that had interests in perpetuating the contrasting images by which they have come to be known.

The name "Pamona" is derived from the mythic kingdom from which all To Pamona, and hence their *adat* (traditions), arose. The name is a Dutch misreading of the word *Pamuna*, which translates as "the origin" (Sigilipu 1990; and Kruyt 1950, p. 16). The kingdom was said to have been a single large village located across the river from Tentena, at the site of a new, similarly named village (Sigilipu 1990, p. 2). This village was ruled by a king who was ultimately conquered by the kingdom of Luwu, and led off in servitude. Since they no longer had a leader, the people of the kingdom decided to disperse, each group leaving behind a stone as a remembrance of their origin there. The saliency of Pamona was thus marked by their common subjection to Luwu, a symbol which simultaneously *emphasized their diaspora*.

The name "To Pamona" (people of Pamona) is of recent origin. The first ethnographer of the area, A.C. Kruyt, used the name "*Bare'e* speaking Toraja", where "Toraja" was a lowland term for "highlander". His ascriptive choice of "Toraja" was due to the absence of any pre-existing sense of "To Pamona" ethnicity among those who tied their group origins to the mythic kingdom (Kruyt 1950, p. 16). Kruyt emphasized that those who traced their origins to Pamona defined their identities in terms of their named *lemba* (cf. Indonesian *suku*, meaning "extended family", "ethnic group"), for example, the To Pebato, To Wingke mPoso or To Lage. Each of these groups was said to share a common set of ancestors and *adat* (tradition). Their differences were often underscored, such that Kruyt's uniform linguistic group of "*Bare'e* speaking Toraja" was, to them, broken up into "*are'e*", "*ae'e*", "*iba*" and "*aunde'e*" speakers. This pattern of supposed common origins but with distinctive identities can be tied to the way they were incorporated in the segmentary state of Luwu. The myth emphasizes their shared origins in terms of their common subjection to Luwu. But since Luwu utilized a strategy of divide and rule, distinct segmentary groups were of greater saliency than any sense of overarching unity.

The development of the current nomenclature by the government is largely ascriptive and applied to those living within the administrative boundaries. It contrasts to some degree with popular usage, which varies by context. A "To Pamona" may refer to a person from the village of Pamona; to a resident of the *kecamatan* (subdistrict) of Pamona Utara or Pamona Selatan; to a person living in the *puse lemba* (centre of the valley/territory), the territory of the To Wingke mPoso at the head of the river Poso; or to a person speaking a dialect of *bahasa Pamona* (language of the To Pamona, an amalgam of the dialects noted above). Thus, a number of villagers from Tentena expressed confusion when I referred to the To Onda'e from the Laa River basin (but still within Pamona Utara), as To Pamona. The To Onda'e lived outside the *puse lemba*, my informants' primary referent. This widespread confusion on the appropriate application of the term is indicative of the mainly bureaucratic origins of the ethnic terminology as it is utilized in discussions of *adat* (traditional) law. Despite government attempts to unify the "To Pamona *adat*", some residents of the *puse lemba* perceive the To Onda'e as having a different *adat* and hence exclude them from the designation "To Pamona".

The creation of "To Pamona" ethnicity is thus at the expense of these various smaller, acephalous kinship groups, or *lemba*, each of which had its own distinctive *adat* (cf. Henley [1996] for a discussion of a similar case in Minahasa). Since 1905, the state has progressively sought to amalgamate these *lemba* into larger districts each governed by a district headman subordinated to the newly appointed *raja* (king). Since the kingdom was ruled according to *adat* law, and each district was an amalgam of several *lemba*, each with its own *adat*, a process of government rationalization of *adat* law began almost immediately and has continued until today. In 1990 a government-sponsored *musyawarah* (conference) was called to attempt, once again, to rationalize and unify the *adats* of the To Pamona (*ada mPamona*). No more successful than earlier attempts, the *musyawarah's* report lies in bureaucratic limbo.

The Role of *Adat* Studies in the Netherlands East Indies

The peoples who have come to be called the To Pamona were incorporated in the Netherlands East Indies (NEI) under the Ethical Policy in 1905. The Ethical Policy, introduced by Dutch religious parties in 1901, represented a major shift in colonial policy. It is the implications of, first, the actions of the Dutch religious parties, and, secondly, the Ethical Policy and its theological subtext that we will explore here.

The religious political parties which introduced the Policy can be characterized by their attempts to prevent state interference in the "religious sphere" in the Netherlands, within which they included education, welfare, health care and family law (Stuurman 1983). While in power, these parties provided the legislative basis by which denominational social organizations could fulfil their religious mission of directing their adherents' spiritual development through denominational schools, unions, newspapers, hospitals, political parties and a host of other services. The vertical division or "pillarization" (*verzuiling*) of Dutch society on a religious basis ministered to the social and religious needs of Orthodox Calvinists and Catholics from cradle to grave. Secularism, as an ideology, was marginalized. This movement has historically been characterized as an "emancipation movement" similar to the democratic nationalist struggles of other European "nations" (*volk*) (Stuurman 1983, pp. 72–75). The easiest way in which to summarize this politico-religious formation is by reference to a better known concept — that of apartheid — a policy which also has its roots in Dutch Calvinism. What the Dutch call social "pillarization" by religion is a religious rather than racial apartheid. Like apartheid, it allows for the separate existence of a number of "nations" within a single state.

The moralizing tone of the religious political parties is clearly evident in the Ethical Policy, a variation of the "white man's burden" (Locher-Scholten 1981). Highly critical of the Liberal Party's policy of open-door capitalist expansion in the archipelago and the abuses it engendered, the confessionals (following the socialists) accepted the *Ereschuld* (Dutch, meaning "debt of honour") that the Netherlands owed the Netherlands East Indies for the millions of guilders extracted from the colonial economy. They did not, however, abdicate the Netherlands' right to rule the archipelago, nor the basic form of private capitalist exploitation. The policy was marked, rather, by new concerns for "native welfare" and "development," and the repatriation of some of the funds regularly transferred from the colony. The paternalistic development policies instituted in Java, where most of the abuses had taken place, were accompanied by a new and contrasting "ethical imperialism" in the Outer Islands, where the "white's man's burden" replaced a "hand's off" policy and led the Dutch to depose "despotic" indigenous leaders for the greater good of their subjects (Locher Scholten 1981, pp. 194–99). The Rev. Abraham Kuyper, the Dutch Prime Minister under whom the Ethical Policy was introduced, emphasized that the Netherlands East Indies were not an integral part of the Kingdom of the Netherlands (Locher Scholten 1981, p. 178). They were, rather, an obligation inherited from the bankrupt East Indies Company. Subject peoples in the NEI were *not* Dutch citizens, and had no rights under the Dutch constitution. The Dutch did, however, inherit a responsibility for the archipelago, an ethical call to protect and shepherd the colony until it had matured enough for independence. The ethical responsibility of the Dutch was explicitly formulated in terms of *state formation*, which was, however, to be a Dutch prerogative. State formation in the colony by the Dutch was contrasted with the existence within the colony of numerous "nations" defined by a shared *adat*, or legal tradition.

State formation in the NEI was consequently equated with ethical responsibility, and this meant the introduction of modern liberal, administrative techniques. Indirect rule through indigenous "nations" were to be rationalized along the lines of Western statecraft. This spatial extension of the state was accompanied by an expansion in the number of governmental departments and their programmes:

> Education, religion, irrigation, agricultural improvements, hygiene, mineral exploitation, political surveillance — all increasingly became the business of a rapidly expanding officialdom, which unfolded more according to its inner impulses than in response to any organised extra-state demands (Anderson 1983a, p. 479).

The rapid expansion of the state apparatus raised its own problems. Lacking manpower, the NEI government was increasingly forced to turn to the religious missions to implement specific programmes, especially in education and health. State formation in the Netherlands East Indies thus began to mirror that of the mother country itself, with each religion serving the "social needs" of its members (in the Indonesian literature, these blocs came to be called *aliran*; see Geertz 1965, Gunawan and Muizenberg 1967, Gunawan 1971, McVey 1970, Wertheim 1973).

Such an easy parallel, however, is confused by specifically East Indies issues, in particular a militant Islam. Indigenous opposition to Dutch rule in the archipelago was increasingly phrased in terms of Pan-Islamic unity and the call for observance of *shariah* law (in effect, a call for a unified legal-bureaucratic system for the East Indies in East Indian hands). The NEI state sought to limit the political claims of Islam. The recognition of numerous "nations" within the state, indirect rule through indigenous élites and the codification of *adat* law were, in fact, aimed at curtailing Islam's unifying power within the colony as a whole (Lev 1985, p. 66). By strengthening traditional non-religious (that is, ethnic) élites and inventing them where none existed, the process of divide and rule continued in a new guise. The rigour with which the Dutch sought to preserve "traditional law" within the colonial state, legitimated by its obligation to "develop" its subject peoples, is a clear indication that it was the practical, administrative logic of state formation which determined the content of the Ethical Policy, not vice versa. Under the Ethical Policy, this pluralist approach was advanced through *adat* law studies — ethnographic studies which were utilized to define "tradition", and hence the structure of indirect rule. Importantly, many of these *adat* law studies were written by missionaries influenced by the theological underpinnings of pillarization and its alternate conceptualization of the relationship of "nationhood" to the state. The NEI state and the missions thus had differing interests in preparing these studies.

In the case of Central Sulawesi, the separation of "religion" from indigenous government was unclear; secular governance was unknown. By strengthening the position of *adat* law for the non-Islamic peoples among whom the missions had been granted permission to work, the government worked against mission efforts at *religious* conversion since these peoples made no distinction between *adat* and religion. This left the missions with two options: the first, to oppose the policy of indirect rule through indigenous *adat* would have meant an alliance with Islam, and hence was untenable. The second option was to embrace *adat* studies as a means of defining "religion" in the East Indies social formation. This second option was adopted by the ethical theologians who utilized "secular liberal" social sciences in the service of missions. A.C. Kruyt, the missionary ethnographer of the To Pamona, stood at the forefront of such developments, his "sociological method" becoming a standard in Dutch missions during the early twentieth century. Their ethnographic work thus took place within the framework established by *adat* law studies, indirect rule and their own attempts to delimit a "religious" sphere distinct from *adat*.

Indirect rule required the codification of "tradition" in such a form that it could be administered as law. As just noted, the abstraction of "law" from "religion" was frequently problematic. It was this administrative problem which gave rise to the Dutch theoretical debate about the universal features of "religion". This ideologically charged debate was influenced not only by the administrative logic of the colony, but also by the prevailing political debate in the Netherlands. Since "religion" and "law" were administered by two different departments of the NEI state, the ultimate resolution of the theoretical debate in turn determined departmental competence. Mission ethnography played an important role in determining this competence. The division of religion from law, however, invoked more than questions of departmental division of labour. It simultaneously evoked long-standing theological concerns about the relation of religion and the *volk* being established by legal means. Their adoption of *adat* studies redefined the meaning of "conversion".

Earlier missions had often treated religious conversion as the first step of the social conversion of the "native" into a Dutch citizen. This meant the use of non-native languages (*Bahasa Malayu* [Indonesian] or Dutch) in church services, the strict adherence to Dutch liturgies, individualized conversion and attempts to "civilize" the new converts. The ethical theologians argued that such converts simply acquired a Christian "lacquer"; there was no real transformation of the essential being of the new converts, the end result being a syncretic and impure Christianity. In contrast, the ethical theologians conceptualized the role of the Church specifically in terms of a spiritual community, a *volkskerk* (Dutch, meaning "people's" church, in a sense, defining nationhood). This conceptualization of the Church involved a relativization of its tenets, a recognition that cultural norms should not be confused with Biblical principles; different peoples could have different cultures and different churches, but still dwell in God's truth as long as those traditions were evaluated from a Biblical perspective (van Randwijck 1981, pp. 146–49). "Ethical Theology" emphasized respect for indigenous cultures, and missions in the vernacular. Conversion to Christianity thus created an alternate "nationalist" discourse — a discourse which also drew on the "emancipatory" politics of the churches in the Netherlands, which sought to contest the demands of the state on their "nations".

There are three aspects of "Ethical Theology" pertinent to the colonial setting. First, its conceptualization of the Church as *volkskerk* implies a "people." The word "*volk*", like "nation" was based on cultural or "racial" criteria, and hence stood in opposition to the state. In the colonial setting, indigenous political divisions could be ignored and a "people" defined even where no indigenous sense of ethnic identity existed; such was the case with the To Pamona. Such cultural categorization worked hand in hand with *adat* studies in that the "people" were said to share an *adat* and hence became an administrative unit in the NEI bureaucracy. The second implication of "Ethical Theology" was its paternalism. The emphasis on individual reformation and the disregard for denominational organization ensured that the *volkskerk* so defined remained under mission control. This paternalism was masked by mission relativism; it insisted that the transformation of the *adat* under Christian principles had to emerge through self-examination and self-reformation and would lead to a distinctive form of indigenous Christianity. This ignored, of course, Dutch control of church administration, and mission efforts to document "Christian" *adat* within the larger legal-administrative system of the NEI. The third implication of "Ethical Theology", its cultural relativity, gave rise to a widespread attempt to understand other cultures in their own terms. Missionaries were thus an integral part of the development of anthropology in its pre-professional phase in the Netherlands.

Mission ethnographies, as empirical studies, explicitly sought to situate their ethnographic subjects in universalist (usually evolutionist) terms, and hence bear no outward sign of these politically charged colonial debates; the uses of ethnography were separated from the *act* of ethnography, thus validating their objectivity and universal conclusions. We have seen, however, that such abstract theoretical considerations had practical implications for administrative competence within the bureaucracy, as well as for defining the rights of missions *vis-à-vis* that bureaucracy within the larger state formation. In particular, the definition of religion and the establishment of ethnic boundaries (*adatrechtkring*) were not simply abstract theoretical issues, but an exercise of power by which subject "peoples" (as collections of individuals, yet as a *volk*) were co-opted and integrated within the emerging NEI state and the mission church.

The "Sociological Mission Method"

In 1890, the Netherlands Missionary Society and the Netherlands Bible Society, in consultation with G.W.W.C. Baron van Hoevell,

Assistant Resident of Menado, settled upon Central Sulawesi as a new mission field (Arts 1985, p. 86; and J. Kruyt 1970, p. 56). Two missionaries, then in training, were designated for the field: Albert Christiaan Kruyt (1869–1949), the son of a Netherlands Missionary Society missionary in Java (Brouwer 1951, p. 11–16), and Nicolas Adriani (1865–1926), son of the Director of the Utrecht Missionary Association and nephew of the Director of the Netherlands Missionary Society (Kraemer 1935, p. 12). These two men, each from a strong mission background, embodied the new currents which affected missions in the Netherlands East Indies. "Ethical Theology" and "Ethical Policy" were combined in these men to produce a new mission methodology, the "Sociological Method", in which ethnography played a key role. Between them, Kruyt and Adriani produced no less than four lengthy ethnographies of the *"Bare'e* speaking Toraja" who were later to be known as the To Pamona (Kruyt 1895–97; Adriani and Kruyt 1912–14; Adriani 1919; Kruyt 1950), theoretical studies on "animism" (Kruyt 1906; Adriani 1919), two dictionaries (Kruyt 1894; Adriani 1928), an extensive grammar (Adriani 1931), as well as articles too numerous to mention (see the bibliographies in Brouwer 1951; Adriani 1932). This flood of information about the previously unknown To Pamona provided a showcase for their new missiological method. It also provided "objective" data which backed mission definitions of the boundary between *adat* and religion within the colonial formation, and hence fixed the cultural markers by which the To Pamona would come to be defined.

The figure linking the key players and organizations which led to Kruyt and Adriani's placement in Central Sulawesi was Prof. P.D. Chantepie de la Saussaye. Saussaye was a prominent ethical theologian who was the Chairman of the Board of both the Netherlands Missionary Society and the Netherlands Bible Society. He was an ardent opponent of the enlightenment and liberalism. His doctoral thesis, entitled *Methodological Contributions to the Study of the Origins of Religion* (1871), was one of the first comparative studies of religion in the Netherlands, and made heavy use of ethnographic studies (Rasker 1974, p. 235). He was named to the Chair in Comparative Religion at the University of Amsterdam in 1878. It was his knowledge of comparative religion which led to his involvement in mission organizations, and his academic position which guaranteed his influence in the continuing debate on the nature and boundaries of "religion" in the NEI. Saussaye thus gave the missions of the Netherlands Missionary Society and the Netherlands Bible Society their ethical imperative, as well as directed their "ethnological" studies. It was he, in consultation with Assistant Resident G.W.W.C. Baron van Hoevell, who decided to open the mission field in Central Sulawesi, and as chairman of both the Netherlands Missionary Society and the Netherlands Bible Society ensured the close co-operation between the two missions.

Kruyt and Adriani's adoption of a common "Toraja" category for all the highland peoples was based on a number of factors. First, as with the term it replaced, *Alfuru*, the name was to differentiate those groups which were not Islamic from the coastal peoples who were. Kruyt, however, did not see their unity in strictly negative terms, but identified a number of shared cultural traits, primarily a common "animist" religion focused on "feasts of merit" and head-hunting. Somewhat more problematical to Kruyt was the division of this universal category into smaller units of greater cultural consistency. Kruyt outlined a threefold division of the highlanders of Central Sulawesi into the *Bare'e* speaking, the West and the Sa'dan Toraja in two multi-volume ethnographies (1912, 1938). Kruyt's division was based on a combination of factors such as language and the presence or absence of specific cultural traits such as the mutilation of teeth. As the division was somewhat arbitrary, Kruyt's division was contested by some, in particular Adriani (in Vol. 3 of Adriani and Kruyt 1912–14), who based his division on a more refined linguistic analysis; and Walter Kaudern, a Swedish anthropologist who divided the area into four, rather than three subgroups (1925). It was Kruyt's ethnic categories, however, which were to provide the basis of C. van Vollenhoven's analysis of the "Toraja traditional law area" (*adatrechtkring*).

Van Vollenhoven was a Dutch law scholar who played a central role in the creation of the system of indirect rule in the Netherlands East Indies. Van Vollenhoven divided Indonesia into nineteen traditional law areas, utilizing "indigenous law" to define administrative divisions. The Toraja traditional law area was subdivided into three sub-districts, matching Kruyt's three groups. The Poso-Tojo traditional law sub-district corresponded with Kruyt's *"Bare'e* speaking Toraja". It was further subdivided into two kingdoms (autonomous regions) in the Dutch colonial administration, one under Islamic influence, and the other under the guidance of Christian missions. The traditional ties of political dependency of the highlands on the Islamic coastal kingdoms of Luwu, Mori, Tojo and Parigi were thus severed. Since the new "kingdom" of Poso lacked any form of indigenous political unity, the Dutch imposed a *raja* (Indonesian, king, ruler) who acted as intermediary between the indigenous peoples and the colonial administration (Arts 1985, pp. 106–9; J. Kruyt 1970, pp. 99–104). The term "To Pamona" roughly applies to the peoples living in the now defunct kingdom of Poso.

Although Kruyt's division of the Toraja peoples found ready acceptance in colonial Dutch scholarly and administrative circles, we must question the broader basis for his decision. Kruyt and Adriani adopted the term "Toraja" as a substitute for *Alfuru,* an ascriptive ethnic categorization based primarily on religion. Kruyt and Adriani had been invited by the NEI government to begin their mission in the Poso area in 1892 as a means of asserting a Dutch presence in the area, as well as creating a Christian bulwark against the spread of a politicized Islam in the highlands (Arts 1985, p. 86). All the highland peoples had extensive ties with Islamic coastal kingdoms, which, though Islamic, were characterized by many of the cultural features which guided Kruyt in his categorization. Thus, the primary criteria in Kruyt's ethnic categorization were based on his own needs as a missionary. The military invasion of Central Sulawesi by the NEI in 1905 was justified in large part by Kruyt's call to sever the tie between the Islamic coastal states and the highlands because they hindered mission activities (Engelenberg 1906, p. 14). His scholarly separation of the non-Islamic highland peoples from the coastal kingdoms mirrored this political division on a cultural level. The imposed unity of this culture area, as well as its administrative unification, thus became the reason for establishing a single Toraja church for the Toraja *volk* under the Netherlands Missionary Society (van den End 1992, p. 23). Kruyt's project was no less than a "nationalist" one, predicated upon the rational (theological) reformation of "primordial" ethnic sentiments.

Kruyt's mission methodology was thus based on a series of oppositions: of the rational Dutch versus the irrational Toraja; of universal theological truths versus a culturally specific animism; of valid nationalist sentiments versus a particularist chauvinism. Successful conversion thus involved the "evolution" of the Toraja from one pole to the other. The sociological method was to be a means of "inculturating"[1] Christianity within a non-Christian people in such a way that their culture was Christianized (rationalized, nationalized) without necessarily losing its distinctive ethos.

> How must we approach the *adat*? When we truly recognize the *adat* as the form wherein the Indonesian shows his inner being, when we view the *adat* as the result of a perhaps age-old history and development, if we know that the *adat* is the formulation of the most appropriate rules of living for the people, then we stand with respect towards the *adat*, even if it does differ from our opinions. Then we will study it to understand how it works, and that which people cannot retain as Christians we do not cut off in rough fashion, but rework the thoughts and feelings of the native Christian through preaching the Gospel, through Christian education, so that when their circumstances have changed, become Christian, they themselves will alter their *adat*, so that they in their Christian state, become an expression of what lives within them. (Kruyt 1937, p. 48, author's translation).

Study of the *adat* was considered essential to understanding the religious feelings and thoughts of Indonesians, since these emotions and symbol systems were rooted in "pre-logical" thought (see, for example, Kruyt 1937, pp. 22–39; Kruyt 1925, p. 182). Kruyt recognized that the message of the Gospel was not self-evident, and that Indonesian converts often interpreted the message in their own cultural terms. Kruyt saw such attempts as encouraging, as a sign that converts were seeking to find the relevance of the Gospels within their cultures. He did not view conversion as an all-or-none phenomena, but as a developmental process. This process was characterized by preaching the Gospel, its reception and the evocation of questions about its application in their lives, followed by the selective reworking of the *adat* by the Indonesians themselves. Kruyt refused to issue a set of rules, a ready-made "Christian *adat*", but insisted on the reformation of the old *adat* through a dialogue with the mission (Kruyt 1925, pp. 134–57).

It was within this dialogue that the group which now defines itself as To Pamona came to acquire and internalize a sense of common identity under Kruyt's tutelage. Many of the regional variations in *adat* were eliminated in the process of purging it of "unChristian" elements. More important, however, was the sense of "imagined community" which the "Brotherhood of Christ" provided (cf. Anderson 1983b). The mission specifically propagated itself as a "people's church", as community-based and inclusive rather than exclusive. This ideology took root among the new indigenous ministers, who received better than average education, worked in a supra-local organization, and who were actively involved in refor-mulating the *adat* according to Christian principles. It was through the institutional incorporation of ministers and church elders that the "nationalist" project of church building took place.

The Christian Church of Central Sulawesi grew out of the mission established by Kruyt among the To Pamona, To Mori and a third more diffused group composed of the To Bada, To Besoa and To Napu in the Lore River valley. Each cultural and linguistic group was incorporated on its own cultural terms, and hence different ritual orders emerged within the church. *Padungku* (Thanksgiving), the *Sura Magali* (Pamona-language translation of the New Testament) and the *Sura mPongayu* (Pamona-language hymn book) have become powerful symbols of To Pamona ethnic identity. Yet these symbols have been carefully tempered with an emphasis on the "brotherhood of Christ" to ensure that ethnic strife does not emerge within the Synod. The Synod has frequently failed to prevent this strife, resulting in the schism of ethnic churches. Since its founding in 1947, the Christian Church of Central Sulawesi has splintered, forming the independent churches of Gereja Kristen Luwuk Banggai, Gereja Protestan Indonesia Donggala, and the Gereja Protestan Indonesia Buol Toli-Toli. The inability to maintain the unity of the Synod makes the issue of ethnicity important for the church.

Adat Law and the State

Although ethnic divisions in Central Sulawesi have their roots in Kruyt's definitions of *adat* communities, and his attempts to reform and unify them under a common "Christian *adat*", the *adat* came to play a second, and not wholly consistent role as *adat* law. *Adat* law, administered by the state, has thus served as a second locus in defining To Pamona ethnicity. *Adat* law was tied to specific administrative boundaries. The name "To Pamona" was first used in about 1973 (Pakan 1977; 1986, p. 19) and later applied to the two districts around Lake Poso which had been the heartland of the kingdom created by the Dutch after 1905. Thus, their new sense of ethnic identity has grown out of a legal fiction, the *resurrected* colonial kingdom of Poso/Pamona which had been used by the Dutch as a means of indirect rule. As noted earlier, however, the state has had little success in amalgamating the *adat* law of the area. It has been far more successful in marginalizing its importance. Differences in *adat* have been attenuated throughout almost ninety years of state intervention as the colonial, and now New Order state, attempts to coerce the highlanders along a unilinear development path which has served to homogenize differences between them. The process of homogenization and resettlement has been central to the internalization of administrative boundaries as ethnic identity by the To Pamona. Within this forced march to "modernization", *adat* has been incorporated in a larger, Indonesian nationalist discourse.

The "Ethical Policy" mandated that the colonial government shepherd its wards along what they saw as a unilinear evolutionary path. Swidden agriculture, longhouses and "communal" ownership of property were considered inferior, necessitating policies designed to encourage a freeholding peasantry of nuclear family, wet rice farming households. Following the consolidation of their control of the highlands between 1906 and 1908, the Dutch began a massive resettlement plan, forcing all the highlanders to abandon their hilltop hamlets and construct larger villages in the few alluvial plains suitable for wet-rice agriculture (Kruyt 1970, pp. 91–105, 144–55). These villages were to be situated along a single road. The implementation of these policies has resulted in the consolidation of a number of different groups in the same or neighbouring villages, often at a great distance from their traditional lands. New relations of production, new technologies, and the banning of the religious rites associated with head-hunting have all reduced the scope of *adat* from "the way of the ancestors" to just a part of the wedding ceremony, the bridewealth transactions.

The state's failure to unify the *adat*, and the weakening of its relevance in daily life has not, however, made for a strong ethnic consciousness. In the first phase of contesting representations of the To Pamona, it was the mission which succeeded in establishing a clear, religiously-based identity for the peoples of the highlands. This Christian identity, this sense of Christian community (*volkskerk*) was "represented" in the Soekarno era by a religious political party, Parkindo (Indonesian Protestant Party). In other words, Christianity in the Outer Islands formed an *aliran* similar to that of the Islamic groups described by Geertz in Java. In turn, the *aliran* phenomenon closely resembles the political situation in the Netherlands, where confessional parties dominated the legislature for much of the first half of this century. This commonality of politico-religious trajectories can be tied, I would argue, to the introduction of Dutch definitions of religion to Indonesia through the "Ethical Policy".

The birth of the New Order state in 1964 is well documented, and need not be elaborated on here. Of importance is the position the New Order has taken with respect to the old *aliran* that it inherited after the decimation of the Communist Party. The Generals of the New Order earned their rank in putting down the Islamic *Darul Islam* (Islamic state) rebellions of Sumatra, Java and Sulawesi. Themselves committed to a pluralistic society, they have consistently sought to de-politicize religious identities. A uniform policy has been hindered, however, by a contradictory fear of regional, ethnic separatism as manifested, for example, in the PERMESTA rebellion of North and Central Sulawesi. The colonial policy of utilizing local *adat* to weaken the political power of Islam has thus been made untenable. The New Order has responded by, on the one hand, subordinating the political aspirations of religious groups to the state ideology, the Pancasila. On the other hand, it has further marginalized the importance of *adat* law, thought to foster ethnic separatism, through the creation of a uniform civil bureaucracy operating according to national law.

The isolation imposed on the highlands of Central Sulawesi by regional revolt in the 1950s and 1960s and the destruction of the major means of transport and communication have slowly been eroded by five Five-Year Development Plans (REPELITA). The New Order has strengthened its control of the regions through the professionalization of the civil service at the expense of the older system of *adat* law. Most government departments now have offices at the regency or district level, and many of these have displaced the *adat* processes. This is particularly true of the Ministry of Justice which has established civil courts. The elected village *adat* council (*dewan adat*) now functions as a "poor man's court" rather than as the civil service. This council is directly subordinated to the village mayor who is its chair, and who conducts most *adat* ceremonies. The elected mayors (*kepala desa*) of the six villages that make up the "city" of Tentena have been replaced with appointed civil servants (*lurah*), making the primary *adat* functionary a civil servant whose rulings are increasingly moulded by state policy. Cases which cannot be resolved by the *adat* councils are brought to the district head (*camat*), a civil servant and superior to the mayors.

The marginalization of *adat* law and the new development of a professional civil service has been matched by increased government tutelage of *adat* as "culture" (*kebudayaan*) through new village governmental institutions. The village *adat* law council is now facing new competition in defining local ethnic identity from the "Village Coordination Board" (Lembaga Ketahanan Masyarakat Desa) which sponsors regional competitions of defunct songs and dances. These regional arts competitions are themselves situated within larger national programmes which are broadcast through the state television network, TVRI. *Adat* is being redefined from law to tradition, and in particular, an outdated tradition of little day-to-day saliency. The founding of the Lake Poso Festival and the large-scale construction of traditional *lobo* at the Festival grounds must thus be examined from this perspective, as part of a policy to marginalize the political saliency of religious and ethnic identities except insofar as they are subordinated within the state. Alternative expressions of ethnicity which might prove to be a source of social conflict, such as religion or "race" (or more accurately, Chinese and Papuan ethnicity), have no place in these forums. Hence, it is the dead "animist" tradition, the authentic (*asli*) "origins" of the To Pamona, which is incorporated within the state's ethnic arts discourse, and not the politically salient Christian arts tradition.

This is a new strategy of ethnic management which emphasizes "ethnic blindness and showcase cultures" (Kipp 1993, p. 108). It specifically defines each ethnic group as a part of the cultural mosaic of a state which is officially "Various, but One". Kipp notes that mandatory government identity cards list religion but not ethnicity, and that no statistics are collected on an ethnic basis. Ethnic languages are not repressed, but the utilization of Bahasa Indonesia increasingly marginalizes those languages in public life. "Schools and government are ethnically blind, at least in principle" (ibid., p. 109). This refusal to delimit ethnic groups contrasts with the government's active promotion of "showcase cultures" or "*adat* spectacles" (cf. Acciaioli 1985). By encouraging the mounting of such spectacles, traditional leadership and *adat* discourse are locked into "traditional concerns" and made irrelevant to the normal operations of the state. The emphasis on *adat* as culture marginalizes ethnic politics while simultaneously granting ethnic identity a high profile in a limited sphere which in turn emphasizes its relational aspects. This is the crux of the process which Pemberton describes as "mini-ization", in which the "authentic" origins of each ethnic group are captured in timeless fashion within the overarching unity of "Beautiful Indonesia" as a whole (1994).

Conclusion

I began this article by questioning the essentialist roots of expression of To Pamona ethnicity which claim to represent the group's authentic "origins". By focusing upon how these "representations", in both the sense of "image of" and "speaking for", have been constituted, I have tried to underscore the political, economic and cultural discourses which made the ethnic category "To Pamona" salient. To Pamona ethnicity cannot be rooted in some "primordial sentiment" and opposed to nationalism. Rather, the two divergent ethnic discourses related here are themselves part of emancipatory nationalist discourses. One nationalist discourse is tied to the theological conceptualization of a *volkskerk*; the other to the Indonesian nationalist project, "Various but One". Both discourses can be traced back to their colonial roots, "Ethical Theology" and the "Ethical Policy". Both projects posit unique and sometimes contradictory solutions to the problem of the relationship between nation and state. The New Order's cultural policies specifically aim to depoliticize both ethnic and religious identities. But by redefining the self-image of the "To Pamona" in terms of "animist" songs and dances, their Christian identity is challenged. The New Order's definition of *adat* in terms of pre-Christian traditions and the Church's own definition of a Christian *adat* are inherently contradictory. Government policy is thought to encourage communalism within the Church, threatening Christian unity and abetting the creation of ethnic churches. The Church has already undergone a number of painful ethnic secessions. Driven by its own imagined community, the "Brotherhood of Christ", the Church has shored up its identity by directly contesting the state's representations. These contests only confirm the state's fears of religion as a destabilizing force, and strengthen its resolve to root ethnicity in an alternate depoliticized "cultural" arena.

The Lake Poso Festival is thus much more than an attempt to develop the local economy through tourism. Measured in terms of the billions of rupiah that have been invested in these competing visions of the To Pamona, the stakes are high for both Church and State. Yet it is important to emphasize that the To Pamona are not a monolithic entity, but an internally differentiated group to whom one element or another of these strategies of incorporation appeal. For those encompassed in the name, the choices remain limited. In providing this genealogy of the To Pamona, in "returning to the origin", I have not striven to provide a portrait of their "authentic" culture, but sought to delimit the major boundaries within which individual To Pamona have been led to identify themselves. These boundaries are contested and overlapping, playing particular definitions of ethnicity depending on religion.

Note

1. "Inculturation" is the current missiological expression for a process which Kruyt called "toeëigening", or appropriation.

References

Acciaioli, G. "Culture as Art: From Practice to Spectacle in Indonesia". *Canberra Anthropology* 8, no. 1 and 2 (1985): 148–71.

Adriani, N. *Posso (Midden-Celebes)*. Den Haag: Boekhandel van den Zendingsstudie-Raad, 1919.

———. *Bare'e-Nederlandsch Woordenboek met Nederlandsch-Bare'e Register*. Leiden: Koninklijk Bataviaasch Genootschap van Kunsten en Wetenschappen, 1928.

———. *Spraakkunst der Bare'e-Taal*. Bandoeng: A.C. Nix & Co, 1931.

———. *Verzamelde Geschriften van Dr. N. Adriani*. Haarlem: De Erven F. Bohn N.V., 1932.

Adriani, N. and Albert C. Kruyt. *De Bare'e-Sprekende Toradja's van Midden-Celebes*. Batavia: Landsdrukkerij, 1912–14.

Anderson, B.R.O'G. "Old State, New Society: Indonesia's New Order in Comparative Historical Perspective". *Journal of Asian Studies* 42, no. 3 (1983a): 477–96.

———. *Imagined Communities: Reflections on the Origin and Spread of Nationalism*. London: Verso, 1983b.

Arts, J.A. "Zending en bestuur op Midden-Celebes tussen 1890 en 1920. Van samenwerking naar confrontatie en eigen verantwoordelijkheid". In *Imperialisme in de Marge: De Afronding van Nederlands-Indië*, edited by J. van Goor. Utrecht: HES Uitgevers, 1985.

Brouwer, Dr. K.J. *Dr. A.C. Kruyt: Dienaar der Toradja's*. Den Haag: J.N. Voorhoeve, 1951.

End, Th. van den. "Rencana Gereja Kesatuan Sulawesi Tengah pada Masa Zending". In *Wajah GKST*, edited by Pdt. Dj. Tanggerahi et al. Tentena: Gereja Kristen Sulawesi Tengah, 1992.

Engelenberg, W.G. "Bijdrage voor de memorie van overgave van den Resident S.J.M. van Geuns, voorzoover betreft de afdeeling Midden-Celebes, bevattende een overzicht van de gebeutenissen van 13 Mei 1903–1 Juni 1906". MMK 302, Algemeen Rijksarchief, 'S-Gravenhage, 1906.

Geertz, C. *The Social History of an Indonesian Town*. Cambridge, Mass.: MIT Press, 1965.

Gunawan, B. and O.D. van den Muizenberg. "Verzuilingstendenties en Sociale Stratificatie in Indonesie". *Sociologische Gids* 14 (1967): 146–58.

Gunawan, B. "Aliran en Sociale Structuur". In *Buiten de Grenzen*, edited by W.F. Wertheim. Meppel: Boom, 1971.

Henley, D.E.F. *Nationalism and Regionalism in a Colonial Context: Minahasa in the Dutch East Indies*. Leiden: KITLV Press, 1996.

Kahn, J.S. *Constituting the Minangkabau: Peasants, Culture and Modernity in Colonial Indonesia*. Providence: Berg Publishers, 1993.

Kaudern, W. *Migrations of the Toradja in Central Celebes.* Gotenborg: Elanders Boktryckeri Aktiebolag, 1925.

Kipp, R.S. *Dissociated Identities: Ethnicity, Religion, and Class in an Indonesian Society.* Ann Arbor: University of Michigan Press, 1993.

Kraemer, Dr. H., ed. *Dr N. Adriani.* Amsterdam: H.J. Paris, 1935.

Kruyt, A.C. "Grammaticale Schets van de Bare'e-Taal". *Bijdragen tot de Taal-, Land en Volkenkunde van Nederlandsch-Indië* 42 (1893): 203–33.

———. *Woordenlijst van de Bare'e Taal.* Den Haag: Martinus Nijhoff, 1894.

———. "Een en Ander aangaande het Geestelijk en Maatschappelijk Leven van den Poso-Alfoer". *Mededeelingen van Wege het Nederlands Zendelingen Genootschap* 39 (1895):3–36, 106–53; 40 (1896):7–31, 121–60, 245–82; 41 (1897):1–52.

———. "Van Paloppo (I) naar Posso". *Mededeelingen van Wege het Nederlands Zendelingen Genootschap* 42 (1898): 1–106.

———. *Het Animisme in den Indischen Archipel.* Den Haag: Martinus Nijhoff, 1906.

———. *Van Heiden tot Christen.* Oestgeest, Netherlands: Zendingsbureau Oegstgeest, 1925.

———. *Zending en Volkskracht.* 's-Gravenhage, Boekhandel en Uitgeverij voor Inwendige en Uitwendige Zending, 1937.

———. *De West Toradjas op Midden Celebes.* 4 vols. Verhandelingen der Koninklijke Nederlandse Akademie van Wetenschappen, Afdeling Letterkunde, new series, Vol. XL. Noord Hollandsche Uitgevers Maatschappij, 1938.

———. *De Bare'e Sprekende Toradjas van Midden Celebes (de Oost Toradjas).* 3 vols., second edition. Amsterdam, Verhandelingen der Koninklijke Nederlandse Akademie van Wetenschappen, Afdeling Letterkunde, new series, Vol. LIV. Noord Hollandsche Uitgevers Maatschappij, 1950 (1912).

Kruyt, J. *Het Zendingsveld Poso: Geschiedenis van Een Konfrontatie.* Kampen: Uitgeversmij J.H. Kok N.V., 1970.

Lev, D.S. "Colonial Law and the Genesis of the Indonesian State". *Indonesia* 40 (1985): 57–74.

Locher-Scholten, E. *Ethiek in Fragmenten.* Utrecht: HES Publishers, 1981.

McVey, R.T. "Nationalism, Islam, and Marxism: The Management of Ideological Conflict in Indonesia". In *Nationalism, Islam, and Marxism*, edited by Ruth McVey, pp. 1–33. Ithaca, NY: Modern Indonesia Project, Cornell University, 1970.

Noorduyn, J. *A Critical Survey of Studies on the Languages of Sulawesi.* Leiden: KITLV Press, 1991.

Pakan (Suryadarma), P. "Orang Toraja: Identifikasi, Klasifikasi dan Lokasi". *Berita Antropologi* 9, no. 32–33 (1977): 21–49.

226 Albert Schrauwers

———. "Bibliografi Beranotasi Folklor Toraja". *Berita Antropologi* 12, no. 42 (1986): 1–195.

Pemberton, John. *On the Subject of "Java"*. Ithaca, N.Y: Cornell University Press, 1994.

Randwijck, S.C.G. van. *Handelen en Denken in Dienst der Zending: Oegstgeest 1897–1942*. 's-Gravenhage: Uitgeverij Boekencentrum bv, 1981.

Rasker, A.J. *De Nederlandse Hervormde Kerk Vanaf 1795: Haar Geschiedenis en Theologie in de Negentiende en Twintigste Eeuw*. Kampen: Kok Uitgeverij, 1974.

Sigilipu, P. *Mabaresi Polimbayo Lemba mPamona i Piamo*. Tonusu, Central Sulawesi: privately published, 1990.

Stuurman, S. *Verzuiling, Kapitalisme en Patriarchaat: Aspecten van de Ontwikkeling van de Moderne Staat in Nederland*. Nijmegen: Socialistiese Uitgeverij Nijmegen, 1983.

Wertheim, W.F. "From Aliran towards Class Struggle in the Countryside of Java". In *Dawning of an Asian Dream: Selected Articles on Modernization and Emancipation*, edited by W.F. Wertheim, pp. 94–115. Amsterdam: Afdeling Zuid- en Zuidoost Azie, Antropologisch-Sociologisch Centrum, Universiteit van Amsterdam, 1973.

chapter nine

NATIONAL DIFFERENCE AND GLOBAL CITIZENSHIP

WENDY MEE

Introduction

A key insight in the work of Roland Robertson (1990, 1992) is the idea that to be modern is necessarily to be global, or in other words, that modernity is characterized by the process of "globalization". Robertson identifies a long historical process of global compression, and with this, an attendant consciousness of the world as a singular place, with its own processes and forms of integration. Many commentators have highlighted the role played by telecommunication and information technologies within the process of globalization. Such technologies are considered crucial to globalization, given the way they enable and shape global capitalism and the circulation of symbolic messages and images. This, however, should not be read as evidence of the dissolution of the nation-state, or nationalist sentiment. Claims that advanced information and telecommunication technologies undermine the nation-state and people's close identification with their nation are simplistic. At the very least, such technologies can intensify nationalist sensibilities, even through the process of building extra-national relations.

To understand this seeming paradox requires a reconceptualization of nationalism. Johan Arnason has observed the generalized failure of current conceptions of nationalism to deal with the realities of contemporary modernity. As he forcefully argues:

> It would be an understatement to say that the theory and practice of nationalism have not kept in step. A failure to progress beyond classical models and a preference for reductionist versions of them have been characteristic of otherwise different perspectives on the modern world.... (Arnason 1990, p. 207)

Consequently, discussions of contemporary modernity are marked by an excessive preoccupation with economic and technological aspects of modernity, on the one hand, and an unwillingness to engage with new formulations within nationalism which may indicate developments and a reorientation within modern national culture and identity, on the other. This conceptual challenge will not simply resolve itself in the theoretical move towards a post-national, global culture. As Wee (1994) notes, we have still to account for the continuing attractions of modernization, development and nationalism within global capitalism. Furthermore, in the context of post-colonial nation-states, we need to understand this attraction in terms of anti-imperial discourses and actions (ibid, p. 229), and not simply assume that these nations will be convinced by the rhetorical force of a post-industrial, anti-nationalist globalism.

The overwhelming sense one gets from writings on post-industrialism and the information economy is that culture is subordinate to the logic of inevitable economic and technological changes (Archer 1990). Post-industrial theorists, such as Daniel Bell (1980) and Alvin Toffler (1981), suggest that the processes of post-industrialism will result in a uniformity of socio-cultural systems following the demise of the nation-state. Part of the reason why most post-industrial accounts fail to see a continuing presence of national cultures is that they implicitly work within a classical model of nationalism. According to this model, nationalism and national culture are viewed as a reflection of an essentialist, almost autochthonous, cultural tradition. This cultural tradition is codified in the institution of the nation-state to such an extent that, in an ideal sense, the contours of a world system of nation-states can be used to map a world system of cultural differentiation. For theorists such as Anthony Smith (1990) who derive nationalism and national culture from an abiding ethnic core, the reorientation of the nation-state towards a global arena must necessarily threaten the nation-state. Such an orientation introduces exogenous cultural and social influences which threaten to weaken the nation's foundation — the supposed cultural core.

I want to suggest an alternative view of the nation, where the nation is a highly adaptive and always multicultural entity. As the case of Malaysia demonstrates, modern nationalism is not dependent on cultural homogeneity. In contrast to the myth of the culturally homogenous nation-state, the Malaysian nation-state was based on the institutionalization of at least three ethnically "absolutist" divisions and developed in response to a system of British colonial rule and racial classification. These "racial" categories which, in any event, shifted over time, never exhausted the multiple sources of identity for many Malaysians. The experience of English language fluency, overseas education and a range of cultural commitments such as Islam, Western humanism, Catholicism, urban life-style, *kampung* heritage, and so forth, further defined the individual within the national landscape. While most of these markers are in some sense extra-local in origin, they have nevertheless helped shape the many nationalisms that exist within Malaysia. As Roff (1967) has detailed, an openness to exogenous ideas and forces was central to the emergence of the different forms of Malay nationalism. It seems probable, therefore, that a contemporary openness, or global orientation, does not signal the demise of the nation-state or national cultures in Malaysia. Rather, I will argue, modern Malaysian citizenship is irredeemably nationalist, and is constituted by the continuing relevance of a primary identification with the nation-state *in conjunction* with an orientation to the global arena.

Nationalist Imaginings and Economic Themes in Malaysia

This argument is more convincing if we consider not only Anderson's suggestion that we treat nationalism in the same way we treat kinship or religion and not as an ideology such as liberalism or fascism (Anderson 1991, p. 5), but also Chatterjee's (1993) argument that we attend to the emotional and affective bonds of nationalism which emerged in response to relations of colonial subordination and constructions of (non-Western) cultural inferiority.

Chatterjee's analysis of the emergence of a nationalist imagination in colonial India signals the importance of appreciating the powerful and creative attachment that post-colonial peoples display to their nation. He argues that during the colonial rule of India, a sense of national community and moral solidarity first emerged in a "spiritual", "inner" domain, around a concept of *difference from*, not identification with, the West: "If the nation is an imagined community, then this is where it is brought into being" (Chatterjee 1993, p. 6). According to Chatterjee, it was in this private domain, marked by cultural difference, that the anti-colonial "national" was defined and defended as autonomous and uncontestable by the colonial power. I have some difficulty, however, with both his public–private dichotomy and his assertion that the first was marked by conformity with the principles of modern Western government (ibid, p. 74) and the latter, by cultural difference. Firstly, the public and private dualism is often unhelpful in that it disguises the degree to which the so-called public and private are mutually determining, and secondly, in Malaysia (and I suspect elsewhere), there is a melange of notions around sameness and difference, universality and specificity, in constructions within the public and private spheres, and these categories themselves are unhelpful in that they disguise the degree to which the so-called public and private are mutually determining.[1] Nevertheless, I am drawn to his identification of the co-existence of the defence of difference and moral solidarity, on the one hand, and struggles premised on the right to establish Western-styled institutions of self-government, on the other. A similar co-existence can be found in Malaysia, where, for example, individuals trained in science, technology, management, and state-craft at Western centres of learning and commerce, hold to a belief that national development based on these principles is nevertheless local and specific. This conviction, in a sense of *difference from* the West, is, I believe, the key to understanding Malaysians' commitment to the Malaysian nation in the face of cultural heterogeneity and external orientations.

As presented here, Chatterjee's thesis attempts to situate nationalist responses in the context of historical and ongoing global power blocs. Anderson's suggestion, however, directs us to consider the internal relations of nationalism and the connections between the idea of the nation and the materiality of the nation-state. His call that we analyse nationalism in terms of kinship or religion reorients us from the abstraction of nationalism towards an appreciation of nationalism as a set of relationships and meanings interpreted and redesigned over time by members of the community. It encourages us to explore the material and social relationships which bind individual destinies to the shape and fortune of the nation. National systems of language, education, governance and legislation are primary relations here, but so too are the economic ties of patronage and political influence which are selectively extended to certain groups within Malaysian society. This shift has particular relevance to the study of post-independence nationalism, which must take into account the taken-for-granted status of the nation-state in the minds of contemporary Malaysians. The sense of nationalism felt by Malaysians born after independence is very different from the nationalistic striving of pre-independence Malaysians. Few (if any) of the Malaysian Internet users I discuss would claim to be intentionally acting out of a sense of nationalism. The reality of the nation-state and the experience of nationalism has informed their sense of identity from a young age. Consequently, we should not be surprised that nationalistic expressions do not take the form of political pamphlets and didactic literature (characteristic of pre-independence nationalists) and are not limited to more formal and collective expressions introduced by the early post-independence national government.

This does not mean, however, that contemporary national culture bears no relationship to early nationalist imaginings and themes, but it does suggest that we attend to more mundane, "everyday" engagements with national identity and culture. In a different context, Lash and Friedman argue for the recognition of "*another* modernity":

> The vision in this book is that of *another* modernity. ...of the fleeting, the transient. ...of the sensual in the baroque allegory. ...of the

> disruption of classicisms and neo-classicisms by Hieronymus Bosch.
> ...of Simmel's aestheticisation of everyday life in turn-of-the-century
> Berlin. ... It is a modernism of the popular, of — in a thoroughly
> globalized context — das Volk. ... It is not a high modernism, but
> rather a low modernism (Lash and Friedman 1992, p. 2–3).

Following from this, I want to make space for the analysis of
what could be called more popularistic and mundane nationalist
representations. This is not to deny that more literary and formal
representations of national culture are found on the Internet or distributed via computer-mediated communications, but to argue that
an understanding of contemporary nationalism needs to consider
other forms of nationalist expression. Certainly, collective nationalistic
symbols, celebrations, myths and neo-traditions are represented by
Malaysians on the Internet, but they tend to be displaced by the
informality and humour of vernacular representations of Malaysia.
While one can download from the Internet the Malaysian national
anthem and flag, these digitalized icons compete with electronically-
reproduced drawings of colonial shophouses, cartoon caricatures of
durian buyers and photographs of "KL by night" and "Sunset on
Batu Ferringhi".[2]

Increasing numbers of mostly middle-class and technologically-
literate Malaysians are participating on the Internet.[3] Once the preserve of overseas Malaysian students, other Malaysians, including
information technologists, journalists, public servants, researchers and
professionals now regularly access the Internet. By doing so they
have established a wide variety of transnational relationships, as in
the case of technologists who subscribe to international professional
forums, Muslims who participate in pan-Islamic News groups, and
conservationists and human rights activists who garner international
support via electronic networks. Yet this globalism is only part of
the picture. An analysis of Internet communications by professional
and technologically-literate Malaysians reveals a host of socio-
cultural and geographic referents which reinstate the nation both
as cultural identity and territory. Through their Internet interactions,
these Malaysians construct "modern" Malaysian identities and
representations of Malaysia which are both self-reflexively global
and particular — that is, premised on the concept of the world as

a global, interrelated system, but differentiated in terms of national and cultural specificities.

There has been considerable speculation over the economic status and cultural role played by the middle-classes and techno-logically-literate professionals. Theorists have pointed to the rise of the transnational profession (Hannerz 1990; King 1990), the "service class" (Lash and Urry 1987), and the development of "third culture" specialists who mediate between persons from different national cultures (Gessner and Schade 1990). With perhaps the exception of Lash and Urry,[4] these approaches tend to focus either on the role of these professionals in binding local economies to the global economy or the emergence of supranational cultures that are derivative of many national cultures (for example, Hannerz's notion of the "cos-mopolitan"). Less attention has been paid to the question of how this loose grouping of professional and technologically-literate Malaysians contribute to the ongoing development and maintenance of nationalism and national culture. Less recognition has been given to the fact that their status as experts and their mediation of local–global economic relations have *local* implications.

Those familiar with Malaysia will know of the government's strong push to see Malaysia become a fully industrialized country by the year 2020. "Vision 2020" — as this policy is referred to — has become the mission statement of the ruling coalition government. The mission is to create a united, tolerant, economically just and ethical Malaysia, underpinned by an advanced, competitive and dynamic economy. A key strategy in "Vision 2020" is the promotion and adoption of advanced technologies as a means of accelerating the rate of industrialization and of leap-frogging to a more eco-nomically competitive status. Information technology is one of five government priority areas together with biotechnology, electronics, advanced materials, and automated manufacturing technology (Council for the Coordination and Transfer of Industrial Technology, 1990). Terms such as information economy, information society, global village and information superhighway are widely circulated by the government, the media and in public forums. Malaysia's Prime Minister, Datuk Seri Dr Mahathir Mohamad, is an articulate pro-ponent of the transformational effects of information technology in an information age, as demonstrated by the following statement which was made by him during a speech given to the Malaysian Business Council in 1991:

> [i]n the information age that we are living in, Malaysian society must be information-rich… Increasingly, knowledge will not only be the basis of power but also prosperity… no effort must be spared in the creation of an information-rich Malaysian society. (Cited in Karthyeni and Azzman 1995, p. 141)

The close connection posited here between information and the global economy places those members of Malaysian society who provide an interface between local and global information flows in a crucial position with regard to the nation's economic well-being. Not only do these professionals mediate between the local and global levels of the economy, but they are seen as a critical national resource in terms of future national development and economic competitiveness. In addition, government privatization and corporatization policies have further strengthened the close relationship between the "nation" and the economy by providing members of Malaysia's business community with significant, local economic opportunities. Policies and concepts, such as the "Privatization Masterplan" (1991) and "Malaysia Inc." (popularized during the 1980s), have led to the development of a financial and business interdependency between the government and the corporate sectors. Within the telecommunications sector, for example, the privatization and liberalization of Jabatan Telekom Malaysia have led to the concentration of great wealth in the hands of a small group of politically well-connected Malaysians (Sussman and Lent 1991, pp. 175–81).[5]

The status of "expert" accorded to some of these professionals is closely tied to both their mediation of the global economy and their control of knowledge, education and science (a relationship also noted by Lash and Urry [1987] in their review of the service class in Europe and the United States). The Malaysian Government's commitment to a policy of science- and technology-led modernization makes the government itself dependent on the "expert" advice of technologists and other professionals in policy decisions. This emphasis on science and technology has also been a cause of anxiety for the government, given Malaysia's skilled labour shortage, particularly in the areas of technology and research and development.[6] Technological expertise is thus at a premium, and the expert status and economic roles of technologists and other professionals have combined to give them a heightened profile in the ongoing debate within Malaysia over the nature of Malaysian society and its relationship to the processes of globalization. This is not to argue that all technologists, business analysts or management experts share the same set of assumptions or outlook, but it does suggest that such people are given a legitimated and prominent role in local government, business and media circles.

It is in the context of "economic nationalism" (Jomo 1994) that we most clearly see how Malaysia's professionals and technologists can assume a cultural, even intellectual, role. The appeal to economic autonomy as the means to achieve political sovereignty has been a recurrent theme in proto-nationalist and nationalist debate since at least the late nineteenth century (see Roff 1967; Shaharuddin 1988; and Milner 1993). Issues of economic nationalism continue to be integral to the discussion of nationalism, with the government drawing upon economic nationalist sensibilities for public support of its development policies and concepts (see Jomo 1994). It is not surprising then that the opinions and interests of those professional, technological and educated middle-classes who are central to the conduct of such policies, are in a position to shape and inform broader discussions of nationalism in ways reminiscent of Anderson's "professionalised intelligentsias" (1991).

A recent interview in a local Malaysian newspaper exemplifies the close connection between some Malaysian professionals, economic nationalism and social change. The interview profiled the Chief Executive Officer of Malaysia's Multimedia Super Corridor (MSC). Recently announced as Malaysia's "cyber leap", the RM50–100 billion MSC has been tagged Malaysia's first "super information technology hub" and is to spearhead Malaysia's entry into the information age (*The Star*, 1 August 1996, p. 2, 2 August 1996, p. 1). Dr Mohamad Arif Nun, who has a degree in engineering from the University of London and a Ph.D. from Loughborough University of Technology, moved from the Malaysian Institute of Microelectronic

Systems (MIMOS)[7] to take up this planning and development position. According to Dr Arif, the MSC is emblematic of the emerging information age and "borderless world" which will transform the way Malaysians work and live:

> The MSC is expected to change the way we think, live and work. As such, it will be a 24-hour day operation linking and shrinking the world through the use of a personal computer. ... The MSC will be a place where good things can take place ... there, professionals from all walks of life will try new paradigms. Work will not be a chore. People will enjoy what they are doing and keep on creating for others to enjoy their fruits of labour. (Quoted in *Sunday Star*, 25 August 1996, p. 21)

Dr Arif's endorsement of the MSC goes beyond an economic or technological justification. In an important way, as an informed and expert adviser, he can translate for the general public the meaning of such technological developments. His enthusiasm for a McLuhanesque "global village" and his optimism regarding Malaysia's post-industrial future are most striking. Finally, in case this view of the future is too far removed from the experiences and desires of the Malaysian public, he goes on to outline a more popularist multimedia application:

> For example, a CD-ROM of P. Ramlee[8] could be created. At the click of the mouse you will be able to hear his melodious *Getaran Jiwa*, find the list of his classics and synopsis of it. Find out about the man himself and even how many times he was married. (Quoted in *Sunday Star*, 25 August 1996, p. 21)

Only a limited number of this loose grouping of Malaysians are active users of the Internet to date. According to JARING (Joint Advanced Research Integrated Networking),[9] there were an estimated 100,000 JARING subscribers by August 1996, including 3,500 organizations (http://www.jaring.my/jaring/faq/). The actual number of Internet users in Malaysia is likely to be higher, however, as a number of Internet users access the Internet through their Internet Access Provider's or their corporate network's JARING account. In terms of growth, Malaysia's rate of Internet adoption has been substantial. A JARING press release from October 1995 reported an average growth rate of more than 20 per cent per month over a three-month period. At that time, JARING anticipated that its subscriber base would reach more than 100,000 users within twelve to eighteen months and announced plans to extend the number of Internet nodes from seventeen to around one hundred (http://www.jaring.my/jaring/info/press.html). It appears that the growth of Internet in Malaysia has already overtaken the estimates made less than twelve months ago.

From my observation, the majority of Internet users in Malaysia are male, professional and under forty years of age. In this, Malaysia follows the general pattern of Internet adoption experienced elsewhere. Unfortunately, it is difficult to obtain reliable user demographics which would allow us to chart how these might be changing over time. There are increasingly more women on the Internet, but it is still the case that economic resources, gender, education, ethnicity, and English language skills determine access to this technology. In one of the JARING mail lists that I subscribed to in Malaysia, the following comment was made by one of the few women who posted messages,

> Cyberspace is 85% male, and somewhat intimidating to a lot of women … maybe you can help change that by your sensitivity [to the use of sexist language]. (PCBASE, subscriber)

In response to an earlier posting from a man that no female information technology consultants had replied to an on-line survey regarding consultancy rates, and that this could lead one to assume that there are no "women consultants", she said:

> No — they're are just too shy to participate in surveys. Also we are obviously under-represented in cyber space. (PCBASE, subscriber)

The definition and shaping of national sentiment on the Internet may thus represent a narrow range of viewpoints, reflecting the similarity in education, gender, age and occupation of users. It is important to acknowledge, therefore, that this discussion of Malaysian Internet users is not an adequate basis for a general theory of Malaysian nationalism. At the very least, such a theory would need to account for the involvement and investment of a broad spectrum of Malaysians in the processes of nationalism.[10] Kemper

(1993) is right to criticize theories of nationalism which deny agency to all but an élite group of intellectuals. Nevertheless, appropriating Anderson's kinship analogy once more, there is nothing necessarily equitable or democratic in the socio-cultural, economic and political relations of nationalism. It is precisely that cohort of professional, technical and business groups — well-placed in terms of Castells' "materiality of networks and flows" (1996) and over represented on the Internet — who have a disproportionate influence over the design and redesign of nationalism.

Malaysians on the Net

Internet services on offer in Malaysia include electronic mail, mailing lists, Usenet News groups, Bulletin Boards, Internet Relay Chat, Multi-User Dimensions (MUDs), the World Wide Web (WWW), and commercial on-line networks such as CompuServe and Malaysia On-Line. Electronic mail,[11] or e-mail, allows anyone with an e-mail address to send and receive "mail" through a computer, often at a fraction of the cost of a phone call. Mailing lists, Usenet News groups and Bulletin Boards provide electronic forums for the discussion of every conceivable topic. Many of the earliest Usenet groups were computer-oriented (reflecting the professional interests of the early users), but a surprisingly large number were also concerned with social, political and regional issues from around the world. Internet Relay Chat (IRC) provides real-time interaction between people through a computer. The "chat" actually refers to an exchange of text that each participant types in turn. MUDs are electronic storylines where players assume a persona in order to participate in adventure and fantasy games.

The World Wide Web is a comparatively recent development on the Internet (which has been around in some form for over twenty years). The development of easy to use Web browsers and search engines have popularized the use of the Internet beyond the small cohort of early Internet savants. The World Wide Web potentially gives the user access to coloured photographs, graphics, sound and video. It allows people to create colourful Web pages and electronic magazines (e-zines) by linking a series of Web pages. The WWW has encouraged people and organizations to create "home pages" on their Web site, and many have invested a considerable amount of time (and computer skill) to create home pages that are a reflection and/or representation of themselves or their organization. It is the attractiveness of this platform for the development of highly individualized, iconic self-representation that has given the World Wide Web so much of its colour and character.

The following discussion focuses on a selection of WWW home pages created by Malaysians and two Malaysian-based mailing lists. The aim is to indicate the persistence of a sense of nationalism and the ongoing relevance of national culture as an interpretive filter for Malaysia's technologically-literate professionals through a review of their Internet communications and representations. This analysis reveals the intensification of nationalist sensibilities that accompanies the process of building extra-national relations, and the parallel processes of differentiation from, and identification with, a global order exhibited by their electronic communications.[12]

Personal home pages and Web pages can be a lot of fun and at times a bit confusing. There is no space on a home page for lengthy introductions and descriptions. There is only room for a line or two by way of a greeting or biographical snapshot, a photo, some indication of hobbies and taste in music, and a few links to favourite Web sites. The page is designed to allow readers to use their keyboard mouse to select and click on the topic of interest to them. This will send them, via a hyper text link, to another Web page where more details are listed. According to "Malaysia's Home Page", in July 1996 there were 267 Malaysian personal home pages; by September the number was more than 460 (http://www.jaring.my/msia/msia-link/lo-menu.html).[13] This list, moreover, is far from complete and does not account for all the personal home pages and Web sites constructed by Malaysians, many of whom are overseas students.

A fairly typical example of an overseas Malaysian student's home page is that of "David Chai", a computer science undergraduate in the United States. At the top of his home page is his name in both English and Chinese characters. Beneath this is his photo, which is followed by four categories of links which the reader can follow. The first set of links is to Malaysian-related Web pages, including images of "Fascinating Malaysia", "Malaysian Business Pages" and

"Welcome to Malaysia" (information in English on Malaysia provided by the Malaysian Government). The second and third categories relate to his studies — there are details on his course work and a beginner's guide to HTML (the computer language that makes hyper text links possible). The fourth category is a list of personal details, such as links to Hong Kong-related Web sites, his resume, and a list of Christian resources available on the Web. At the very end, there is an e-mail address for those who would like to contact David and a blue ribbon. This is the emblem of the anti-censorship campaign that has been raging in the United States over the perceived threat to free speech on-line by the Federal Government's Communications Decency Act.

It is not only students who establish home pages. "Eric Loo" is a computer analyst working for a multinational corporation in Penang. There is a photograph of himself together with his wife on holidays at the top of the page. His home page offers a number of links to other Web pages, including links to information on his former school in Penang; his favourite Web sites; friends' Web pages; sound clips from his favourite Western musicals (which can be down-loaded and listened to if your computer has the necessary equipment); and digitalized photographs of Penang (one of the ferry with the City of Georgetown in the background and one of a Batu Ferringhi beach).

As suggested above, the author's "Malaysian-ness" is typically a feature of these home pages. This is a place to state one's private (for example, favourite band) as well as community affiliations. Such community-based affiliations do not have to be formalized in the sense of membership to a Malaysian student association. They are just as likely to be Malaysian jokes and advice in Malaysian–English slang, or on where to find the best fish-head curry in Penang. People pilfer a range of graphics, cartoons, and photographs from books, magazines, and other Web pages to enhance the visual display of who they are and where they come from. In the case of Malaysian personal home pages, there is a bias towards postcards of Malaysia ("my home town of Kuala Kangsar" and the Malaysian flag). This orientation towards photographic representations suggests an expectation that the audience is likely to be unfamiliar with Malaysia and Malaysians. Obviously, the home page also provides an arena where one can demonstrate one's computer skills (such as the incorporation of graphics and photos), but the fact that the majority of home pages are written predominantly in English reflects an inherent expectation of a potentially world-wide audience. These computer- and English language-literate home page designers act as ambassadors for Malaysia, demonstrating the technical and cultural competence of Malaysians for both a local and global audience.

There is often a sense of homesickness and a desire to recreate and revive a sense of "home" in many personal home pages. This is particularly evident in the home pages of overseas Malaysian students and Internet mailing lists which attract a large number of overseas students and immigrants. However, it would be wrong to conclude from this that the tendency to reveal something of oneself and one's nation through the cultural iconography of a home page is an exclusively diasporic or post-colonial phenomenon. Let me briefly describe an Australian home page to offset this impression. "Bruce's Page" is composed of four computer-generated, gilt-framed graphics. They are the logo of an Australian Rules football club; a Rugby League football; the cap worn by a surf life-saver; and the General Motors Holden logo. Each icon is linked to another Web page which gives details of the specific sporting clubs Bruce supports and his love of old Holden cars. There is nothing about Bruce which suggests that he is anything other than a "born and bred" Australian, so how are we to understand this cultural and national assertiveness? The approach I favour is to locate the Internet in its global and globalizing context. From this perspective, personal home pages can be seen as a response to the expansion of globalizing pressures which, by enhancing our self-awareness of the world as interconnected and global, raise the question of the individual's place in this world-wide web. After all, the act of constituting (or reconstituting) the local is explicable only in a context of the extra-local.

There are increasingly more Malay-language Web pages, signalling a process of appropriation of a predominantly English language electronic medium. In one Malaysian-based Web site, constructed by a Malay man, only the introductory home page is in English, and even then not exclusively as there is a Malay language index to further links. The home page introduces us to an IRC channel for

Malay language speakers to exchange greetings and photos. It is a popular web site for local Malaysians as well as the occasional Malaysian visitor from abroad. The presentation is suggestive of a village house where visitors are welcome to chat and exchange photographs. There are a number of links on the home page including links to albums of past Internet visitors or "villagers", to a coffee shop, and to instructions (in English) on how to download IRC software. In the first album, the seven men and nine women are predominantly Malay (identifiable by either their photo or name). The sense of largely Malay participants is reinforced by the welcome page which is dominated by a Hari Raya[14] greeting.

Both the village and the coffee shop are recurrent themes in Malaysian World Wide Web home pages. For example, the Malaysian.Net Home Page welcomes visitors to the Malaysia.Net Cyber Coffeeshop, the cyber version of the good "ol coffee-shop".

> Come in. Sit down. Get yourself a cup of coffee (Ah Chong's out today so you'll have to run to the kitchen and do it yourself). Don't mind the spittoons. Overhear your buddies in the next table. Join in (yes, everyone's welcome to add their 2 cents to everyone else's views). (http://www.malaysia.net/)

The home page of MalaysiaNet, an electronic magazine compiled by a Malaysian freelance journalist in London, picks up the theme of the village, and likewise, transports it into the World Wide Web:

> If you stand long enough in the kampung you'll get all the rumours you want to hear. This is your kampung on the web, a repository of news, views, stories, cartoons, and the occasional encounter. (http://www.MalaysiaNet.com/about.html)

This imagery came up during a discussion on a JARING mailing list over the value of the information that is found in newsgroups. One subscriber was concerned about the potentially misleading information available on the Internet:

> The advent of a free-for-all open forum as exemplified by internet newsgroups has set me thinking. Sure with these newsgroups you become richer — information wise. But the question is whether the information is useful, or is it just full of noise. ... If it's full of noise,

you could end up stupider and more ignorant than before. That's fine if that person is on his own, but he also has access to the Internet and could easily propagate his ideas and mislead others in the process. (GENERAL subscriber)

The sense of danger associated with the anonymity (who is qualified to voice an opinion? how would one know?) and pervasiveness of the Internet was diffused by another subscriber who invoked, firstly, the familiar, and secondly, technology as mechanisms for managing the Internet:

> I think the usenet newsgroups are more analogous to "kedai kopi" [coffee shop] rather than conference room.[15] When discussing in kedai kopi, you'll soon learn who to welcome to your table, and whose opinion needs to be taken with a grain (or a big bag) of salt. Good usenet newsreaders have such a filter. It is normally called a kill file. You can "kill", that is not see at all, postings from persistent null-content offenders. ... Now, the question is who to kill? You just have to make your own mind up... (GENERAL subscriber).

Home pages belonging to organizations generally lack the chatty approach and individualized appeal of the personal home page. In the case of government and semi-government home pages, the focus is the promotion of Malaysia to an international audience. For example, one of JARING's activities is to co-ordinate the "Malaysia's Home Page" (http://www.jaring.my/). This home page links to a number of other Web pages, including JARING's own home page ("JARING — Connecting you to the Global Information Superhighway") and a Research and Development Web page. This page acts as a linked index to Malaysian research and development-related sites, including information on the Multimedia Super Corridor, Malaysian research institutions, and the role and status of research and development in Malaysia. "Views on R&D" (http://www.jaring.my/msia/rnd/view.html) presents excerpts from the speeches of Mahathir Mohamad (the Prime Minister), Anwar Ibrahim (the Deputy Prime Minister), Rafidah Aziz (the Minister of International Trade and Industry), and Law Hieng Deng (the Minister of Science, Technology and Environment) on the value of research and development in Malaysia. A photograph of each speaker accompanies the English text. There is nothing in the speeches to surprise a Western or East Asian audience as the speakers plainly endorse the views that research and development are critical to industry and that countries need a strong research and development knowledge-base. References to the cultural specificity of Malaysia are not found in the speeches as much as in the dress of the Malay ministers: Mahathir and Anwar wear *songkok* and *baju melayu*, and Rafidah wears *baju kurung*.[16] The Chinese Malaysian, Law, wears a suit and tie.

In the case of JARING's Web pages, the focus was on demonstrating Malaysia's commitment to post-industrial formations and a global political economy. Other government home pages take a different focus and provide, for example, tourist-oriented information and "fast facts and figures" on Malaysia, designed for a general audience. There is even a "Dr Mahathir Mohamad Home Page". There are obvious promotional aspects inherent in these Web pages, and this is consistent with other government "advertising campaigns" in newspapers and on television. Through its promotion of Malaysian industry and technological competence, the Malaysian Government is in effect celebrating and advertising itself. The achievements of the nation become merged with the achievements of the government, and this is a key mechanism by which the state can harness nationalist feelings to engender popular support for its cause. The close connection between advertising and nationalist sentiment is reinforced by the high proportion of Malaysians who include hypertext links to a range of JARING Web pages from their own home pages. The majority of Malaysian home pages would link to at least one JARING Web page, typically to those sites which provide images of Malaysian landscapes, monuments, and maps, or general information on Malaysia's history, business, industry and government. Kemper (1993) has observed a similar phenomenon in Sri Lanka, where he argues that rising nationalist feelings are tied to the state's celebration of its own role. Advertising is central to this celebration to such an extent that Sri Lankan advertising agencies receive more than half of their revenues from the national government.

Raymond Williams calls advertising the "official art" of capitalism. In postcolonial societies, advertising has become the "official art" of government (ibid: 380–81).

In addition, in Malaysia, such "advertising" is often explicitly focused on locally-made products and consumer items. The "national car" (the Proton Saga), skyscrapers (see Goh Beng Lan in this volume), Islamic banking, and icons of advanced science and technology are routinely implicated in an economic/consumerist nationalism where products "are good to think the nation" (Kemper 1993, p. 381). National products are lauded as national achievements in such a way as to link desire, social imaginary, socio-economic relations and political practice. This has obvious significance for nationalism and nationalist culture:

> In the emergence of national identity in Third World countries, goods are put to new purposes. They allow people to think the nation ... blurring the distinction between consumption and citizenship. (Kemper 1993, pp. 381–82)

Of particular relevance to this chapter is the influence that technology industry professionals, communication consultants, telecommunication policy-makers and business consultants have in the design of infrastructure and content of electronic media which contribute to the distribution and institutionalization of nationalist imaginaries in Malaysia. In this context, the Internet is an important communication tool which allows such professionals to reinforce, construct, question and imagine national cultural practices in relation to both a local and global audience.

The projection of a strong national direction and the celebration of Malaysia's advances in science, technology and international trade found on JARING's Web pages seek to capture more than just the confidence and imagination of the local citizenry. They are fundamentally targeted to attract foreign investors, tourists and transnational capital to Malaysia. In a supranational context, "where rich[er] nations seek to direct the development of poor[er] nations" (ibid, p. 381), the Malaysian Government has pursued a policy of appropriating the forces of development. The state's endorsement and adoption of information technology is both the medium and the message of Malaysia's global advertisement campaign. Through JARING's Internet promotion of national development, the Malaysian state attempts to strengthen its own position as well as Malaysia's relative position *vis-à-vis* the supranational context.

In addition to hosting the Malaysian Government's Web pages, JARING also provides a number of electronic forums for its subscribers. During early 1995, I subscribed to two Malaysian mailing lists: pcbase@jaring.my and general@jaring.my. Both mailing lists were complementary services offered to JARING subscribers. PCBASE was a forum for the discussion of personal computing hardware, software, applications and developments, while GENERAL was oriented towards general discussion. Sometimes the lines were crossed and a subscriber would ask that those involved in a particular discussion thread move from PCBASE to GENERAL (it did not happen the other way). Many of the subscribers who regularly posted messages at that time were on both mailing lists and, from their Internet addresses, were professional technologists, consultants, journalists and managers within the computer industry, government departments and leading Malaysian companies such as Hicom, MIMOS and Telekom Malaysia. There were also high school and university students, as well as a few overseas subscribers from North America, Singapore and Australia. From their addresses and comments, it appeared that they were mostly computer professionals and consultants as well.

PCBASE was predominantly a forum for discussing technical issues and problems. This was the place to turn to for advice on e-mail, modems, operating systems, connection difficulties, and for information on new products, applications and software releases. The volume of traffic on PCBASE was at times a burden (it was more popular than GENERAL). One subscriber complained that when he subscribed to PCBASE a year before he had received between 10–20 messages a day, but of late he sometimes had to deal with over a hundred messages a day. Some of the less technical issues discussed over a three-month period included: the number of high school students ("children") on PCBASE; flaming (see below) on the Internet; a debate over the morality of hacking; opinions on Bill Gates' Microsoft presentation in Kuala Lumpur; sexist language in computer science; cellular mobile phones (cost, coverage, billing frauds, etc.); current affairs (for example, Intel's pentium chip flaw); and computer games. The following examples of discussion threads from PCBASE are only two of a number of discussions that were relevant to this chapter.

The first discussion centred on a new project to establish Internet access to Malaysia's rural and remote towns and villages. This example reveals the slippage between "vested interest" and "national interest" that many information and computer technologists experience. This merger is neither merely selfish nor altruistic, and directs us to explore "the imagination as social practice" (Appadurai 1990, p. 5). The "Jantung Project" was introduced to the PCBASE mailing list as an Internet-based forum for the discussion of technical and practical issues on the establishment and administration of Internet nodes throughout Malaysia. The proposal was framed to attract those PCBASE subscribers who are disadvantaged by higher telephone charges and/or keen to improve their network skills to enlist in the project. However, the initiative was also placed within the nationalistic development goal of "wiring up" Malaysia.

> Jantung will be relevant to you if you live outside the area covered by existing Jaring nodes, ie you have to make a trunk call to connect to Jaring, resulting in high telephone charges [or if you] just want to learn about running Internet or any Wide Area Networks for that matter, so that you can add to your C.V. "WAN Administrator", "Unix Sysadmin OK", "Member of ABC Internet Sysop Club". The solution is to set up a Jaring node in your place. ... Information society sounds great. But to make it happen in Malaysia, we need at least one Unix guru in every kampung, capable of running a Unix Internet workstation. ... In the next Jantung update, I will describe in detail how ... to achieve a common goal, ie to extend Jaring. (PCBASE Guest, UK-based, "The problem of making Singapore an intelligent island is trivial. Wiring up all the fishing villages in Malaysia IS what I call intelligent.")

Replies to this posting were positive, and in particular, responded favourably to the goal of extending the JARING network for the benefit of Malaysia,

> What is attractive in the proposed Jantung concept is the idea of extending the information super highway to as wide an area as possible in the country. ... Any delay in making available the information network will be a handicap. (PCBASE subscriber, Malaysian public service)

The second example suggests something of the equivocal relationship some Malaysian technologists feel towards "Western technology". As well as dispelling the notion that all Malaysian technologists think alike, this debate on "flaming" was fascinating for making explicit what is sometimes hidden: the connection between culture and technology. Anyone familiar with Internet newsgroups will have come across the problem of "flaming", that is, responding angrily or abruptly to a particular posting. Flaming can be deliberate or unintentional (when one mistakenly perceives a personal insult in another's message) which at times leads to "flame wars". PCBASE was by and large a friendly and open forum, where members were generous with their help (even if sometimes a little keen to show off their own cleverness). An incident of flaming did, however, arise over several postings by a high school student which were deemed irrelevant to PCBASE by some subscribers. The matter cleared up within a couple of days, but it did lead to some interesting comments on Malaysians' relationship to technology, and via technology, on the nature and quality of Malaysians in general. One subscriber attempted to subdue the flaming by arguing that such behaviour was contrary to Malaysian culture:

> The Internet is part of the Western culture that we have found ben-
> eficial. Along with the Net we have adopted some Net culture that
> may not be so beneficial ie. flaming. If people are more considerate
> towards each other and learn to accept Western technology only in
> the best of its manifestations problems like flaming will not arise. ...
> Therefore we should learn the "art of sifting, during the receiving". It
> may amuse the flamer to flame someone, but it is not the same for
> the other guy. (PCBASE subscriber, International Islamic University)

This was too much for another subscriber, who disputed the claim that the Internet was "Western" and further argued that technology (and technologists) cannot be held accountable for users' "irresponsible behaviour":

> What's the internet and *western culture* got to do with people
> flaming? If I flamed you verbally, would that be ok, since I am using
> nature and not *western culture*? Let's not confuse the issues with
> the facts and separate irresponsible behaviour from the technology

that carries it. ... By the way, the internet is not *western culture*. In my opinion, it's technology which has been developed by a lot of people, be they from western or asian or african or european or animistic countries. Misuse of the technology should not be blamed on the developers of the technology. (PCBASE subscriber)

The discussion more or less came to an end after the high school student originally "flamed" apologized for the flame war. His appeal to "Beautiful Malaysia" and his apology were no doubt central here, but it is interesting to speculate whether his reminder that non-Malaysians may be reading PCBASE had any impact:

> Now, it comes to that touchy topic again... [flame wars]. Actually, from my point of view, I think that both parties were at wrong (including myself). This was mostly due to misunderstanding and misinterpretation of the postings here. I hope this has all been forgiven. We are all humans and we all err once in a while. ... I made a few mistakes — such as posting about Lake Toba/Medan in here. But it was a misunderstanding. ... The original topic of the thread was about Beautiful Malaysia, and I'm sure everyone will agree on that. Malaysians are known to be unique because several different races can live and work together. I don't see why that shouldn't be so in PCBASE either. If we all work hard and bear with each other's mistakes, I'm sure we can work together in harmony. Malaysia is a rapidly progressing country, and others may soon be reading our newsgroups. We don't want to give them a bad impression of Malaysians do we? (PCBASE subscriber, Form 2 student)

The issue of Malaysian sensitivity to criticisms from outsiders also arose in a discussion about corruption on the GENERAL mailing list. As the name suggests, the GENERAL mailing list provided a forum for postings on just about any topic, including an impressive list of best places to eat in Penang; a list of episodes of "The X Files"; debate on the United State's Communications Decency Act; and a discussion on the value of Internet newsgroups ("is it just full of noise?"). The matter of corruption developed out of a number of complaints that the traffic police always pick-on motor-bike riders rather than car drivers. This thread started out as a complaint against Malaysian traffic police from a subscriber, which in turn led to a few anecdotes about police corruption. At this time in Malaysia, there had been widespread media reporting of bribery in football, resulting in some well publicized arrests and convictions. A subscriber from North America then asked whether in fact "coffee funds" did exist for traffic cops. One Malaysian subscriber diplomatically suggested that this was a problem everywhere, and one which he had faced when studying in Australia; another remarked that no-one could be blamed for thinking that such funds existed in the light of the investigations into bribery in football. The inquiry, however, resulted in a rather heated response from one Malaysian subscriber:

> The last thing we want is a foreigner insinuating that our country is full of corrupt cops. In my day-to-day business dealings, I do come across a lot of foreign businessmen who think that everybody here from the parking attendant to the PM is bribable, which is truly insulting. (GENERAL subscriber, Hicom)

There was a general perception that these mailing lists were for local Malaysians. This was reinforced by JARING's insistence that its mailing lists were for JARING subscribers and not for free distribution on other bulletin boards. This obviously opened up space for the discussion of Malaysian-related topics and generated the expectation that views expressed on these mailing lists would generally reflect a Malaysian perspective (albeit an élitist perspective in that these were English language mailing lists). As a consequence, these forums were highly particular. Many of these Malaysians were active in other non-Malaysian Internet groups at the same time (and sometimes cross-posted relevant news items and computer industry up-dates from them). It is doubtful that the same open identification with Malaysian society and development expressed in PCBASE and GENERAL would be observable in electronic forums with an international membership.[17] However, despite broad consensus regarding the status of JARING's mailing lists as "local", subscribers regularly made contingent and shifting assessments as to what constituted the local in relation to a wider network of national, regional and transnational relations. While these boundaries were often assumed to be relatively stable and enduring, the concept of the "local" was in fact always in flux. Local could stand for the nation-state, a particular neighbourhood, or even the mailing list itself. Sometimes a local quality was attached to the global context (for example, reference to the global community of information technologists), while at other times the global context was broken into more or less local (anti-Western) affiliations.

> The fact is that this dinosaur [US computer industry] is getting irrelevant. Most of the PCs are produced by Taiwanese. And the top ends are produced by Japanese (NEC, FUJITSU are giving IBM a fair fight). The Koreans are tops on memory chips. The Indians are shaking the software arena. Pretty soon, Asians will call the shots! Even though hard disks are produced by MNCs in Singapore and Penang, most of the workers/technicians are local. The technical capabilities of Singapore design teams are proven in Macintosh design, HP Deskjet, Philip's Matline TV. (PCBASE subscriber)

Conclusion

The observation that the "local" is in a state of flux has been used to argue that the nation — as a particular form of locality — is itself increasingly unstable and permeable. Such a position, however, warrants critical evaluation on the grounds that it relies upon a culturally essentialist definition of the nation. In the case of Malaysia, a strong sense of the nation has developed within the context of an external orientation and acknowledged ethnic (or "racial") differences.[18] The extra-local global and regional associations of Malaysian Internet users do not of themselves threaten Malaysian nationalism. Certainly, Malaysians' Internet activities have an impact on their nationalist imaginaries and affiliations, which in turn, influence the formation of nationalism and national culture within the broader community. But it is an oversight to consider and give weight only to these global exchanges and interactions, without attending to the relations and interpretive practices which bind these individuals to Malaysian society and nationalism.

In part, this oversight is symptomatic of the failure to differentiate between the bonds of *place* and the bonds of *presence*. No one would deny that electronic networks enable individuals to develop a sense of presence with respect to virtual and globalized worlds. However, this sense of presence developed through participation on an electronic network falls far short from that sense of place that is built-up over time through everyday interactions and constantly affirmed by dense and overlocking social, cultural, economic and political processes. While information technology can be used to extend a sense of presence across a global arena, it is doubtful whether Internet affiliations can by themselves undermine that sense of place — or nation — that develops through interactions with national institutions and systems of government, education, language and culture. A formative influence here is the sense of difference which is a legacy of the historical experiences of colonialism and reaffirmed by a global political economy which insert a hierarchy of difference in our post-colonial world.

Nevertheless, it is important to remember that an individual's experience of the nation is largely conceptual. As individuals, we only directly experience particularistic units which we then imaginatively connect to form a concept of the nation-as-whole. In order to maintain this linkage, we must continue to extend a sense of the nation as place to a sense of the nation as presence. The above discussion of Malaysians constructing Malaysia through their personal home pages and mailing lists shows the effect that information technology has within the context of the nation-state: through highly personalized representations, the Internet confirms the existence and specificity of the nation by reinstating its sense of presence for these Malaysians.

From the perspective of Malaysia's post-colonial nationalism, the nation-state has delivered not only the promises of economic well-being but also a level of independence and participation within an international arena. These have not been necessarily delivered evenly to all Malaysians, but certainly large numbers of today's professional and technologically-literate classes are, and will continue to be, major recipients of favourable government policies and economic opportunities which lead, in turn, to their active engagement with and mediation of global relations and processes. No doubt, participation in globalized processes will continue to inform people's experience of the nation (as it has done in the past) and research into the effect of global influences on nationalism and nationalist practices remains a priority. However, such interaction with global processes and politics has also contributed to a sense of the importance of the nation-state as a source of autonomy and distinction within a global world. It is no surprise, therefore, that the international audience of Internet users has brought into focus issues of Malaysia's specificity within and allegiance to a global world order. Certainly, as noted above, the Internet has served to heighten nationalist sensitivities and anti-imperialist rhetoric in relation to perceived "Western" criticism. On a more positive note, as demonstrated by the celebratory tone of home pages, the intensification of globalizing pressures draws in response a greater awareness of the nation and what this represents (for example, through the inclusion of national monuments, cartoons and cultural icons), even while signalling an active participation in global processes (for example, rock music, post-industrial formations and global religions). While information technology, such as the Internet, remains firmly in the service of Malaysia's ongoing nation-building, I find little evidence to support the claim that the nation is being superseded by an emerging transnationalism.

Notes

1. A somewhat facile example is the discussion of so-called "scientific principles" of Western management in the daily newspapers in Malaysia. There are two regular columnists whose main preoccupation is to take current Western management principles and seek complementary approaches in the writings of early Islamic and Chinese philosophers. Such discussions are obviously directed at the public sphere (the world of business and commerce) but incorporate notions of cultural specificity and difference.

2. Batu Ferringhi is a popular resort area in Penang.

3. Many of the observations I make in this paper about Malaysians' use and adoption of information technology are based on research I conducted in Malaysia from July 1994 to May 1995. During this time I interviewed a number of Malaysian professionals and technologists in the information technology sector, surveyed a range of users and students on their use of information technology, and attended conferences on the themes of computerization and Internet adoption in Malaysia.

4. I am hesitant to give too much credit to Lash and Urry (1987) here. Their concept of the service class relies heavily on a notion of cultural capital, and would ultimately defend the service classes' power and authority to influence national culture in economistic terms. It is

instructive to refer to Kahn's criticism of recent attempts to accommodate these new groupings within the rubric of class and class formation:

> The process of political, social and cultural differentiation that characterise modernity must be analysed as separate from the dominant process of class formation, and not, as a number of revisionists have done, be subsumed under an increasingly elaborate, but ultimately sterile conceptual apparatus of 'new' classes. (ibid, pp. 149–50)

5. For more general discussions of Malaysia's "statist capitalists" and the government's involvement in the ownership and control of Malaysia's largest corporations, see Jomo (1988) and Lim Mah Hui (1981) respectively.

6. According to the 1994 report from the Malaysian Science and Technology Information Centre (MASTIC),

> Malaysia is suffering a shortage of skilled scientists and technologists. Currently it has 20,000 engineers, and by the year 2000, considering expected growth rates and continued industrialisation, it will need 56,000. The current stock of students in the 'education pipeline' in Malaysia cannot satisfy demand. The percentage of students electing for a science subject declined from 24.7% in 1991 to 22.3% in 1992. Similarly, Malaysia's current ratio of 350 scientists per million population compares poorly with developed nations' ratio of 4000–6000 per million population." (*Science and Technology Awareness*, MASTIC, Ministry of Science, Technology and the Environment, Malaysia, August 1994, p. 2.)

In response, this report recommended a number of promotional activities to foster a "science culture" in Malaysia to ensure that the "nation [maintains] the current rate of growth and fulfil the aims of Vision 2020..." (ibid.).

In another report compiled by MASTIC, concern was expressed over the comparatively low number of research and development (R&D) personnel and R&D expenditure in Malaysia by international standards. For example, total R&D expenditure in Malaysia was RM550.7 million, or almost 0.4 per cent of GDP in 1992. This was significantly less than Singapore (over 1 per cent) and Taiwan (1.7 per cent). There were about 2.1 researchers per 10,000 of the work-force in Malaysia in 1992, compared to 39.8 in Singapore and 50.0 in Australia (*1992 National Survey of R&D*, MASTIC, Ministry of Science, Technology and the Environment, December 1994, p. 17).

7. Among other things, MIMOS controls the Internet gateway in Malaysia, JARING. MIMOS has been called the "brain-child" of the Prime Minister, Dr Mahathir Mohamad (Sussman and Lent 1991) and has been a tireless promotor of computerization in Malaysia, particularly through the efforts of its Director General, Tengku Mohd. Azzman Shariffadeen. Through

JARING, MIMOS has stated its support of the MSC and committed itself to provide a fully integrated Internet network to the new Putrajaya Intelligent City and MSC developments (http://www.jaring.my/jaring/info/press.html).

8. P. Ramlee is a hero of the Malaysian film industry. He was celebrated as creator, musical director, producer and actor in Malay-language dramas in the post-independence era.

9. JARING is an acronym which also means "net" in Malay. JARING was developed by MIMOS to establish a computer network throughout Malaysia and to operate Malaysia's international Internet gateway.

10. I am conscious of the need for a more detailed feminist analysis here, in particular, one that explores the masculinist nature of Malaysian nationalism and recent nationalist constructions, such as the "New Malay". My oversight is highly problematic, given the attention in this chapter to notions of economic nationalism. As Maila Stivens has noted, gender has never been absent from Malaysian constructions of nationalism and nationalist symbols. As she has written, "women's issues" have played a prominent role in national development within the context of Malaysian modernity (Stivens 1991; 1994). What is required, therefore, is a feminist analysis of the centrality of gender in recent (re)constructions of the nation and Malaysian identities, in line with futuristic visions of a global, informational and post-industrial Malaysia. I am currently pursuing this line of research.

11. The following definitions are derived from the highly accessible descriptions provided by Senjen and Guthrey (1996).

12. The convention in anthropology is to ensure the anonymity of all informants. Ethical reporting of informants' comments from the Internet is yet to form anything like a "convention". Some researchers prefer to include names and identifiers, and consequently get permission from the individuals before quoting the communication. Other researchers observe that users are aware that when posting to an Internet forum they are making a public posting and thus argue that any material drawn from the Internet's public forums can be treated and quoted in a manner similar to a "letter to the editor" in a newspaper. I have chosen a compromise. For discussions and quotes drawn from newsgroups, I have removed all identifying names but kept organization markers where I felt this was relevant (and would not result in identifying the individual). The fact that users must subscribe to newsgroups may give some people a (false) sense that the newsgroup represents a fairly closed community. This was certainly the case with the JARING newsgroups I subscribed to while in Malaysia. Predominantly computer-oriented newsgroups, everyone was well aware of the openness (and

potential leaks) of the forums. However, the small (but growing) number of registered subscribers, coupled with the low number of Malaysian-based newsgroups at the time, reinforced a sense of a closed, "known" group of discussants. In some cases, it may still be possible to track the actual individual by referring to the newsgroups' archives, but public access to the details of discussions generated 2–3 years ago is limited. With regard to the WWW home pages, while I personally think that they are the billboards of the Internet, I have changed the names of all personal home pages, but have not maintained the anonymity of home pages belonging to public organizations and electronic magazines.

13. In addition to 462 Malaysian personal homepages, JARING listed 64 Malaysian electronic publishing sites, 58 tourist sites, and 36 science and technology sites.

14. Hari Raya is the national holiday to celebrate the end of the Muslim fasting month of Ramadan.

15. This figure is known as an "emoticon" smiley. Emoticons are used on the Internet to express a range of emotions and explanations. ;) implies a good-humoured joke, in contrast to :-(which conveys a sense of sadness or disappointment.

16. The *songkok* is a Muslim/Malay cap worn with the *baju Melayu*, which is a Malay shirt worn with trousers and a sarong. The Malay *baju kurung* is a loose-fitting dress worn over a long skirt.

17. The important exceptions here are the Bulletin Boards, newsgroups and electronic magazines with a focus on Malaysian subject matter.

18. It has been noted by Jomo (1994) that Malaysia has a relatively weak sense of nationalism because of the people's stronger ethnic, religious and regional affiliations. He bemoans the fact that Malaysia has yet to develop "a progressive nationalist, as opposed to ethno-popularist or neo-colonial globalist agenda" (Jomo 1994, p. 86) which would enhance national unity. The emergence of terms such as the "New Malay" during the early 1990s, however, represents a shift away from this ethno-popularist nationalism towards a greater acknowledgment of a *Malaysian* economic nationalism. Furthermore, I would argue, that the sense of nation is nevertheless strongly marked in all communities, despite the exclusionary boundaries sometimes erected out of ethnic chauvinism.

References

Anderson, B. *Imagined Communities: Reflections on the Origin and Spread of Nationalism*. Revised edition. London: Verso, 1991.

Appadurai, A. "Disjuncture and Difference in the Global Cultural Economy". *Public Culture* 2, no. 2 (1990): 1–24.

Archer, M. "Theory, Culture and Post-Industrial Society". In *Global Culture: Nationalism, Globalization and Modernity*, edited by M. Featherstone. London, Sage, 1990.

Arnason, J. "Nationalism, Globalization and Modernity". In *Global Culture: Nationalism, Globalization and Modernity*, edited by M. Featherstone. London: Sage, 1990.

Bell, D. "The Social Framework of the Information Society". In *The Computer Age: A Twenty-Year View*, edited by M. Dertouzos and J. Moses. Cambridge, Mass.: MIT Press, 1980.

Castells, M. "The Net and the Self: Working Notes for a Critical Theory of the Informational Society". *Critique of Anthropology* 16, no. 1 (1996): 9–38.

Chatterjee, P. *The Nation and Its Fragments: Colonial and Postcolonial Histories.* Princeton: Princeton University Press, 1993.

Council for the Coordination and Transfer of Industrial Technology. *Industrial Technology Development: A National Plan of Action.* Malaysia: Ministry of Science, Technology and Environment, February 1990.

Featherstone, M. "Global and Local Cultures". In *Mapping the Futures: Local Cultures, Global Change*, edited by J. Bird, B. Curtis, T. Putnam, G. Robertson, and L. Tickner. London: Routledge, 1993.

Gessner, V. and A. Schade. "Conflicts of Culture in Cross-Border Legal Relations". In *Global Culture: Nationalism, Globalization and Modernity*, edited by M. Featherstone. London: Sage, 1990.

Hannerz, U. "Cosmopolitans and Locals in World Culture". In *Global Culture: Nationalism, Globalization and Modernity*, edited by M. Featherstone. London: Sage, 1990.

Jackson, P. "Towards a Cultural Politics of Consumption". In *Mapping the Futures: Local Cultures, Global Change*, edited by J. Bird, B. Curtis, T. Putnam, G. Robertson, and L. Tickner. London: Routledge, 1993.

Jomo, K.S. *A Question of Class: Capital, the State, and Uneven Development in Malaya.* New York: Monthly Review Press; and Manila: Journal of Contemporary Asia Publishers, 1988.

———. *U-Turn? Malaysian Economic Development Policies After 1990.* Queensland: James Cook University Press, 1994.

Kahn, J. *Culture, Multiculture, Postculture.* London: Sage, 1995.

Karthyeni, S. and Tengku Mohd. Azzman Shariffadeen. "Information Technology, Office Work and National Development". In *Keying into the Future: The Impact of Computerization on Office Workers*, edited by C. Ng and A. Monro-Kua. Kuala Lumpur: WDC Sdn. Bhd, 1994.

Kemper, S. "The Nation Consumed: Buying and Believing in Sri Lanka". *Public Culture* 5 (1993): 377–93.

King, A. "Architecture, Capital and Globalization of Culture". In *Global Culture: Nationalism, Globalization and Modernity*, edited by M. Featherstone. London: Sage, 1990.

Lash, S. and J. Friedman, eds. "Introduction". *Modernity and Identity.* Oxford: Basil Blackwell, 1992.

Lash, S. and J. Urry. *The End of Organized Capitalism.* Cambridge: Polity Press, 1987.

Lim Mah Hui. *Ownership and Control of the One Hundred Largest Corporations in Malaysia.* Kuala Lumpur: East Asian Social Science Monographs, Oxford University Press, 1981.

Malaysian Science and Technology Information Centre. *1992 National Survey of Research and Development.* Malaysia: Ministry of Science, Technology and the Environment, December, 1994a.

———. *Science and Technology Awareness.* Malaysia: Ministry of Science, Technology and the Environment, August, 1994b.

Milner, A.C. "Islamic Debate in the Public Sphere". In *The Making of an Islamic Political Discourse in Southeast Asia,* edited by A. Reid. Monash Papers on Southeast Asia, No. 27. Clayton, Victoria, Australia: Monash University, 1993.

Robertson, R. "Mapping the Global Condition: Globalization as the Central Concept". In *Global Culture: Nationalism, Globalization and Modernity,* edited by M. Featherstone. London: Sage, 1990.

———. *Globalization: Social Theory and Global Culture.* London: Sage, 1992.

Roff, W. *The Origins of Malay Nationalism.* New Haven: Yale University Press, 1967.

Senjen, R. and J. Guthrey. *The Internet for Women.* Melbourne: Spinifex, 1996.

Shaharuddin Maaruf. *Malay Ideas on Development: From Feudal Lord to Capitalist.* Singapore: Times Books International, 1988.

Smith, Anthony. "Towards a Global Culture". In *Global Culture: Nationalism, Globalization and Modernity,* edited by M. Featherstone. London: Sage, 1990.

Stivens, M., ed. *Why Gender Matters in Southeast Asian Politics.* Monash Papers on Southeast Asia, No. 23. Clayton, Victoria, Australia: Monash University, 1991.

Stivens, M. "Gender and Modernity in Malaysia". In *Modernity and Identity: Asian Illustrations,* edited by A. Gomes. Bundoora, Victoria, Australia: Comparative Asian Studies Series, La Trobe University Press, 1994.

Sussman, G. and J. Lent, eds. *Transnational Communications: Wiring the Third World.* Newbury Park, Calif.: Sage, 1991.

Toffler, Alvin. *The Third Wave.* New York: Morrow, 1980.

Wee, C.J.W.-L. "Framing the 'New' East Asian Anti-Imperialist Discourse and Global Capitalism". *Southern Review* 28, no. 3 (1995). Special Edition: "Framing Post Colonial Cultures", edited by David Birch and Central Queensland University.

Internet URLs

JARING Home Page	http://www.jaring.my/jaring/welcome.html
Malaysia's Home Page	http://www.jaring.my/
Malaysia.Net Cyber	
Coffeeshop	http://www.malaysia.net/
MalaysiaNet	http://MalaysiaNet.com/about.html

Index

THE EDITOR

Joel S. Kahn is currently Professor in the School of Sociology, Politics & Anthropology at La Trobe University in Melbourne, Australia. His most recent book is *Culture, Multiculture, Postculture* (London: Sage, 1995).